Akira K
and Moo

MW01090101

Akira Kurosawa
and Modern Japan

DAVID A. CONRAD

McFarland & Company, Inc., Publishers

Jefferson, North Carolina

This book has undergone peer review.

ISBN (print) 978-1-4766-8674-5
ISBN (ebook) 978-1-4766-4637-4

Library of Congress and British Library
cataloguing data are available

Library of Congress Control Number 2022015416

Front cover: Film director Akira Kurosawa (Photofest);
background image: Japanese style illustration (Shutterstock/Artbox)

Printed in the United States of America

*McFarland & Company, Inc., Publishers
Box 611, Jefferson, North Carolina 28640
www.mcfarlandpub.com*

To the friends, neighbors, teachers, students, and strangers who made Japan my home away from home.

Acknowledgments

My first thanks is to my wife, Kathryn. One day, after I came home and launched into an unasked-for monologue on *No Regrets for Our Youth*, I asked her whether I should make a series of short videos about the historical contexts of Kurosawa movies. She has a lot of experience with video, so I knew she would give me good advice. "Why don't you write a book?" she replied. It was good advice indeed, but she should have asked, "Why don't we write a book?" Her editorial contributions were critical and her support for the project tireless. She made the fun parts of the process more fun and the other parts not so bad. We welcomed two children before the manuscript went to press, and many of our precious free hours went toward the book instead of, say, sleep. I look forward to all of our future projects together, as soon as we've recovered from this one.

Next, thank you to the Flickchart community, the best friends a movie fanatic can have. Flickchart co-creator Nathan Chase was the first person to give me a platform to write about movies, and it was the gig that kept me sane(ish) through graduate school. The friends I've made in the Flickcharters Facebook group, some of whom have become offline friends as well, continue to expand my cinematic horizons, and every day they pull off the extraordinary feat of making social media fun. This book would not exist without them.

When I was a teenager putting my very own, brand-new video rental card to full use, my dad recommended that I check out a movie called *Seven Samurai*, which he had seen in his freshman year of college. I was mesmerized from the first drumbeat of the opening credits. Every time I rewatch it, the opening score transports me to that upstairs study with the VHS player where I saw my first Japanese film. Dad's love of history early on became my love of history too, so it is fitting that he helped edit this book that combines two of our longtime shared interests. Thanks for everything, Dad.

Thank you also to the teachers, researchers, journalists, film programmers and critics, peer reviewers, and everyone else who knowingly or unknowingly gave me questions, answers, guidance, and ideas. I take from you with gratitude and differ from you with trepidation.

Finally, thanks to all of Kurosawa's fans around the world, many of whom were not yet born when he made his last film. You help keep these movies relevant and accessible. My hope for this book is that it will do the same, both for the movies and for the times in which they were made.

Table of Contents

On Names, Transliteration, Titles, and How to Read This Book

Outside of the title of the book, which uses the familiar "Akira Kurosawa," Japanese names in this book appear in Japanese order with surnames first and given names second (e.g., Kurosawa Akira). The exceptions are citations for English-language sources, in which names and words appear as they do in the original texts.

To render Japanese words and names in the Latin alphabet, I have used a variation of the Hepburn transliteration system with macrons above long vowels, m and n used variably for ん, and no apostrophes. I omit macrons in familiar place names like Tokyo, Kyoto, and Osaka, and in words like judo and Shinto where the English and Japanese words for the concept are otherwise identical. The commonly-used Noh appears instead of *nō* for the theater style whose aesthetics inspired several Kurosawa characters and films.

I have opted to use Japanese titles for some of Kurosawa's films (e.g., *Ran, Yōjimbō*) and English titles for others (e.g., *Drunken Angel, Seven Samurai*) in accordance with which is most familiar to English-speaking audiences. In a few cases, however, I have chosen to use my own translations and transliterations instead of the most common ones. In the spirit of accuracy I use *Record of Living Things* rather than *I Live in Fear* for *Ikimono no kiroku*, *Spiderweb Castle* rather than *Throne of Blood* for *Kumonosujō*, and *Heaven and Hell* rather than *High and Low* for *Tengoku to jigoku*. For readability I prefer *Redbeard* rather than *Red Beard* for *Akahige*, and *Dodesukaden* rather than the clunky and artificial *Dodes'ka-den*. For other Japanese movies I give the common English title first, if different from the Japanese, followed parenthetically by the Japanese title and a more literal translation if necessary. When quoting dialogue I am indebted to the work of previous English translators, but I have made occasional minor changes. When quoting dialogue I am indebted to the work of previous English translators, but I have made occasional minor changes.

It is possible to appreciate this book without having seen any of Kurosawa's 30 films. However, the book spoils many plot points, and my recommendation is to watch each film before reading its associated chapter. If a picture is worth 1000 words, imagine what a great movie is worth.

Introduction

Kurosawa and the Japanese Century

In 1941, the American magazine *TIME* declared that the world was in the midst of "the American Century." *TIME*'s owner, Henry Luce, had been born in China to missionary parents at the end of the last century. A proselytizer of power, he believed that the United States should assume a leading role in international affairs, especially Asian affairs. Judging by events like the Philippine-American War (1899–1902), the American occupation of Japan (1945–1952), and American interventions across Asia from Korea and Vietnam to the Middle East, that's exactly how "the American Century" played out. Yet in another century or two or ten, historians might have a new name for the era. If "the Asian Century" still lies ahead of us as China continues its ascent and Korea anticipates reunification, then the 20th century was a taste of things to come—a time when a nation on the edge of Asia created the Japanese Century through political power, an economic miracle, and its culture and media, particularly its movies.[1]

The Japanese calendar divides the 20th century, plus a few decades to either side, into four *jidai*, translated as "periods" or "eras." Each *jidai* takes its name from the reign name of the emperor who was on the throne at the time: the Meiji *jidai* (1868–1912), the Taishō *jidai* (1912–1926), the Shōwa *jidai* (1926–1989), and the Heisei *jidai* (1989–2019). When a new emperor ascends the Chrysanthemum Throne, a new era begins. The word *jidaigeki*, "period drama," is familiar to international movie buffs because so many acclaimed Japanese movies belong to the genre: director Kurosawa Akira's award-winning samurai movies *Rashōmon* (1950), *Yōjimbō* (1961), and *Ran* (1985) all take place during long-ago *jidai*. Many movie lovers also know that George Lucas, director of *Star Wars* and friend of Kurosawa, came up with the word "Jedi" as a play on *jidai*. The opposite of *jidaigeki* is *gendaigeki*, "present-day drama," a category that includes influential titles like *Drunken Angel* (1948), *Stray Dog* (1949), and *Ikiru* (1952), also by Kurosawa. Both *jidaigeki* and *gendaigeki* reveal much about the *jidai* in which they were made. Regardless of when their stories take place, they are all products of the *jidai* that make up Japan's dramatic, painful, inspirational, contradictory 20th century.

The Meiji *jidai* began in 1868 when a group of samurai waged a successful rebellion against the *shōgun*, whose government had controlled Japan for centuries, and began to rule in the name of the Meiji emperor. This period was marked by purposeful Westernization and modernization, including the speedy adaptation of European government models, education standards, business methods, and military organization. The Meiji emperor's mentally-ill son, the Taishō emperor, reigned during the Taishō *jidai*. This era saw more Westernization, rising living standards, popular demonstrations for greater rights, and the rise of distinctively modern urban subcultures.

In the first two decades of the Shōwa *jidai*, which lasted from the enthronement of Emperor Hirohito in 1926 until his death in 1989, a backlash against Meiji- and Taishō-era change brought fascist military leaders to power. Defeat in World War II ended their regime, and the postwar Shōwa decades were defined by relative peace and undreamed-of prosperity as Japan exported its art, culture, and technology to the world. Economic growth slowed during the Heisei *jidai* (1989–2019) as Japan's population declined, but a tourism boom and persistent interest in Japanese culture abroad kept Japan a significant player in world affairs.

Japanese political power reached its maximum extent between the years 1895 and 1945, from the latter part of the Meiji *jidai* through the Taishō and early Shōwa *jidai*. At one time or another during those decades, the Japanese flag flew from New Guinea off the coast of Australia to the Aleutian Islands near Alaska, and from Burma on the border of India to the isle of Kiribati southwest of Hawai'i. In 1895, in a one-sided naval battle against Russia, Japan became the first East Asian nation to defeat a European nation in war since the Mongolian khans of the 13th century, and as spoils it received Russia's outposts in northern China. Japan seized Korea in 1910, fulfilling a long-held ambition of the samurai caste. During World War I Japan declared on the side of Britain, France, Russia, and America, and with victory in 1918 Japan took control of Germany's numerous Asian possessions. More of China fell to the Japanese army in 1931 and 1937, and Southeast Asia and a series of Pacific islands followed between 1940 and 1943. The name the Japanese government gave to its overseas territories was "The Greater East-Asia Co-prosperity Sphere," a euphemism that hinted at the empire's economic purpose. Japan profited from the unfortunate nations that ceded their best lands to Japanese colonists, their natural resources to Japanese industries, and whose people gave up their bodies and lives to the conquerors.

Japan's hemispheric empire ended when the United States, responding to attacks on its own imperial possessions in the Pacific, used its air and naval superiority to push Japan back inside the borders of its home islands. In 1945 Japan's leaders, from the Shōwa emperor to the politicians who governed in his name to the businessmen facing uncertain prospects, had no recourse but to put the nation's destiny in the hands of the enemy. For seven years the United States military occupied Japan and radically redirected its political, economic, and social structures. After that the two countries became firm Cold War allies, though aspects of their relationship remained controversial. After Japan regained its sovereignty in 1952, protests and riots over the permanent American military presence in Japan occurred with regularity.

In the 1950s and '60s Japanese businesses found that a commercial empire could be more profitable than a political one. The production of affordable, high-quality cars and electronics provided Japan with valuable export goods and powered an "economic miracle" that transformed Japanese cities from piles of rubble and ash into futuristic metropolises. Rural communities did not lag far behind as farmers shifted to work in industry or commerce and acquired the same radios, televisions, cars, and appliances as their urban counterparts. When the long Shōwa *jidai* ended in the 1980s, a middle-class lifestyle—exemplified by a "salaryman" husband, a wife who worked in the home or outside it, and children who received high-quality public education as well as public healthcare—was an attainable and pervasive norm throughout the country.

Japan's cultural influence grew apace with its economy. Japanese architecture and traditional arts gained admirers and practitioners around the world, and Japanese fashion and entertainment enjoyed waves of faddishness and emulation in Western society. In the United States and elsewhere, "Japanophiles" fueled a demand for Japanese TV shows, video games, and food, and their appetites increased during the Heisei *jidai* that bridged the 20th and 21st centuries.

Japanese movies were pivotal cultural exports during the postwar era. Films made in Japan were not always widely screened in Western movie theaters, and when they were they were often dubbed into English and heavily edited to minimize their foreignness. The prime example is 1954's *Godzilla* (*Gojira*), which most Western audiences saw only after an American production company inserted new footage featuring American actor Raymond Burr. Yet in more rarified circles, unfiltered Japanese dramas regularly contended for and won prestigious movie awards like the Palme d'Or, the Golden Lion, and the Oscar for Best Foreign Language Film. At the same time, filmmakers in Europe and America eagerly consumed and copied Japanese cinema. In France in the mid–1950s, budding auteurs like Jacques Rivette, Francois Truffaut, and Jean-Luc Godard attended the private theater of obsessive celluloid collector Henri Langlois to view the works of Kurosawa, Mizoguchi Kenji, Ozu Yasujirō, and other Japanese filmmakers. Mizoguchi and his frequent star Tanaka Kinuyo went on a much-publicized European tour in 1953, one of the first trips of its kind for Japanese screen celebrities. During the next several decades Kurosawa and his costars flew to Europe and America many times to introduce their films, accept awards, and convene with their peers. The effects rippled through world cinema. Bergman, the Swedish master, said that his movie *The Virgin Spring* (1960) was a "wretched imitation of Kurosawa." *A Fistful of Dollars* (1964), the first part of Italian director Sergio Leone's "Man with No Name" trilogy starring Clint Eastwood, is a close remake of Kurosawa's *Yōjimbō* (1961), just as the Hollywood western *The Magnificent Seven* (1960) is a remake of *Seven Samurai* (1954). George Lucas has acknowledged the influence of Kurosawa's *The Hidden Fortress* (1958) on his screenplay for *Star Wars* (1977). Francis Ford Coppola, who directed *The Godfather* (1972), helped produce Kurosawa's 1980 film *Kagemusha*, and cineaste director Martin Scorsese made an on-screen appearance in Kurosawa's 1990 film *Dreams* (*Yume*). Steven Spielberg, who cast Kurosawa's 16-time star Mifune Toshirō in the 1979 blockbuster comedy *1941*, contributed to *Dreams* as well.

Kurosawa's films are uniquely effective at conveying the 20th-century Japanese experience. Unlike his contemporaries Ozu, Mizoguchi, and Naruse Mikio, all of whom died comparatively young in the 1950s and '60s, Kurosawa lived a long life and remained active into the 1990s. Mizoguchi, Ozu, and Naruse were prolific during the 1920s and '30s, but the bulk of their early work is lost; fairly few films from Japan's silent and early sound era survived the devastation wrought by American bombs and Japan's frequent natural disasters. Kurosawa got started later, and all of his films survive at least in part. Though not uniformly productive—his output surged, fell, then surged again—Kurosawa made enough films over a long enough period of time to capture the spirit of many different political and cultural moments.

Inagaki Hiroshi (1905–1980), Ichikawa Kon (1915–2008), Kobayashi Masaki (1916–1996), Honda Ishirō (1911–1993), and Kinoshita Keisuke (1912–1998) are five directors whose lives and output more closely parallel Kurosawa's. Inagaki's colorful *jidaigeki* like the *Samurai Trilogy* (1954–56) starring Mifune were popular with critics and audiences, but late in his career he seldom departed from the samurai movie tropes that he helped establish. Kurosawa's body of work is more diverse. Ichikawa was originally an animator before finding success with grim live-action dramas, dark comedies, and the occasional documentary. He often left writing to others, notably his wife Wada Natto who wrote the screenplays for several of his most famous movies including the multiple-award-winning *The Burmese Harp* (*Biruma no tategoto*, 1956). Kurosawa wrote or co-wrote all of his screenplays, and they reflect a consistent worldview even as they adapt to major changes in Japanese society. Kobayashi missed his chance to contribute to the filmography of the war years when he was drafted into the army; his resulting commitment to pacifism and his interest in Marxism strongly color his films like the *Human Condition* trilogy (*Ningen no jōken*, 1959–1961) and *Harakiri* (1962). Kurosawa did not serve in the military, and though he shared Kobayashi's ideals to an extent, his movies reflect a wider array of concerns. Honda is well known for sci-fi and monster movies like *Godzilla* and its sequels, and he served as an assistant director or advisor on six of Kurosawa's films, including all five made between 1980 and 1993. Kinoshita's work is characterized by a lingering fixation on the war and on violence in general, especially violence among juveniles. He drew on kabuki traditions for 1958's *Ballad of Narayama* (*Narayama bushi kō*). Kurosawa's work also contains elements from Japanese theater and allusions to the war and youthful discontent, and it has been more successful than Kinoshita's in transmitting Japanese aesthetics and ideas to a worldwide audience.

The ideas expressed on film by Kurosawa and his cowriters took shape in a specifically Japanese context—a context that encompassed slow-changing cultural norms, breakneck economic and political metamorphosis, and new social dynamics. Kurosawa's four wartime movies deal with Japan's martial history, with themes of duty and sacrifice, and with the meaning of total war to civilians' lives. His next nine features, released during the American occupation, take cold, hard looks at postwar realities like crime, poverty, inflation, the black market, and the challenges of democratizing or re-democratizing rural and urban Japan. The ten movies Kurosawa released between 1954 and 1965 include his most well-known and well-regarded works, but their relationship to Japan's "economic miracle" of the 1950s and '60s is couched in *jidaigeki* metaphor and has received scant attention from critics. In the last phase of his career, from 1970 to 1993, Kurosawa used new cinematic techniques to make seven sprawling films of unprecedented visual and emotional power. They offer a window not only into the mind of a seasoned creator near the end of his life, but into a nation's collective reckoning at the end of a tumultuous century.

All 30 Kurosawa films are products of their specific place and time: Japan in the Japanese Century. All but one were filmed in Japan, and most of them were either original works or adaptations of works by Japanese authors. When a Western work provided the inspiration, as in the Shakespeare adaptations *Spiderweb Castle* (*Kumonosujō*) and *Ran*, Kurosawa modified the stories and characters to suit a Japanese setting. Most significantly, Kurosawa grounded his narratives in the immediate concerns of Japan's wartime and postwar generations, whether overtly in his early *gendaigeki* or subtly in the *jidaigeki* epics of his middle and late career. "I live in modern society," Kurosawa once reminded an American film scholar, "thus it is normal that my historical films contain modern dimensions." From a certain point of view, all of them entered the world as *gendaigeki*. Now they are all *jidaigeki*, portals to the past.[2]

Kurosawa's 30 films have much to teach us about Japan's 20th century. This book explores the connections between the Japan that Kurosawa made famous on screen and the Japan that existed behind the scenes. His well-known movies, and the few that have lingered in obscurity, reveal deeper layers and become more resonant when understood in the context of their *jidai*. By the same token, the Japanese Century comes into focus as tragedy, adventure, and epic thanks to the stories Kurosawa told in and about it.

PART ONE

The War Years

CHAPTER 1

Sanshirō Sugata

Except for the rookie director, the young star, and the even younger love interest, nearly everybody on the set of *Sanshirō Sugata* (*Sugata Sanshirō*) could remember the Meiji *jidai*. The man in charge of recreating its look and feel for the camera, Kurosawa Akira, was only two years old when the Meiji emperor died in July 1912, but like everybody else in Japan he knew exactly what the *jidai* had meant. It was the longest reign of any emperor in recorded history, surpassed only by the legendary ancients over 2000 years earlier. During the Meiji *jidai*'s four and a half decades, Japan changed more radically than during whole centuries before. The suits and slacks that Kurosawa's cast and crew wore to and from the set, the concrete and steel buildings they worked in, and the very existence of the Japanese film industry that sustained them were evidence of the Meiji era's grand project of "Westernizing" and "modernizing" the country. The film *Sanshirō Sugata* took place at the dawn of modern Japan, and Kurosawa's team worked hard to do justice to those memorable years that were so formative for them and for the nation.

They also had another objective even more important than making a good *jidaigeki*: they had to make a movie that spoke to Japan's current era, the Shōwa *jidai*, a period that thus far entailed depression, war, and great sacrifice. What nobody involved with *Sanshirō Sugata* knew was that the Shōwa *jidai*, then only in its second decade, would eventually far surpass the Meiji *jidai* in length and in dramatic change, and that Kurosawa would become its greatest chronicler.

The Meiji *jidai* began with a civil war that swept away Japan's old regime. When the last *shōgun* proved too weak to resist American and European demands for access to the Japanese market, his enemies banded together and revolted in the name of the young emperor. The rebels won the war through sheer military superiority, using swords and spears but also rifles, machine guns, and ironclad ships. They championed national purity ("Expel the barbarians!") and traditional virtues ("Revere the Emperor!"), but once in power they copied wholesale from America and Europe. Increasingly, so did ordinary citizens. While the government remade itself, building up the country's military and education system and introducing a host of new laws based on examples from overseas, more and more of the emperor's subjects began to dress, eat, and entertain themselves like their counterparts abroad.

The values of the Meiji *jidai*—strength and Westernization—are also the

A Tokyo street in the late Meiji *jidai*, 1910 (from National Diet Library Digital Collections).

themes of Kurosawa's debut film. *Sanshirō Sugata* begins in the year Meiji 15, which is 1882 in the Gregorian calendar. The text that informs the audience of the year is almost unnecessary, because from the first shot of his first movie Kurosawa displays a knack for period-specific storytelling. The camera travels along the center of a busy urban street. On the left of the screen are low, Japanese-style buildings with tiled roofs and wooden store signs. There are metal light fixtures, gas or electric, on or near each structure. On the right side the skyline is dominated by a tall, steepled structure, a prominent example of Western architecture. Women and men in *kimono* and wooden sandals called *geta* walk along the street, but some of the men wear top hats as well. A policeman who would not look out of place in Chicago or London crosses the road near a group of children in light *kimono*, while two horse-drawn carriages pass a rickshaw. The time period can only be Meiji, and in a single shot the essence of the *jidai* condenses into a single busy street.

The foreign elements of *Sanshirō Sugata*'s world are evident in every facet of the film except the dialogue. The characters, taken from a novel by Tomita Tsuneo and based loosely on historical figures, never remark upon them. Rather, their words are weighted with Shinto, Confucian, and militarist overtones—ideologies that wartime movies like *Sanshirō Sugata* had to endorse in order to win approval from government censors. The first spoken words in Kurosawa's directorial career come as his camera veers off the cosmopolitan street and enters a narrow alley where several women are singing a song:

This narrow road,
Where does it go?
This narrow road belongs to the Tenjin god

"The Tenjin god" is a god of scholarship in Japan's Shinto religion, so it is appropriate that the alley is home to a teacher—in this case, a *jūjutsu* instructor, the father of one of the singing women. Before deification Tenjin was a flesh-and-blood, 9th-century court figure, the kind of studious official held up as an ideal in Confucian philosophy. Over a millennium after Tenjin's death, Japan's government made him a symbol of national pride; paper money issued in 5- and 20-yen denominations between 1888 and 1946 bore Tenjin's image. Meiji leaders revered him as a faithful supporter of the emperor, and they anachronistically attributed the slogan "Japanese spirit, Western knowledge" to him in order to show that their policies had both history and heaven on their side. By 1943, the government used the ideologies of Shinto and Confucianism to demand loyalty to the divine emperor and to give a sense of sacredness to Japan's ongoing war against the world.

Japan had been at war in Asia for years when Kurosawa first took the director's chair, but the recent entry of the United States into the fray had turned the tide against them. In June 1942 the Japanese fleet, theretofore unchallenged in the Pacific, suffered a major defeat at Midway Atoll thanks to American aviation. Later that same year, American and Australian forces under General Douglas MacArthur began to liberate the islands of New Guinea from their Japanese occupiers. The Allies took back Guadalcanal in the Solomon Islands early in 1943, and U.S. Marines stormed Tarawa in the Gilbert Islands at the end of the year. Japan had no answer to these losses. Its once-great navy was on the retreat, its pilots were outclassed, and on island after island its soldiers were cut off and dying by the thousands. The military-dominated government in Tokyo began to lose the support of Hirohito, the Shōwa emperor. It could not afford to lose the support of the people as well. Controlling the narrative through propaganda became more and more essential, and government censors looked closely at each new movie to determine whether it met the needs of the moment.

Censorship influenced Kurosawa's first film before the cameras ever rolled, and even before he wrote the script. By 1942 Kurosawa had a good reputation as an award-winning screenwriter and a hardworking assistant director on films like *Uma* ("Horse," 1941) but the Interior Department's censors rejected at least three scripts he proposed for his solo directorial debut. They saw signs of "Western influence" in each of them, particularly in their romantic scenes. Kurosawa finally won approval to adapt the popular novel *Sanshirō Sugata*, whose story, at least on the surface, was the sort that the militarist government looked upon with favor. It highlights the Japanese martial arts of *jūjutsu* and judo and follows an earnest young man's quest to hone his fighting skills and bring honor to his *sensei*, his *dōjō*, and himself. Taken at face value, the story could inspire soldiers and civilians to fight harder and work more diligently for the glory of the nation. Yet in the finished film there is still enough "Western influence," and enough of an impulse more nuanced than propaganda, to complicate the message.

The character Sugata Sanshirō (Fujita Susumu) enters the narrow alley in search of a martial arts *sensei*. The *jūjutsu* master Monma (Kosugi Yoshio), is sneering and slovenly, with a slouched bearing unbecoming a man of his position and influence. Sanshirō later watches from the shadows as Monma and his students ambush their rival, a judo master named Yano (Ōkōchi Denjirō). Though they outnumber Yano seven to one and try to use a weapon against him, Yano calmly defeats them by throwing each attacker into a canal. Sanshirō falls to his knees and begs Yano to teach him judo. Yano is the visual inverse of Monma; the latter is bent, bare-headed, and roughly shaved, while Yano stands erect and wears a neatly-trimmed mustache and trilby hat. Sanshirō's first lesson is that the world of Japanese martial arts is fractious and contains cowardice as well as courage.

The depiction of a *jūjutsu*/judo rivalry is true to life. Many Japanese pursuits, from flower arranging to poetry to martial arts, spawn competing schools whose differences seem esoteric to outsiders but are critically important to practitioners. During the Meiji *jidai*, judo experts like Saigō Shirō, the inspiration for Sanshirō, regularly defeated *jūjutsu* masters in highly-publicized bouts, and their sport gained new fans in Japan and abroad. Still, the movie's vilification of followers of *jūjutsu*, an old and venerable fighting style, was a risk at a time when censors hoped to encourage people's fighting spirits across the board. Even more risky was the movie's depiction of Yano as a hero in a Western hat—a hero, moreover, who has less to teach Sanshirō about fighting than about living.

After becoming a disciple of Yano, Sanshirō struggles to prove his worthiness. He makes a good start by removing his *geta*, unsuitable for running, in order to pull Yano's rickshaw. As co-editor of the film, Kurosawa conveys passage of time through a montage sequence, following one of Sanshirō's discarded sandals as it experiences a year's worth of seasons. When we rejoin Sanshirō at the end of the montage, he is as unchanged as his wooden shoe. Too eagerly, he picks fights in a crowded street until meeting his match in the form of a large sumo wrestler. He returns to Yano's school, the Shūdōkan, with torn clothes and head hung in shame.

Sanshirō's maturity happens not over the course of time, but in an instant that is tinged with political and religious significance. Two other students beg Yano to go easy on Sanshirō, but Yano chastises the protagonist for his reckless and aimless bullying. By way of apology Sanshirō declares his willingness to die, then jumps dramatically into the Shūdōkan's garden pond. He clutches an upright branch and remains there, half-submerged, late into the night. The image of Sanshirō and the branch suggests a soldier carrying a rifle through one of the jungles of "the South," the term people in Japan used for the Pacific theater of war. The notion of a young man seeking validation through death had special significance for wartime audiences whose brothers and sons were spread across the Pacific, dying for their country. Unlike so many of Japan's young men, Sanshirō does not die. After hours in the pond he spots a floating lotus flower, a Buddhist symbol of purity and perfection, blossoming and shining in the light of the full moon. Finally humbled by a vision of something greater than himself, Sanshirō emerges from the water a wiser man, ready to submit to the teachings of his *sensei*.

Sanshirō's moral education draws on multiple ideological traditions. Buddhism and Shinto are Japan's dominant faiths, and most people practice both in different circumstances. They each figure in Sanshirō's life as reminders of how far he has to go in his journey of self-improvement. The Shūdōkan's Buddhist priest (Kōdō Kokuten) smirks at Sanshirō's undisciplined and therefore impotent strength, but he offers the protagonist only cryptic guidance; Buddhism's focus lies beyond the self and the world, and Sanshirō must shed pride and ambition in order to discover greater truths. Shinto, "the way of the gods," explains the world and people's relationship to it. It is present from the opening scene's invocation of the Tenjin god and appears again indirectly when the sumo wrestler defeats Sanshirō; the sport of sumo is itself a Shinto ritual once connected to harvests, and before the development of Western-style arenas its tournaments took place at shrines. Two key moments in Sanshirō's life occur on the grounds of a shrine.

More than either of these religions, though, it is Confucianism, a social philosophy that originated in China and spread to Japan in antiquity, that most clearly illuminates Sanshirō's path. Confucianism emphasizes loyalty to those above you in the social hierarchy and benevolence to those beneath you. The teacher Yano, a serene and fatherly figure, is a model Confucian man and Sanshirō's most useful guide. When Sanshirō bows to Yano after his experience in the pond and begins to take his role as a student seriously, Yano upholds his end of the Confucian contract by instructing him in both comportment and combat.

Yano teaches Sanshirō that humanity and sensitivity to beauty are greater virtues than mere strength. He stresses to Sanshirō the importance of "filial piety"—the loyalty and obedience that children owe to their parents, a key concept in Confucianism. The line about filial piety was not originally in Kurosawa's script, but Japanese censors required it. They intended to remind audiences to remain loyal to the government, whose relationship with Japanese citizens was, they believed, comparable to the relationship between parents and children. There is a gulf between the enlightened, humanistic philosophy of Yano and the aggressive, destructive agenda of the early Shōwa government, but the government would not have admitted the contradiction. They always declared that their actions overseas were justified, and that their soldiers were creating a "Greater East Asian Co-Prosperity Sphere" for the mutual good of Japan and its neighbors. Even as they raped and pillaged in Asia, educated officers of the Japanese military emulated medieval warrior-poets by writing *haiku* and practicing calligraphy, and many soldiers believed they were spreading the benefits of Japan's superior culture through conquest. *Sanshirō Sugata* insists on compassion's moral superiority to combat, but by phrasing the message in terms of loyalty and duty it leaves little room to question whether Japan's wartime government measures up to the ideal.[1]

Female students at Taihoku Imperial University, a university for Japanese colonists in Taiwan, practice martial arts in 1940 (from Taiwan Image Database).

Sanshirō is dutifully channeling his strength toward a menial task when he meets the movie's antagonist, Higaki Gennosuke, a character Kurosawa called "my Mephistopheles." Played by Tsukigata Ryūnosuke, Higaki is tall, thin, gloved, draped in a Western-style jacket, and topped with a mane of slicked-back hair beneath a bowler hat. Film scholar Stephen Prince describes Higaki's Occidental wardrobe as "a sop to the militarism" of 1943, but the irreproachable Yano is also seen in Western garb, and Sanshirō's fellow students wear a mix of sartorial styles. Kurosawa's vision of Meiji contains the *jidai*'s multitudes.[2]

When Higaki appears, calmly lighting a cigarette and speaking barely above a whisper, the wind howls desolately. Displaying what scholar Paul Anderer calls "an unmistakable sympathy for the devil," Kurosawa uses Higaki to charge the film with a dark and seductive energy. Higaki is a *jūjutsu* master, and he demands a match against Yano or his best pupil. Here, for one of the first times in his career, Kurosawa uses a kinetic editing technique, the screen wipe, to convey Higaki's intensity. A rapid slide to the right takes us from a view of Higaki to a shot of a Shūdōkan student crashing into a wall. Higaki is an overwhelming force whose strength seems to move the very film itself.

There is an equivalence between Yano, the studious master of judo, and Higaki, the shadowy champion of *jūjutsu*. In their clothes and aristocratic bearing they recall Meiji-era internationalists, liberals, and bourgeoisie: the kind of people Japanese militarists assassinated during their rise to power in the 1930s. Higaki and

Yano are both more richly characterized than Sanshirō, betraying Kurosawa's abiding interest in their class of men—a class he would examine more directly after the war (see Chapter 5). In sharp contrast to them is Monma, who lives on the street of Tenjin and wears exclusively Japanese garb but is the weakest and most vulgar character in the film.

Ever watchful for political sins, censors reportedly required the removal of seventeen minutes from Kurosawa's debut film. What most troubled them was not the movie's reflection of Meiji-era Westernization or its gentle critique of violence as an end unto itself, but its depiction of women. Other Japanese films from the war years provoked censors' wrath by showing actors kissing on screen, a "British-American" way of showing affection. Even without a kiss, scenes between men and women could run afoul of wartime entertainment policies. Two of *Sanshirō Sugata*'s deleted sequences, only partially restored years later, both involve women in Sanshirō's life. One is called Sayo (Todoroki Yukiko). She is the daughter of Higaki's *jūjutsu* teacher, a drunk named Murai (Shimura Takashi), and she is disturbed by "Higaki's dark side, his snakelike shadow." In the deleted footage Higaki behaves quite coarsely toward Sayo, slipping money into her *kimono* and comparing her beauty to a Chinese woman he once saw. This was too much for a hypersensitive historical moment when policing morality went hand in hand with encouraging correct political thinking.[3]

Another redacted sequence involves Monma's daughter, who reenters the story for the first time since singing about the Tenjin god in the opening scene. She attends Sanshirō's match against her father, a *jūjutsu* versus judo showdown. At the end of the fight, Sanshirō flings Monma into a wall, killing him. Kurosawa uses slow motion to accentuate the crowd's dumbstruck reaction. Monma's daughter watches from a window, and Kurosawa cuts in on her twice, closer and closer, until her face fills the frame. Her eyes smolder with hatred and determination. Later she goes to the Shūdōkan with a knife to kill Sanshirō, but fails. It is here that another substantial sequence was cut from the finished film, including Sanshirō's "disturbed" reaction to the assassination attempt and his "lifeless" moonlit training session with Yano afterward. Kurosawa did not approve of the changes to his movie, but the studio he worked for, Tōhō, probably did not mind them. From the studio's perspective there was a financial advantage to a shorter film, since it could run more times each day in theaters. Tōhō likely cut material from *Sanshiro Sugata* for this reason, as there are a handful of missing scenes that contained nothing likely to have offended government censors.[4]

Despite different religious and political contexts, Japanese films' depictions of sex and relations between men and women followed a similar trajectory to their Hollywood counterparts. Neither Japan nor the United States put explicit sexual content on the big screen, but they both presented more salacious content in the silent and early talkie films of the 1920s and early '30s than in the comparatively conservative movies of the next couple of decades. *A Page of Madness* (*Kurutta ippēji*, 1926) is one of the rare Japanese silents to survive the bombing raids and natural disasters that doomed most of the volatile silver nitrate film stock of the era. Taking place in an insane asylum, its sexually-charged exploration of fantasy and psychosis probably would not have passed censors' inspection in 1943. The flirtation between a married man and his jazz-loving female neighbor in Japan's first talkie, *The Neighbor's Wife and Mine* (*Madamu to Nyōbō*, "The Madam and the Wife," 1931), likely would have faced greater opposition as well had it come out later. The wartime government had an existential dread that defeat in war would mean the defeat of their preferred patriarchal cultural norms at home—a fear that was not wholly unjustified, as the early postwar years would prove. In their own ways, when Monma's daughter seeks vengeance for her father and shakes Sanshirō's confidence, and when Sayo pits her integrity against her drunken father and his sinister student, they complicate the prevailing social order that valued strong men and obedient women.

A lengthy, romantic montage of Sanshirō and Sayo meeting on the steps of a Shinto shrine remains in the film. The leads fall in love before learning each other's identity or that Sanshirō will one day have to fight Murai. Sayo, in full *kimono*, carries a parasol down the winding stair like a figure from a 19th-century woodblock print. Sanshirō courteously uses his handkerchief to fix the strap of Sayo's *geta*. Sayo later tries to return the handkerchief on the same steps, but Sanshirō declines and walks swiftly away. The formal politeness of their courtship, which Kurosawa stages on the grounds of a sacred building, shields the movie's romantic sensibilities from official censure.

The Japanese government under General Tōjō Hideki, prime minister from 1941 to 1944, was deeply paranoid about the politics of moviemakers and actors. A few years before playing Murai in *Sanshirō Sugata*, Shimura Takashi, who would appear in more Kurosawa films than any other actor, was detained for several weeks on suspicion of being a radical leftist or communist. It surely did not help Shimura's case that he had been an avid student of English at Kansai University. In the end Shimura's friend Tsukigata Ryūnosuke, who would play his student Higaki in *Sanshirō Sugata*, vouched for him to secure his release. Shimura and Tsukigata, who came of age in more liberal *jidai*, bring depths to their characters that help make *Sanshirō Sugata* feel like more than a story about a muscular youth in a manly avocation. Sanshirō's encounters with Murai and Higaki help him evolve from a mere brawler, a new Monma, into a disciple of humanity, an aspiring Yano.[5]

In the movie's climactic bouts, Sanshirō defeats Murai and Higaki but takes no pleasure in it. Murai's vision is blurred by age and drink, and only reluctantly does Sanshirō press his advantage against him. Higaki and Sanshirō's hand-to-hand duel on a windswept knoll comes next, and in the end both hero and villain leave the fight changed for the better. It was meant to be a fight to the death, but Sanshirō chooses life. The ending of the film closes this chapter of Sanshirō's career but suggests the possibility of more to come.

Kurosawa's first production walked a fine line, rankling censors with its treatment of gender dynamics and presenting a cosmopolitan view of Japan shot through with humanism. Yet when established director Ozu Yasujirō spoke to skeptical censors in praise of Kurosawa's debut, a sequel became an early possibility. Before continuing the story of Sanshirō, however, Kurosawa helmed a movie that addressed the war and its effect on notions of Japanese womanhood directly, without the veil of a *jidaigeki.*

CHAPTER 2

The Most Beautiful

The most significant innovation of 20th-century warfare was not a tactical maneuver, like the logistically-mindboggling amphibious assaults that allowed Allied troops to gain footholds in northern France and the central Pacific, nor a weapon like the incendiary bombs that created hell on earth in German and Japanese cities. It was not even the atomic bomb, which was soon eclipsed by even more powerful kinds of nuclear weapons. It was the transformation of industrial societies into "total war" economies—economies in which practically every factory and useful pair of hands contributed to the war effort. For combatant nations, increasing factory output meant expanding the labor force. In large part this was achieved by employing more women in industrial roles than ever before.

Japanese women had never been wholly excluded from the workforce. In urban areas like Osaka in the 18th and 19th centuries, practical economic needs trumped religious and ideological doctrines that sought to confine women to the home, and there were women who ran *sake* breweries and other businesses either officially or on a *de facto* basis. During the Meiji *jidai*, the modernizing government mandated public education for girls as well as boys, and the nation benefited enormously from female textile workers who made the fabrics that were Japan's first major export goods. Yet women could not vote or hold political office, and Meiji politicians held firm to the idea that women's first duties were to home and family. The governments of the Taishō and early Shōwa *jidai* maintained this stance throughout the 1910s, '20s, and '30s even as other industrialized nations granted women the vote.[1]

The Taishō *jidai* lasted just 14 years from July 1912 to December 1926, but for Japanese women the significance of the period was profound. World War I fueled an economic boom in Japan that contributed to the rise of consumer groups, labor movements, and rural organizations, and women led many of these. Women played a major role in the "rice riots" of 1918, a series of protests against high rice prices that constituted "the greatest mass disturbances in Japan's modern history." The Japanese media in the 1920s seized on the popular image of the "Modern Girl" or "New Woman," a parallel to the American flapper, who represented sexual and economic power for women outside of home and family. Such women exchanged ideas with international women's groups, embraced Western fashion, traveled more widely than their foremothers, advocated legal and social gender equality, and prompted

Women work with machinery at a garment factory in the mid–Meiji *jidai*, c. 1888 (Wikimedia Commons).

national conversations about divorce, childrearing, and women working outside the home. Magazines and department stores catered to these conspicuously nontraditional women, and businesses increasingly sought female employees to work in offices, behind sales counters, at cafes (including some with erotic themes), and in nightclubs. By 1920 the 3.5 million women in the Japanese labor force were still only a small fraction of Japan's 27 million women, but the number was rising. The generation of New Women embodied the spirit of "Taishō Democracy" for which the era came to be remembered.[2]

The early Shōwa *jidai* was far less liberating. The global economic depression of the 1930s hit Japan hard. A series of assassinations targeted liberal, internationalist politicians and paved the way for militant nationalists to take power. The nation's new leaders tried to slow women's entry into the workforce. Like Nazi Germany, which viewed women as "Mothers of the *Volk*," militarist Japan conceived of women in strictly domestic terms. The government promoted the idea that women, in their proper role as wives and mothers and daughters-in-law, were the basis of an inalterable family system that derived from Confucian and Shinto traditions stressing familial obligation. This idea existed in the Meiji and Taishō *jidai* as well, but the extreme nationalism of the early Shōwa period accentuated it. People who criticized the government's reactionary impulses on this and other topics could find themselves in prison.

When Japan launched all-out war against China in 1937 and against the United

States and Britain in 1941, the government instructed civilians to endure hardship and practice austerity for the sake of the nation. Women absorbed the "masculinist military rhetoric" of the moment. Girls who came of age in the 1930s and '40s did not try to emulate the New Women of the Taishō period, but rather to share the sacrifices of their fathers and brothers in uniform. For many, this meant setting aside personal ambitions in order to stay home and manage frugal, patriotic households. The feminist movements that gained traction in the 1920s "retreat[ed] under the rise of the fascist power," wrote women's rights activist Katō Shizue. It was legal for Japanese women to work outside the home, but during the war fewer did so than in any Allied country. The nations of Russia, Britain, and the United States encouraged or even required women to contribute to the war effort through factory work, but Japan did not do so until the middle of 1944 when defeat was imminent. In August of that year the government reluctantly bowed to necessity and required all single women older than twelve and younger than forty to register for work in munitions factories.[3]

Kurosawa's April 1944 movie about young women in a military optics factory was therefore supremely timely. Critics often describe *The Most Beautiful* (*Ichiban utsukushiku*) as a propaganda film, a movie about patriotic Japanese women who dedicate their lives to the war effort at the moment when their country needs them most. Yet, like *Sanshirō Sugata*, the emotional texture of *The Most Beautiful* is more complex than that description suggests. The film's intimate depiction of working women's lives could not help but reopen perennial questions about women's place in the modern Japanese economy. *The Most Beautiful* does not insist on a particular point of view about the propriety of female employment—whether it is a sad measure of last resort or an option that ought to be available to women at will—but it does demand that viewers acknowledge the existence of working women, empathize with their varied experiences in the workplace, and observe how women control their own destinies and even the destiny of the nation. The movie also undermines its government-approved message by stressing the emotional toll of total war and suggesting that its characters' sacrifices may be in vain.

The Most Beautiful opens with four title cards. One reads "Attack and Destroy" (*uchiteshi tomamu*), a card attached to the front of most Japanese film reels in 1944 comparable to the "V for Victory" logo in wartime Hollywood films. The next two name the production company and announce the film as an "Information Bureau movie of the people." The final card simply gives the title; the nearly all-female cast went uncredited until the final reel, an inversion of the usual credits-first practice for the era. While this may obscure the contributions of the young actresses, it helps the story feel less like a work of fiction and more like an homage to wartime working women.

The movie opens at the Hiratsuka Factory of East Asian Optics as the factory chief (Shimura Takashi) announces a production quota increase. His proclamation, magnified by loudspeakers around the factory grounds, is received attentively by rows of uniformed men and women. To achieve greater productivity, the chief says, each worker must improve his or her spiritual character. The reason for the emergency increase is no secret, and he states it bluntly: American victories in the war have made it necessary for everyone to work harder. However, the work will not be evenly distributed among the factory employees. Male workers must increase their output by 100 percent, but female employees need only churn out 50 percent more war materiel than before.

Kurosawa shot *The Most Beautiful* on location at the real-life Hiratsuka factory in Tokyo. War factories were often close to civilian housing, partly to make them difficult targets

Illustration from a Taishō *jidai* magazine catering to "modern girls" (Illustration by Takabatake Kashō, *Shojo Club* 2, no. 11, 1924).

for American bombers, who until 1943 attempted precision bombing of specific targets rather than the indiscriminate bombings of 1944 and 1945. Yet filming there was dangerous, and Kurosawa's team narrowly avoided disaster in more than one bombing raid. In order to achieve a documentary feel, Kurosawa had his young cast members work and sleep in the factory alongside actual employees, sharing in their daily lives and their dangers.[4]

In a series of short scenes, women chat inaudibly and neglect their work while a couple of male guards walk a beat. When they see the men, the women stop talking and pivot to their tasks. In these vignettes the factory feels like a prison, and the women's work is dull and repetitive. One woman asks her coworkers to be quiet so that she can concentrate on her task, but they disregard her and continue to talk. When male guards chastise them, the women appeal to a higher authority. They ask to speak to their section chief, a woman named Watanabe Tsuru (Yaguchi Yōko).

Watanabe is bent over her task in a room whose door is adorned with a Shinto purity symbol: a twisted rope hung with lightning-bolt-shaped paper that signifies the sacred importance of the lens calibration work happening inside. She breaks from her job to plead her coworkers' case to the male factory bosses. The reason the women are conversing instead of working, Watanabe explains, is that they object to the 50 percent production quote increase. It is not that it is too large an increase, but too small; the women feel they can do at least two-thirds the work of men. The bosses agree to let them try, and in the women-only dining area the young ladies cheer Watanabe for securing them this opportunity. This sequence, with its depiction of women negotiating from a position of weakness in a hierarchical workplace, reflects the atmosphere of a wartime factory and establishes Watanabe as a trusted go-between for the female employees and the male authorities.

The women in this movie, like their real-life counterparts, do not clock out and go home at the end of the day. Even before the war, labor contracts between employers and women's parents or third-party recruiters meant that female workers could not simply leave their workplaces at will. Dormitories and communal eating areas were longstanding features of Japanese factories for both male and female employees. Within gender-segregated living, eating, and working spaces, women relied on each other and advocated for themselves, much like the women in *The Most Beautiful*. How well working women adjusted to these conditions varied based on personality and background. Women from poorer families often found dorms comfortable and appreciated the quality and quantity of cafeteria food, but others were accustomed to more privacy and better food at their family homes. Some tried to run away only to have the police return them to their managers. In the 1941 film *Uma*, co-written and co-directed by Kurosawa with his mentor Yamamoto Kajirō, a young woman absconds from her cotton factory to look after the family horse while her former teacher arranges a time for her to return to work. After the war, the explicitly coercive power of factories decreased, but many continued to provide room and board to their workers. These services were necessities for many employees, whose family homes could be long distances away, and taking advantage of them demonstrated a worker's commitment to the company.[5]

Kurosawa's factory women sing patriotic songs and march around the grounds in lockstep, but this image of group solidarity is complicated by each individual's fundamental loneliness. Watanabe, already set apart from the others because of her position of authority, has a tic that other characters remark on: when she is angry, she carries one shoulder higher than the other. The gesture foreshadows the famous slouch of Kurosawa's samurai hero in *Yōjimbō* (see Chapter 20). Further evidence of the factory women's essential separateness is on display in a room set aside for pictures of their families. At the end of a shift, two young women go to this *tatami*-matted space reminiscent of the ancestor shrines found in many Japanese homes. After they offer greetings to the framed photos, one looks sadly at the picture of her mother and expresses envy that the other girl has a large family.

These moments of individuality and loneliness contrast with scenes of collective indoctrination. A dorm mother named Mizushima is in bereavement after the death of her soldier husband, but she dutifully leads the young women in a chanted oath to start each day:

> MIZUSHIMA: Today, all day….
> WORKERS: We shall be loyal.
> MIZUSHIMA: We shall remember to worship the gods and revere our ancestors.
> WORKERS: We shall not forget our filial duty.
> MIZUSHIMA: Furthermore….
> WORKERS: We shall not be selfish.
> MIZUSHIMA: We shall remember to be kind and modest.
> WORKERS: We shall endure hardship.
> MIZUSHIMA: We are women of the empire.
> WORKERS: We shall do our best to destroy America and Britain.
> MIZUSHIMA: We shall pass these ideals on to our descendants.
> WORKERS: We shall.

Large banners above the women extol them to follow the examples of Admiral Yamamoto Isoroku and Colonel Yamazaki Yasuo, both of whom died in combat in 1943; the women are supposed to work themselves to death if necessary. Yet the items in the women's quarters speak of personal anxieties, not war. "Mountains and rivers separate me from my home. May mother and father be at peace," reads one woman's scroll. It hangs on top of a map of New Guinea, where Admiral Yamamoto died, partially obscuring it.

Thoughts of home consistently overshadow the drumbeat of jingoism. In addition to the family picture room, the women maintain a garden that contains soil from each of their hometowns. When one girl, Suzumura, falls ill and her father comes to take her home, the others are so overcome with emotion that they run to the entryway in their indoor slippers, leaping over their outdoor shoes at the threshold. The women are sad to see their friend leave, but more tellingly, they are envious of her. "Now I want to go home too," says one girl whose smile belies her longing.

In another scene, a woman named Yamazaki defies a rule against walking on the factory roof in order to gaze at Mt. Fuji and her home beyond. Unfortunately, as a coworker laughingly informs her, her home is in the opposite direction from Fuji. Adding injury to insult, Yamazaki falls from the roof and misses several weeks of work while recuperating in the factory hospital. A more nationalist film might chastise Yamazaki for letting down her country through carelessness, but Kurosawa's script creates empathy for her and her coworkers by emphasizing their youth. The 1944 female labor conscription law applied to widows and unmarried women up to the age of forty, but Kurosawa focuses almost exclusively on women in their teens and early twenties. They still have parents to pine for, and they have little interest in news from far-flung places. Though they give their all to the war effort, Kurosawa gives their personal lives a dramatic weight that is at least equal to the importance of their work.

When the women's manufacturing output falters because of accidents like Yamazaki's, Watanabe organizes a game of volleyball for them. As the women's spirits rise, so does production. Yet there is more sorrow than joy in the women's lives. Through a montage of news bulletins, grim faces, and feverish labor, the women react to reports of Japanese losses on the Pacific islands of Tarawa, Makin, Kwajalein, and Roi-Namur. News from the home front is similarly dismaying: Watanabe receives a letter informing her that her mother is ill, but she refuses to request a leave of absence. Word arrives that Suzumura has recovered from her sickness, but her parents in the countryside won't let her return to the factory where she became ill. *The Most Beautiful* does not glamorize wartime factory labor. The physical and emotional difficulties of the protagonists' lives are in the foreground, and in the background is the grim recognition that Japan is losing the war.

There is no overt acknowledgment in the film of the most dangerous aspect of factory work: American bombs. Still, Kurosawa characterizes the factory as a kind of front line by showing Japanese fighter planes flying overhead on their way to intercept enemy craft. Bombing runs ramped up toward the end of 1944 when U.S. military strategists decided that factories, the workers therein, and even the civilians living nearby were valid targets. American B-29 planes appeared regularly over Japanese cities, and their bombs and the fires they caused destroyed over a quarter of a million buildings and killed around 100,000 people in Tokyo alone.

Startlingly, Kurosawa closes the movie without answering the question of whether the women achieve their production goal. Throughout the runtime he cuts to an animated chart showing the dips and peaks in factory output. The final glimpse of the chart shows an upward trend, but its peak is no higher than previous upswings. In a closing shot that lasts over a minute, Watanabe sits crying at her work station, straining to see her tools through her tears. She has just decided not to go home for her mother's funeral. This sacrifice is profound, and like the sacrifices of Japan's soldiers it comes with no promise of eventual victory. It is a grim thought on which to end.

The Most Beautiful dutifully praises sacrifice but shrouds it in an air of futility. During his directorial apprenticeship Kurosawa helped end 1941's *Uma* on much the same note, with the female protagonist staring into the distance after reluctantly selling her beloved horse to the Army; the censors required cuts elsewhere in that movie but allowed the solemn depiction of sacrifice. In the words of film scholar Audie Bock, who decades later served as Kurosawa's translator, what is most remarkable about *The Most Beautiful* and Kurosawa's other wartime productions is that the government ever approved movies "so scant in fanaticism." Kurosawa's ambivalent patriotism stems from his focus on the individual emotional costs of war. As Stephen Prince observes, the last shot of Watanabe "emphasize[s] the contradiction between personal feelings and national duty." She and her coworkers each suffer in distinct and personal ways, without benefit of nearby family, and to an extent that is poorly understood by their male supervisors.[6]

In later years Kurosawa frequently expressed scorn for the wartime government and its censors, but he did not renounce *The Most Beautiful*. The reason may be partly personal; he married Yaguchi Yōko, who played Watanabe, amid the sound of air raid sirens shortly after production wrapped. The shrine where they got married sustained bomb damage the day after their wedding. Decades later, after his wife's death, Kurosawa stated that he owned a print of the film but could not bear to watch it because she was in it. Yet it may also be that *The Most Beautiful*, often dismissed as propaganda, needed no apology in the eyes of its creator. Its emotional complexity gives it a staying power that propaganda rarely retains after its historical moment has passed.

CHAPTER 3

Sanshirō Sugata Part II

A boorish American sailor—tall, unshaven, ridiculous in his tight-fitting Navy blues—bellows as he throws wild punches on a city street. A small Japanese rickshaw driver cowers helplessly at his feet. A crowd gathers, but none have the strength or courage to stop the rampaging American.

The year is 1887 and the city is Yokohama. Yokohama in the Meiji *jidai* was the most international city in Japan, a berth for traders and mission ships from China, Britain, America, and beyond. The port city was a testing ground for Western amusements and technologies, from rugby to beer to Japan's first electrical power company, and what succeeded there soon spread to the rest of Japan with the support of the pragmatic and progress-minded Meiji government. The financial and material benefits of this robust international exchange made drunk sailors an annoyance worth enduring.

Yet by 1945, the year *Sanshirō Sugata Part II* (*Zoku Sugata Sanshirō,* "Sanshiro Sugata Continued") was released, Japan's government was less pragmatic and more xenophobic than ever before. They knew they were beaten; after the loss of key Pacific island bases and the destruction of most of Japan's air and sea forces, all informed people knew that victory against the Allies was impossible. American bombers flew through Japanese skies with numbing regularity. The resignation of hawkish Prime Minister Tōjō after the fall of the Marianas in 1944 could have paved the way for a more moderate faction to seize the government and offer peace terms to the United States. Instead, a succession of prime ministers proved unable to break the deadlock between the hardline military and the increasingly peace-oriented Imperial household. While Japan's soldiers and civilians continued to die in a war that had no hope of success, its politicians could only pontificate absurdly about the inviolability of the national polity (*kokutai*), a concept which conflated the survival of the people with the maintenance of a militarized government religiously dedicated to the Shōwa emperor. This precise form of government had existed only since the early Shōwa *jidai*, and it stood in marked contrast to the reformist and Western-oriented policies of the Meiji and Taishō *jidai*, but historical memory was not a strength of the wartime government.

The peace faction led by Prince Konoe Fumimaro (the Meiji government borrowed titles like Prince, Count, and Baron from the British) believed that a negotiated surrender was the only way to preserve the Japanese way of life. If Japan did not surrender soon, the Soviet Union might scrap the neutrality pact that Konoe secured from them in 1941 and carve out a communist puppet state in the Japanese islands—the same thing that happened to Germany after its surrender. The Russians would not be content just to reclaim the mainland Asian territory that Japan took from them in the 1905 Russo-Japanese War, or to absorb the parts of China and Korea that Japan colonized between the 1910s and the 1930s; indeed, the Soviet leader Josef Stalin already had designs on islands within the Japanese archipelago.

There was also the possibility that Japanese communists and other leftists could rise up to overthrow the government. Right-wing militarists had done it to Japan's liberal internationalist government during the economic depression of the 1930s. Now that their own plans had come to ruin, they worried that leftist dissidents—those not already in jail, anyway—might take advantage of Japan's defeat to steer the country in a radical new direction. In rural China in the 1930s, Mao Zedong's communist rebels had forcibly redistributed land from wealthy landlords to poor farmers. In the chaos of 1945, a Japanese Mao might do more damage to Japan's social and economic foundations than American bombs had done to its infrastructure.

The war faction of the gridlocked government, headed by General Anami Korechika, argued that if Japan surrendered the Americans might put Emperor Hirohito on trial for war crimes; they might even execute him. Many former German leaders were already in Allied prisons awaiting trials and nooses. Neither the Imperial household nor the Japanese military could accept such a possibility for their head of state, and this was the primary reason for the government's paralysis in the last months of the war. The Allies refused to make any promises about the emperor. They planned to impose sweeping political and social reforms in Japan after its defeat, and at the very least those would include weakening the emperor's position. After U.S. President Franklin Roosevelt died in April 1945, President Harry Truman reaffirmed his policy of unconditional surrender. The Americans' successful test of an atomic bomb in July strengthened their already dominant position and made the possibility of a negotiated peace even more remote.

Unable to find a way forward, Japanese leaders moved the war's frontlines to the only place it could still be won: the realm of fantasy. General Anami called for civilians and soldiers to seek glory through death (*gyokusai*). Government radio broadcasts warned people of the cruelty of American soldiers, preparing them to fight for every inch of soil. And in May 1945, the hero Sugata Sanshirō returned to movie screens to do in the past what Japan could not do in the present: defeat the United States.

Appearing suddenly behind the rampaging American sailor on the Yokohama street, Sanshirō grabs the bully by the wrist and leads him away from the crowd. On the dock, Sanshirō performs the same trick his sensei Yano used to defeat Monma's toughs in the first film: with a well-timed move the judo master uses the American's momentum to send the brute flying into Tokyo Bay.

American B-29 bombers fly near Mt. Fuji, 1945 (photograph by U.S. Army Air Force).

This is a crude bit of wish-fulfillment, a one-dimensional piece of anti–American propaganda with none of the nuance of *Sanshirō Sugata* or *The Most Beautiful*, but it reflects the desperate mood of 1945. No increase in factory production could turn the tide now—not when most factories lay in ruins. Encouragement was moot, and complexity and ambiguity were luxuries ill-suited to a nation facing the abyss. The world of fiction offered the only solace, whether it was the fiction of a movie screen or the government's delusion that there was some alternative to unconditional surrender.

In keeping with the unsubtlety of the moment, the silent attention Kurosawa paid to wardrobes in *Sanshirō Sugata* becomes a matter of open discussion in the sequel. In the film's second scene the Buddhist priest from Yano's school consoles Sayo, who is upset that Sanshirō has not visited her since her father Murai died. (Shimura Takashi is the only principal cast member from the first movie who does not return for the sequel.) The monk says that Sanshirō feels responsible for Murai's death, and that Sanshirō's integrity and depth of feeling set him apart from "youth who wear Western fashion."

Elsewhere, Sanshirō receives a visit from a checkered-suit-wearing dandy named Fubiki. Fubiki is Japan's emissary to the United States. There was sensibility and sophistication to the Western clothes in *Sanshirō Sugata*, but the wardrobes in Part II are different. Fubiki's clothes are a chaotic array of gaudy patterns bursting with pointless, decorative handkerchiefs. The emissary himself is both ridiculous and haughty, prancing around the room to demonstrate American boxing techniques one moment and laughing condescendingly at Sanshirō the next.

Fubiki explains that American boxing champion William Lister heard how Sanshirō humiliated the American sailor and now wants to face Sanshirō in a "friendly" match. A *jūjutsu* fighter has already agreed to fight Lister at the American embassy, so judo's honor is at stake as well as the nation's. Sanshirō dismisses boxing as a mere spectator sport and declines the challenge. He tells a prospective student that he no longer seeks fights and does not rejoice in victory. Still, he agrees to go to the American embassy to witness the match between the *jūjutsu* fighter and the boxer.

Never again would Kurosawa shoot a scene featuring so many non–Japanese faces. He would work with foreign actors many times in the decades to come, including in the film *Dersu Uzala* which features no Japanese actors at all (see Chapter 25), but the set of the American embassy's boxing ring in *Sanshirō Sugata Part II* is unmatched for the sheer number of non–Japanese people present, including the boxer, the referee, and a sizeable portion of the men and women around the ring. The actors playing Americans were Japanese residents of foreign (mostly European) descent.

Sanshirō leaves the event disgusted at boxing's animalistic brutality and the ease with which William "Killer" Liston defeated his *jūjutsu* opponent. He returns to the Shūdōkan, where Yano tells him that defeating the American boxing champion isn't a matter of personal honor or even the honor of judo; it is about the honor of Japanese martial arts writ large. This nationalistic argument perfectly echoes the prevailing propaganda of 1945. Official proclamations that year included dire warnings about what American soldiers would do to Japanese civilians during an invasion, and they predicted that the victory of the United States would mean the death of Japan and its institutions in a zero-sum game.

Like part one, however, *Sanshirō Sugata Part II* is primarily about an intra–Japanese rivalry. The judo versus *jujutsu* dynamic was so integral to the first film that something like it had to appear in the sequel. This time Sanshirō's Japanese challengers practice *karate*. They are Higaki Genzaburō and Higaki Tesshin, the two younger brothers of Higaki Gennosuke, the antagonist of the first movie. Actor Tsukigata Ryūnosuke returns to play the dying Gennosuke as well as Tesshin. This was not the only time that Kurosawa would use a favorite actor in a double role (see *Kagemusha*, Chapter 26), but both of Tsukigata's characters pale next to the striking, otherworldly presence of Genzaburō, played by Kōno Akitake.

Genzaburō's aesthetic comes directly from the stock characters of medieval Noh theater, a deep well of inspiration that Kurosawa would draw from again and again. In Noh plays, which often involve mythological and supernatural events, insane characters carry sticks of bamboo called *kuruizasa* ("madness bamboo"). Genzaburō is exactly such a figure: his pale face and shock of black hair suggest a mask from Noh, his plain white robes enhance his ghostly appearance, and the bamboo stick he waves in front of him suggests his mental state and recalls pre-modern shamanistic rituals for the invocation of spirits.[1]

Sanshirō Sugata Part II foregrounds madness, illness, and death—a curious choice for a sequel to a popular action film, but a choice that made sense in the disintegrating Japan of 1945. In place of the coiled power that he exuded in the first film, Gennosuke now has a wracking cough and a sepulchral mien. Yano's health is in decline as well. When the younger, deranged Higaki siblings beat young Shūdōkan students bloody in alleyway ambushes, even the hero succumbs to darkness. Sanshirō glumly drinks *sake* in the *dōjō*, a violation of Yano's rules, and he collapses in a corner as night engulfs the practice room.

Noh plays signify madness with *kuruizasa*, sprays of bamboo like the one seen here in a production of *Miidera* (photograph © Toshiro Morita, provided by www.the-noh.com).

He and Sayo, whose courtship the first film depicted in an idyllic montage, have just one outing together this time, and that is to visit the grave of Sayo's father. The mood of the film is bleak.

Still, nothing can stop Sanshirō from doing what an action hero must do. He fights Lister at the American embassy and silences the American sailors in the crowd by winning handily. He also agrees to fight the Higaki brothers, but has to resign his post at the *dōjō* in the process. In later years Kurosawa became adept at simulating weather in controlled environments, but for *Sanshirō Sugata Part II* he took his cast, crew, and equipment into an actual blizzard for the climactic fight scene, much to the resentment of star Fujita Susumu who had to stand barefoot in deep snowdrifts. Kurosawa had difficulties of his own with the shoot. Due to war rationing, heavy damage to Japan's factories, and an American naval blockade that prevented the import of goods, the Tōhō studio could only provide him with poor-quality, recycled fragments of film for his cameras. Reportedly, when Kurosawa went to edit the film, he could barely make out what his cast and crew endured so much to produce. The final cut runs only 83 minutes, making *Sanshirō Sugata Part II* one of the shortest Kurosawa films.[2]

Sanshirō defeats the Higaki brothers, and after the fight a recuperating Tesshin says to Genzaburō, "We lost." Genzaburō repeats it with a smile: "We lost." A weight lifts from their shoulders and Genzaburō's madness passes. Sanshirō, smiling widely, looks ahead to a new day. Production on the film wrapped amidst electrical blackouts and air raids, and Tōhō delivered the finished film to the handful of theaters in the country still standing.

Meanwhile, the world waited for Japan's leaders to turn to one another and make the same admission: "We lost." But their madness had not yet run its course, and it would not until Kurosawa's next film was halfway through production.

PART TWO

The Occupation Years

CHAPTER 4

The Men Who Tread on the Tiger's Tail

After leading the Japanese fleet in the surprise attack on the U.S. naval base at Pearl Harbor in December 1941, Admiral Yamamoto Isoroku probably did not say "We have awakened a sleeping dragon." The 1970 war movie *Tora! Tora! Tora!*, a Japanese/American coproduction, quotes him as saying it, and the line stuck in history buffs' imaginations. It is a good line, and since Yamamoto was killed in action in 1943 he could not disown it, but there is no evidence that he ever uttered it.

"The men who tread on the tiger's tail" conjures a similar image of a rash action that provokes a ferocious response. Kurosawa wrote the movie by that title (*Tora no o o fumu otokotachi*) in 1945 during a feverish session in which he penned the entire script in a single day. It was an adaptation of an existing work: the 19th-century kabuki play *Kajinchō*, which itself was based on a 15th-century Noh play titled *Ataka*. When Japanese censors accused Kurosawa of butchering the beloved kabuki play, the young director pushed back and exposed their ignorance of the play's long history. One young censor persisted in calling Kurosawa's script "meaningless," at which point the young director shot back, "If a meaningless person says something is meaningless, that's probably proof that it isn't."[1]

Kurosawa could afford to be so bold because the war was finally at an end. Japan surrendered after what Japanese historians call the "twin shocks"—the atomic bomb that destroyed much of Hiroshima on August 6, and the Soviet declaration of war on Japan two days later. In the final land battle of World War II, Soviet troops poured into Japan's northernmost territories, seizing several islands off the coast of Hokkaido. Japan and Russia would argue about the ownership of these islands into the 21st century. The Americans dropped their next atomic bomb on the city of Nagasaki on August 9, which only increased the urgency for Emperor Hirohito to issue a surrender statement, which he did on August 15 through diplomatic channels and in a prerecorded radio broadcast addressed to the Japanese people. Some who heard it stopped what they were doing, left their workplaces, and spent hours or days in numb astonishment. Others felt a deep sense of relief tempered with anxiety about the future. "We didn't show it outwardly, but underneath we were happy," one woman told a Japanese documentarian years later. "We were happy the war was over, but we did not know what would come next." Many people had lost family members, houses, or businesses in the war. They had endured food shortages and the trauma of air raids. Japan had fought nonstop for eight years, and the government had always said that surrender was not an option. Now it was a fact, and nobody knew what it would mean.[2]

The Japanese government disbanded. General Anami, who resisted surrender until the end, committed *seppuku*, ritual suicide. A few months later Prince Konoe, who had pushed for peace but still faced war crime charges, killed himself with cyanide. Former Prime Minister Tōjō shot himself in the chest when American troops came to his door to arrest him, but doctors saved his life so that he could be put on trial and executed.

The new occupiers were surprised, though, that ordinary people greeted them graciously. American propaganda had imagined Japanese men, women, and children fighting to the death, but when occupation soldiers entered Japanese towns they found themselves politely declining as starving locals offered up what little food they had. The Japanese were equally struck when the Americans did not loot or pillage as wartime leaders had predicted. The foreign soldiers "always carried chocolate, soap, and such things" to hand out, remembered a woman who was 15 at the time of surrender. The head of the occupation, General Douglas MacArthur, soon acquired the nickname "blue-eyed *shōgun*," and during his six years in Japan he received a torrent of gifts and well-wishing letters from all over the country. From occupation headquarters to rural villages across the nation, American and Japanese citizens laid the foundation for a strong postwar partnership.[3]

At the Tōhō movie studio, too, international relationships were budding. Production on *The Men Who Tread on the Tiger's Tail* paused when the emperor announced the surrender, then resumed under the new regime. The famous American director John Ford visited Tōhō towards the end of production. Usually a director of Hollywood westerns, Ford spent the war attached to the U.S. Navy making documentaries like *The Battle of Midway* (1942) and propaganda films like *December 7th* (1943). Ford and Kurosawa became great admirers of each other's work, and westerns and *jidaigeki* would borrow much from each other in the postwar decades. British director Michael Powell, who made several films about the British war experience, visited Tōhō not long after Ford. Kurosawa screened *The Men Who Tread on the Tiger's Tail* for Powell and was pleased when the Englishman said repeatedly that it was "wonderful."[4]

Unfortunately for Kurosawa, the end of the war did not mean the end of government oversight of the film industry. The Civil Information and Education section of MacArthur's occupation headquarters included a group of American movie censors, and they did not care what Michael Powell or even John Ford thought about Japanese movies. They cared about what was in them, and *jidaigeki* like *The Men Who Tread on the Tiger's Tail* contained things that troubled them very much.

The first mission of the American occupation of Japan was to make sure that Japan would never go to war again. Even before the fighting ended, the American government's "Far East" specialists brainstormed ways to eradicate "nationalism," "militarism," and "feudalism" from Japanese minds. America's Japan experts, including many who had lived in Japan before the war, believed that these concepts were deeply embedded in Japanese culture and might lead to another war in the future unless "modern," "democratic" ideas could take their place.

General Douglas MacArthur, Supreme Commander for the Allied Powers and top-ranking official in occupied Japan from 1945 to 1951, meets with Emperor Hirohito in September 1945 (photograph by U.S. Army photographer Lt. Gaetano Faillace).

In order to stop the "dissemination of Japanese militaristic and ultra-nationalistic ideology and propaganda in any form," MacArthur's orders from the Pentagon read, his headquarters should censor Japanese "civilian communications including the mails, wireless, radio, telephone, telegraph and cables, films and press." In November 1945 MacArthur's Civil Information and Education staff published a list of thirteen subjects and themes that Japanese films could not endorse. They were:

1. Militarism
2. Revenge
3. Nationalism
4. Anti-foreignism
5. Historical inaccuracy
6. Racism and religious discrimination
7. Feudalism
8. Suicide
9. Mistreatment of women
10. Violence and "evil"
11. Anti-democracy
12. Mistreatment of children
13. Anything contrary to occupation policy

A film could not be released to the public unless MacArthur's censors gave it a certificate of approval. The prohibition on feudalism especially affected movies set in the past; a film about the samurai caste and their medieval battles, for example, was intrinsically feudal and could hardly avoid touching on prohibited themes. Even if a movie's intent was to criticize the political and social order of the past, American censors might not see it that way, and a studio could lose a lot of money if it produced a film that failed to receive a certificate. As a result, Japanese studios produced very few *jidaigeki* during the American occupation.[5]

The Men Who Tread on the Tiger's Tail stood no chance of approval in this environment. Kurosawa believed that the movie never received a proper review because the Japanese censors, who hated it, did not properly forward it to the American censors, but ultimately its content was just too problematic for the moment. In the first place, its production began under Japan's wartime government, so it carried the taint of militarism and nationalism. Secondly, its heroes are a feudal lord and his loyal samurai. Third, one of the samurai honorably attempts to commit ritual suicide. Fourth, the story is associated with a famous kabuki play—almost all kabuki plays contain "feudal" themes, and the Americans banned kabuki performances early in the occupation. Kurosawa would later say that it was easier to work with American censors than the wartime Japanese ones, but *The Men Who Tread on the Tiger's Tail* fell victim to the transition. Before production even wrapped, the director learned that the American censors would not approve the movie for release. Luckily the film was not destroyed, and years later it finally became available to the public.[6]

The story takes place in the late 1100s and is based on true events. A general named Minamoto no Yoshitsune (Nishina Tadayoshi) and a small group of samurai flee the capital after Yoshitsune falls out of favor with his brother, the *shōgun*. They disguise themselves as wandering monks in order to make it past the *shōgun*'s border guards and reach friendly territory. The general's top samurai, Benkei (Ōkōchi Denjirō), goes to extraordinary lengths to maintain the deception when a border guard holds them for questioning. The heart of the story is the ingenuity and loyalty that Benkei exhibits while saving his master's life.

Unseen singer-narrators explain the movie's premise, punctuate its action, and describe characters' motivations—a useful feature when characters hide their feelings behind disguises and pretenses. The idea of hiding one's feelings and changing one's attitude to suit different circumstances is relatable for Japanese audiences, who have specific words for the phenomenon: *honne* are one's innermost thoughts, and *tatemae* is the façade that one presents to the world for the sake of propriety and to increase group harmony. The play about Benkei's legendary deception is one of many examples of Japanese art involving the *honne-tatemae* distinction. Understood in these terms, the American occupation's intense focus on changing the way Japanese people thought was nothing less than an attempt to change the nation's collective *honne*. American authorities worried quite a bit that Japan would demilitarize and democratize in name only, changing its *tatemae* without altering its *honne*.

Changing Japan's government and dismantling its military were surface-level changes, but enforcing strict new standards on the nation's entertainment was a way to try to reach people's souls.

Kurosawa, too, was interested in reaching audiences as directly as he could. His script invents a character who is not in the original plays, but who functions in the movie as an audience surrogate: a simple porter (Enomoto Kennichi) who carries Yoshitsune's baggage. At first the porter appears to be a fool. He does not recognize the fugitives despite many clues, and in his ignorance he mocks Yoshitsune and Benkei to their faces. When he realizes his mistake, however, he proves surprisingly canny. The porter ingrati-

Kabuki actor Ichikawa Ennosuke II in a production of *Kajinchō,* **1951 (from** *Asahi Graph* **1951 New Year Issue).**

ates himself to the samurai with smiling self-deprecation and constructive criticism sugarcoated in winsome cheer. He is jovial and irreverent but a shrewd survivor and quick improviser. In Kurosawa's version of the story, the porter deserves almost as much credit for the group's escape as Benkei. The idea to disguise Yoshitsune as a porter for the "monks" comes from him, and he donates his own spare clothes to the cause.

The presence of a low-class character among the high and mighty helps anchor the story in familiar ground, and the porter is free to express thoughts that proper samurai leave unsaid. The most dramatic instances of this occur near the end. To maintain their deception at the checkpoint, Benkei beats his "porter," actually his lord Yoshitsune, with a stick. The border guard (Fujita Susumu) lets them go, but once they reach safety Benkei offers to commit *seppuku*. An honorable samurai cannot strike his lord and go on as if nothing happened, even if he had a good reason. The benevolent Yoshitsune forgives the sin, and the samurai all choke back their emotions. The warriors keep their emotions in check, but the porter's comical expressions show extremes of despair and exhilaration at every plot twist. He is the *honne* to the warriors' *tatemae*. Each of Kurosawa's later *jidaigeki*, and many of his *gendaigeki* as well, would use characters of different castes and classes to achieve something similar to this dynamic. His stories play out in three-dimensional social worlds, allowing him to explore events and themes from multiple perspectives.

During the Meiji, Taishō, and early Shōwa *jidai*, a patriotic legend circulated in Japan that further modified the well-known story of Yoshitsune's escape. The real Yoshitsune died when the lord he took shelter with in the north betrayed him, but according to turn-of-the-century mythmakers he not only escaped his brother's forces but left Japan entirely. Yoshitsune, they claimed, arrived in Mongolia and took a new identity: Genghis Khan. This attempt to claim Asia's most famous warrior for Japan was entirely spurious, historically, but it was symptomatic of the ultranationalism of the prewar and wartime years.[7]

By the time he made *The Men Who Tread on the Tiger's Tail*, Kurosawa had amassed a stable of Tōhō-affiliated actors. Ōkōchi Denjirō looks younger and fitter as Benkei than he did as Yano in the *Sanshirō Sugata* movies, but he has the same dignified bearing. Fujita Susumu is more restrained as the border guard than as Sanshirō, but his guileless face makes even the antagonist likable. Mori Masayuki makes his second of five appearances for the director, and Shimura Takashi his fourth of 21; both appear as samurai in Yoshitsune's retinue. Conditions in Japan and its film industry were changing daily in 1945, but these men helped create continuity between Kurosawa's wartime movies and his postwar career.

Kurosawa learned to tread more carefully after MacArthur's censors put his first samurai movie on the shelf. It was a setback, but a temporary one. The director and his team quickly adapted to Japan's new reality, and over the next few years Kurosawa would emerge as one of the nation's most topical storytellers. For the foreseeable future, since he could not tell stories about Japan's past, he tackled the controversies of its present.

CHAPTER 5

No Regrets for Our Youth

In October 1945 General MacArthur ordered the release of about three thousand political prisoners, including nearly eight hundred Japanese communists. The wartime government, which feared communist revolution as much as American bombs, had imprisoned them for the crime of disagreeing with national policy. The occupation authorities, by and large, were not sympathetic to communist ideology, and Japanese leftists found much to disagree with about American policy. Yet the Americans insisted on free speech and free elections in postwar Japan, and they released the prisoners over the objections of the imperial household and many Japanese elites. The first postwar Japanese prime minister, whose job was mainly to implement American policy and who happened to be the emperor's uncle, resigned in protest.

Japanese communist Ozaki Hotsumi did not live long enough to benefit from the clemency. In 1944 he became the only Japanese political prisoner executed for treason during the war. He was a child of the Japanese empire—his father was an administrator in occupied Taiwan—but as an adult he dedicated himself to resisting his government's abuses. Ozaki became a communist sympathizer after the Great Kantō Earthquake of 1923. In the aftermath of that terrible quake, one of the worst in history, rumors spread that Korean laborers were starting fires and looting stores. A great many Koreans lived and worked in Japan with no citizenship rights and little economic power, and they endured discrimination from their Japanese neighbors. After the earthquake, right-wing Japanese vigilantes and police killed thousands of Koreans in retaliation for their supposed crimes. Ozaki observed that the Japanese government did little to protect the Korean community or to bring their attackers to justice, and he joined Japanese socialists in criticizing this outburst of violent, racist nationalism. A decade later, while working as a journalist in China, Ozaki witnessed Japanese soldiers commit war crimes. During his stay in China he met a Soviet intelligence agent named Richard Sorge. In the late 1930s Ozaki got a job in the Japanese government and began passing state secrets to Sorge; he never officially joined the Japanese Communist Party, which would have prevented him from working for the government. The intelligence Ozaki provided helped Moscow understand Japan's strategic thinking on the eve of war. In the autumn of 1941 the Japanese secret police—the Kempeitai—cracked Sorge's spy network and arrested both Sorge and Ozaki. The Soviet Union refused to admit its connection to the spies or agree to a prisoner exchange, so the Kempeitai executed Sorge and Ozaki by hanging on November 7, 1944.

Spies seldom become best-selling authors, especially after they're dead, but that's exactly what happened to Ozaki. During his years in prison he wrote hundreds of letters to his wife Eiko and their daughter Yōko in which he outlined his life philosophy and expressed his deep feelings for them, for Japan, and for the human race. The letters survived the war, and in 1946 a women's magazine editor published them under the title *Love is Like a Shower of Stars* (*Aijō wa furu hoshi no gotoku*) with a foreword by Eiko. Ozaki's poetic, intimate correspondence with his wife and daughter was eminently readable, and the book generated a surge of interest in his life and philosophy.

Japan's Communist Party, emboldened by the release of political prisoners, tried to claim Ozaki as one of their own, but it wasn't the dead man's leftist beliefs or his service to the U.S.S.R. that made his letters a sensation. It was the idea—promoted by the publisher and the Ozaki family, and supported by the idealistic and humanistic content of the letters themselves—that Ozaki had a deeper and more authentic love for his country than the militarists who executed him. "I have lived feeling deep human love everywhere," he wrote. In his imprisonment he turned to Zen Buddhism for comfort. He did not write about Marxist concepts like class struggle or revolution, but instead wrote on peace, love, and humanity. These fit in well with liberal, democratic values that Americans sought to cultivate in postwar Japan. Ozaki was a timely martyr for the new Japan, a posthumous champion of the new progressive creed, and Japanese readers embraced the dead man as a symbol of their own hopes for the future. Ozaki's connection to communism and his work as a spy were beside the point for most readers.[1]

Kurosawa contributed to the posthumous repatriation of Ozaki and the reemergence of Japanese liberalism by basing his fifth film on Ozaki's life. *No Regrets for Our Youth* (*Waga seishun ni kuinashi*) is not, however, a work of biography or hagiography. The script by Kurosawa, Matsuzaki Keiji, and Hisaita Eijirō keeps the historical Ozaki at a distance by renaming him Noge, situating him in a community of likeminded Japanese liberals, and making his love interest the focus of the story. The central figure of *No Regrets for Our Youth*, a willful and fickle young woman named Yukie, is not so much a parallel for Ozaki's widow Eiko as a personification of the spirit of Japan. Her tumultuous relationship with Noge is a metaphor for how Japan abandoned and then rediscovered its humanist soul.

A dreamlike opening in a forest outside Kyoto introduces the film's time period, elegiac tone, and a love triangle that motivates the action. Yukie (Hara Setsuko), her well-heeled parents, and a group of male university students are on an outing in the wooded hills that ring Japan's former capital city. In a nearly wordless sequence, Yukie and the boys take a different trail from her parents and come to a swollen stream. Two of the young men, the smiling and near-sighted Noge (Fujita Susumu) and the somber Itokawa (Kōno Akitake), offer to help Yukie leap across. When she hesitates over which boy's hand to take, Noge strides to her, picks her up, and carries her to the other side. Itokawa darkens, but Yukie playfully smiles at him to indicate that her mind is not made up as to which suitor she favors.

The young party continues up the hillside, and nostalgic music plays as they gaze down on the bell tower of Kyoto University far below. Moved by the sight, one young man rises and describes the school in grandiloquent terms: "Academy of freedom, resplendent tower of learning, Mecca of knowledge." He strikes a dramatic pose for humorous effect. The students' fun is interrupted by the sound of gunfire from soldiers training nearby, and Noge grimly reminds his friends that their beloved university has been under pressure from "fascists" ever since the Manchurian Incident in September 1931.

The Manchurian Incident was the lie that led to the Japanese invasion of China. Small detachments from the Japanese army were in Manchuria, in northern China, guarding a Japanese-owned railway. The railway itself had belonged to Russia until Japan's victory in the 1905 Russo-Japanese war. By 1931, the Japanese army was a breeding ground for a right-wing ideology that insisted on Japan's superiority to its Asian neighbors. The military wanted to establish a Japanese empire in Asia in order to spread its culture, acquire valuable natural resources, and open new opportunities for Japanese farmers and businesses suffering due to the global economic depression. In order to create a pretext for invading China, young army officers sabotaged their own

Ozaki Hotsumi (c. 1930s) spied on behalf of the Soviet Union but became a posthumous icon of humanism in early postwar Japan (*Mainichi Shimbun*).

rail line and blamed it on Chinese insurgents. The Japanese government allowed the army to seize all of Manchuria, which they renamed Manchukuo, and govern it as a Japanese puppet state. During its fourteen-year existence from 1931 to 1945, Manchukuo was a major destination for Japanese investors and Japanese farmers seeking new land. The Soviet Union grew worried about the influx of Japanese troops and civilians to this new nation on its southeastern frontier, and the intelligence that Ozaki and Sorge provided Moscow informed the Soviets' troop deployment strategy along the Manchukuo border.

Noge, Ozaki's movie doppelganger, believes that the rising tide of Japanese nationalism is dangerous, but Yukie finds the sound of gunfire thrilling. She runs to the other side of the hill to get a glimpse of the soldiers. There is a stark contrast between the flirty, fresh-faced youth on a picnic lark and the deadly war games going on around them, but Yukie is drawn to the drama of war and disregards the conscientious doomsaying of the academic who wants her heart.

Noge's worst fears come true when the militarist government cracks down on academic freedom and Yukie's father (Ōkōchi Denjirō) loses his professorship at the university. Other professors threaten to resign in protest, and student groups organize demonstrations that the government and newspapers call "riots." Yet even in the privacy of her family home, Yukie is unwilling to criticize the government. When Noge calls Japan's leaders fascists and militarists, Yukie fidgets uncomfortably and averts her gaze. She believes that her father is innocent of wrongdoing, but she insists that she hates radicals. "My father is a liberal, not a Red," she says, drawing a distinction between the progressive, internationalist, humanist thinkers who thrived during the recent Taishō *jidai* and the socialists and communists whom the government sent to prison in the early Shōwa *jidai*. Noge knows that fascists make no such distinction, but Yukie believes that the government will soon correct its mistake. In the meantime she is determined to prove herself a loyal citizen.

Kurosawa based this sequence on the real-life "Takigawa Incident" of 1933. In that year, a Kyoto University law professor named Takigawa lost his job when the Minister of Education accused him of teaching Marxist philosophy. At issue was a lecture Takigawa delivered in which he said that social circumstances like poverty contributed to criminal behavior. This theory was an established part of early 20th-century progressivism, and was not Marxist *per se*, but the political climate of the early 1930s was increasingly hostile to social reformers and intellectuals. As tensions with the Soviet Union rose after the Manchurian Incident, Japanese nationalists lumped their domestic critics in with their foreign enemies; they were all "Reds," and therefore enemies of the state. The professors and students who rallied to Takigawa's defense understood that a dangerous new era was beginning, since "this was the first instance in which government suppression [of thought] was aimed at liberal, rather than Marxist, intellectuals."[2]

Of course, some Japanese intellectuals did use Marxist language. They read Marx, Lenin, and their philosophical antecedent Hegel, and they seized on the theory of "internal contradictions" that emerged from this trio's writings. According to this theory, unrestrained capitalism created wide wealth gaps amidst overall economic growth, and capitalist governments responded to this problem by seeking new overseas markets through imperialism. The theory seemed particularly applicable to Japan, whose rural areas continued to lag behind urban centers despite nearly 70 years of growth and modernization since the start of the Meiji *jidai*. When the depression of the 1930s brought this contradiction into focus and made a solution more urgent, the government pursued new land and new markets in places like Manchuria to stimulate growth.

Yukie is a mass of "internal contradictions" in a more poetic sense. At the very moment Noge uses the term, Yukie is torn by conflicting impulses. She wants to defend her father without offending the government, and she craves the fawning love of Itokawa despite harboring feelings for the more assertive Noge. Hara Setsuko, who was only 25 years old during production but had over 10 years of film acting experience already, displays impressive range in a long, quiet close-up that solidifies the three principals' personalities. When Noge leaves to attend a rally, Yukie commands Itokawa to kneel before her, and her face registers both satisfaction and disgust when he does so. Throughout the film Itokawa plays the part of obedient sycophant while Noge represents conscientious dissent, and Yukie vacillates between the two.

Several years pass. Yukie's father fails to regain his professorship, Noge drops out in protest and joins a leftist movement, and Itokawa stays in school and becomes a public prosecutor. Like the real-life Ozaki, Noge visits China and then secures a job at a Tokyo think tank that gives him access to sensitive information. Yukie also moves to Tokyo for work. She considers marrying Itokawa, whose position offers stability and security, but in her heart she still desires Noge despite his dangerous political beliefs. She warns Noge that if he uses his position to do anything illicit, Itokawa will find out and report it to the authorities. Noge admits to Yukie that he is secretly working against the government, but he assures her that he understands the risks.

Like the publisher of Ozaki's letters, Kurosawa emphasizes the romantic dimension of his characters' lives. Yukie and Noge eventually pledge to live together "with no regrets," and their relationship deepens in a series of nostalgic vignettes tinged with sadness about what is to come. Yukie sews Noge a marriage *kimono* that she knows he might never wear. They picnic together and reminisce about their youth in Kyoto. They go to a cinema, but Yukie cries silently while the rest of the audience laughs. Because of the nature of Noge's work, Yukie fears that their life together will be short. Yukie and Noge are closer than the real-life Ozakis, whose marriage suffered because of Hotsumi's unfaithfulness to Eiko. Unlike Yuki, Eiko apparently did not know about her husband's spying until his arrest, after which the two grew closer thanks to their heartfelt exchange of letters. In Kurosawa's telling, Yukie's love overcomes her reluctance about Noge's politics, and she grows to understand and support his work.

Noge mirrors the popular image of Ozaki as a patriotic, loving martyr. He predicts that "in ten years, the Japanese people will thank us for what we are doing." He shows Yukie a picture of his parents, from whom he is estranged. They are salt-of-the-earth farmers who disapprove of his work, but he always keeps their wellbeing in mind as he strives to redress the country's ills. Noge's devotion to his parents shows his filial piety and confirms that his actions are motivated by love, not dogma. The same was, apparently, true of Ozaki, even in the opinion of the judge who sentenced him to death. After Noge's own inevitable arrest and death, Kurosawa's story moves beyond the realm of fictionalized biography. It does not merely rehash the mistakes of the past, but uses the transformation of Yukie to engage with the question of Japan's future.

Films about women had special significance during the occupation. The American rulers of Japan believed that Japanese women had an important role to play in the postwar era. MacArthur's staff included a 22-year-old naturalized American woman named Beate Sirota, who authored an equal rights clause for the new Japanese constitution prohibiting discrimination based on sex. Sirota and her colleagues believed that Japanese women were among the chief victims of the nation's "feudal" mentality. The Americans viewed the subordination of women in Japanese life—women did the bulk of the housework and could not vote or run for office—as a characteristically Japanese flaw, though women in the United States had had had the vote for barely a generation and also experienced unequal treatment and underrepresentation in a variety of fields. Japanese women were not helpless, of course; during the Taishō *jidai* there were many "modern," independent women who challenged prevailing norms, and they had foremothers throughout history (see Chapter 2). Still, occupation officials made effective use of their power to increase gender

Some of the first women elected to Japanese government, 1946. Among these women were Katō Shizue, Kōro Mitsu, Wasaki Haru, Yamashita Tsune, Kondō Tsuruyo, and Ōishi Yoshie (Wikimedia Commons).

equality by fiat. In 1946 Japanese women voted for the first time, and their votes helped put 39 women in office. Occupation policies also made it easier for women to inherit property and divorce their husbands. Women's organizations, many of which started in the prewar years, flourished with newly-recruited university students, housewives, and professional women. Japanese women did not just passively receive the Americans' "revolution from above" (*okurareta kakumei*), but took full advantage of their new legal freedoms to demand wage increases, more equitable representation in government, and greater social equality.[3]

In the last act of *No Regrets for Our Youth* Yukie becomes an avatar of liberated Japanese women. Her father and Noge remind audiences that liberal humanists existed in Japan before and during the war, but Yukie herself belongs firmly to the postwar moment. She responds to Noge's death not by retreating into widowhood or returning to her parents' house, but by continuing the fight. Like many women in Japan she moves in with her in-laws, who at first cannot show their faces in public due to Noge's infamy. Yukie, though, dares to go out into the village and the fields, braving the neighbors' hateful stares. A lengthy montage depicts her carrying heavy loads of kindling for fuel, readying the wet field for rice planting, and working alongside Noge's mother to place seedlings in the soaked mud. Other villagers destroy the crops, but Yukie does not give up, and her determination inspires Noge's parents to work harder as well.

Kurosawa does not specify whether Noge's parents are independent farmers or tenants who rent their fields, but this was a crucial distinction in the occupation. American policymakers believed that democracy worked best when people owned their own property; otherwise, landlords might pressure their tenants to vote for their preferred political candidates. Despite the prevalence of sharecropping in large parts of the United States, especially in the south where descendants of enslaved people worked under exploitative tenancy agreements, the Americans who ruled Japan agreed that small, family-run farms were the ideal basis for a free society. Moreover, by redistributing farmland before communist organizers could attempt the same thing, the Americans helped ensure that the Japanese Communist Party never gained a strong foothold in the countryside. In an ambitious land reform program carried out by village-level committees, the United States government paid Japanese landlords nominal amounts for their agricultural land and then sold it to tenant farmers at very low prices. High postwar inflation meant that these cash transactions were worth far less than the land itself, so the program amounted to a virtual giveaway of most of Japan's farmland. General MacArthur took great personal pride in this redistribution of rural wealth, which was one of the occupation's most successful and popular achievements.[4]

In *No Regrets for Our Youth* Yukie describes herself as "the shining light of the village cultural movement," terminology that refers to a whole range of improvements in rural areas. Yukie decides to stay with the Noge family after the war and keep working to improve the lives of Japanese farmers, "especially the women." Her father, meanwhile, returns to his position at Kyoto University. His brand of liberalism is once again welcome in Japan, and in a triumphant speech to students and faculty he praises the martyred Noge for his human compassion and commitment to freedom. *No Regrets for Our Youth* perfectly encapsulates Japanese citizens' posthumous rehabilitation of Ozaki and the Americans' reformist zeal regarding women and rice-roots change.

Kurosawa's first occupation-era film paints an optimistic picture of the future, but if American censors expected him to be a cheerleader for their regime, they would soon be sorely disappointed. Kurosawa's next movie, made the following year, proved far less sanguine about actual conditions in defeated Japan.

Chapter 6

One Wonderful Sunday

Numbers are a poor reflection of human suffering, but one telling statistic is that over 50 percent of people in Japan were clinically malnourished at the time of the surrender in August 1945. The previous year, 46 percent of all "economic crimes" in and around the city of Osaka involved food; a common crime was the theft of grains and produce. Japanese soldiers in the field fared no better than their families and friends back home, often emerging from their last bastions in the Pacific as "living skeletons." Japanese factories that withstood the bombing raids saw production decrease when workers disappeared to scavenge for food and fell ill due to insufficient calorie intake. Ersatz "foods" like acorns, peanut shells, orange peels, and sawdust mixed with flour entered the Japanese diet near the end of the war as American naval patrols blockaded the country and sank incoming supply ships. Japanese children caught frogs and grasshoppers to eat, but months or years of poor nutrition meant that those who grew up during the war were physically smaller than kids who grew up in the Taishō *jidai*.[1]

Finding food remained an urgent task in the early occupation period. Well over a thousand people in urban areas died of starvation between August and December 1945. General MacArthur's headquarters requisitioned large amounts of "wheat, flour, corn, legumes, sugar," and "small quantities of rice, powdered milk, and tinned goods such as corned beef" from American suppliers. Japanese farmers had to sell a certain amount of their produce directly to the government so that officials could distribute food in areas that had none. Nearly everything was subject to strict rationing. The maximum amount of food that a person could legally receive from the government contained less than half the calories an active adult needed to survive. To make up the difference, people sold their most precious possessions and went to the black market, where they paid up to thirty times the official price for rice. Cash-strapped farmers could hardly refuse to sell to black market traders, including "evil" middlemen who jacked up prices.

In the first few years of the occupation, virtually everybody took part in the black market. The fate of those who did not was grimly illustrated by a young judge named Yamaguchi Yoshitada, who was responsible for sentencing food thieves to prison. In 1946 he assuaged his guilty conscience by eating nothing that came from the black market. Though he restricted himself to his allotted rations, he let his wife

49

and children continue to eat black market food. He died in October 1947 at the age of 33. The failure to adequately feed the Japanese population was a grievous shortcoming on the Americans' part, but the food they did provide was like "a merciful rain during a drought" according to a contemporary Japanese chronicler.[2]

Another acute crisis was the housing shortage. Around 9 million people out of a total population of 72 million were homeless at the end of the war. This number included many thousands of orphaned children and disabled war veterans. With so many above-ground structures in ruins, homeless individuals and families crowded into subway stations for shelter. Hundreds died of cold and hunger during the occupation's first two winters. The occupation government did even less to address homelessness than starvation. MacArthur's instructions from Washington were to reform Japan; they said nothing about rebuilding it.[3]

The newly-elected Japanese government that existed to carry out MacArthur's staff's orders paid for the construction of over ten thousand new residences, all of which went to occupation officials and American military families. These and other "war termination expenses," a euphemism for the financial cost of the occupation, took up a large share of the Japanese budget every year between 1945 and 1952. The U.S. Congress allocated millions of dollars to the occupation as well, but it spent only half as much on occupied Japan as it did on occupied Germany. Japanese citizens paid a share of everything from the living expenses of the occupiers to the costly reform programs that MacArthur's headquarters kept announcing. At the same time, the Americans forbade the Japanese government from distributing veterans' benefits to ex-soldiers or their dependents. Since many homeless people were veterans or the widows and orphans of veterans, this prohibition exacerbated an already severe problem.[4]

Filmmakers responded to Japan's humanitarian crisis when government officials could not or would not. Like the "neorealist" filmmakers of postwar Italy, where intense fighting in the last years of the war created many of the same problems that Japan now faced, Kurosawa and his colleagues set stories of extreme poverty against backdrops of rubble and dilapidation. Kurosawa later remarked that during the occupation he wanted to make "such a film as *Bicycle Thieves*," the most famous of the Italian neorealist movies. In addition to Kurosawa's work in this period, Ozu's *Record of a Tenement Gentleman* (*Nagaya shinshiroku*, 1947) and *A Hen in the Wind* (*Kaze no naka no mendori*, 1948) stem from the same impulse. Such bleak movies from the early occupation are usually referred to as *shoshimin eiga*, "lower-class urban people movies," but that term is overly broad and encompasses many prewar movies as well. The stories filmmakers told in the late 1940s were about the specific miseries of that period, and they comprise a subgenre unto themselves—a kind of Japanese neorealism centering on the harsh, new realities of the postwar era.[5]

In *No Regrets for Our Youth* Kurosawa expressed optimism about the return of liberalism to Japan and the prospects of great changes to come (see Chapter 5), but as the occupation wore on the road to recovery looked longer and more uncertain.

A Tokyo train station with bomb damage, 1945 (photograph by Nakamura Rikkō).

Jidaigeki were still off-limits under American censorship rules, and to make an honest *gendaigeki* meant addressing the serious problems that existed under American leadership. MacArthur's censors examined each script to ensure that films did not challenge American authority or violate specific rules (see Chapter 4), but for films to depict problems like hunger, homelessness, and crime in a general way was fair game.

One Wonderful Sunday (*Subarashiki nichiyōbi*) opens with a sight that is familiar in Japan even today: a Tokyo commuter train so crowded that passengers have to squeeze up against the windows. Trains have been important features of Japan cities since the Meiji *jidai*, and Tokyoites' reliance on mass transit continued unabated through war and occupation. Extreme crowding increased during the occupation due to wartime bomb damage that reduced the number of operable lines. In December 1945 an infant died of suffocation on a car filled well over capacity. Yet trains remained indispensable to people who traveled the breadth of the city in pursuit of work, food, and shelter. They even provided a form of entertainment; a game among children who grew up in the occupation was play-acting as commuters jostling each other in an imaginary train car.[6]

As a train pulls into a station in the opening scene of *One Wonderful Sunday*, a young man named Yuzo (Numasaki Isao) eyes a discarded cigarette butt on the concrete floor of the station and furtively picks it up as his fiancée Masako (Nakakita

Chieko) disembarks. She sees him do it, and both of them are embarrassed for a moment. Money is in short supply for Yuzo, who dejectedly tells Masako that he has only fifteen yen to spend on their weekly date. Shrugging it off, Masako cheerfully tells him that she has twenty yen. Yuzo balks at the idea of using her money to pay for the date, but after some cajoling he agrees to go out for a "35-yen Sunday."

The lovers' first conversation is about money, and their second is about shelter. Masako sees an advertisement for 100,000-yen prefabricated houses and convinces Yuzo to tour a full-size display model. To Yuzo the idea of buying a house is a useless pipe dream, but Masako insists that they must have dreams or life would be too sad. Standing in a house they cannot afford, though, reminds Yuzo of their current living arrangements, which give the couple little opportunity for privacy. Yuzo lives in a one-room apartment with a friend, and Masako lives in a house with 16 other people. The model home is temporarily unoccupied, and once inside Yuzo wants to seize the opportunity for sex. Masako modestly retreats from him, and another couple soon arrives to tour the tiny home. From them Yuzo and Masako learn about a nearby apartment renting for cheap, so they decide to check it out.

The manager of the apartment is disarmingly honest about its low quality. To begin with, its size is only six *tatami* mats. Japanese rooms are measured in *tatami*, rectangular straw mats about 180 centimeters long and 90 centimeters wide. Six of them fill an apartment 9 feet by 18 feet. In addition to its small size, the manager says that the apartment has no view, no natural light, and unhealthy air that will give its tenants rheumatism in the winter and typhoid in the summer. He also informs Yuzo and Masako that the landlord is a cruel man who will evict them if they miss a payment. Each month's 600-yen rent must be paid in "new yen," not prewar currency, and the deposit is 2000 yen. Yuzo and Masako sadly realize that they cannot afford even this wretched apartment.

The next part of Yuzo and Masako's 35-yen date involves baseball, the American pastime that came to Japan in 1870s and went professional in the 1920s. Japan's wartime government could never stamp out the foreign sport's popularity, but fascists did target it at times. In 1934, sword-wielding nationalists tried to assassinate a Japanese business mogul who invited an American all-star team to play in Japan; the Americans had consistently beaten their Japanese competition in front of sell-out crowds. After the attack on Pearl Harbor, a professional player born in Hawai'i to Japanese parents had to renounce his American citizenship in order to continue playing in Japan. Originally Japanese baseball players and fans used English words like "strike" and "ball," but during the war they replaced them with Japanese equivalents. After the war, American censors encouraged Japanese movie studios to include baseball in their films, hoping that the popularity of the American sport would translate to support for occupation policies. In *One Wonderful Sunday* Yuzo and Masako spot a ragtag group of boys playing baseball in an abandoned lot. Shouting English terms like "play ball," the kids' high spirits stand in juxtaposition to their ruined surroundings; half-destroyed buildings flank the makeshift diamond. Yuzo takes a turn at bat, but when he connects he sends the ball crashing into a nearby shop selling sweet bean treats. By way of apology Yuzo spends ten yen on snacks.[7]

Casting about for something else to do with Masako, Yuzo remembers that he has a war buddy who runs a cabaret. Stylish if somewhat disreputable establishments, cabarets became popular in Japan in the Taishō *jidai*, but during the occupation their aesthetics changed. They clustered in the Asakusa neighborhood of Tokyo, formerly home to an enormous Buddhist temple that burned in the war. To draw in American soldiers, occupation-era cabarets employed tall, curvy Japanese women with "Caucasian" skin tones. The cabaret in *One Wonderful Sunday* even advertises a "Valentine's Day dance party" many years before the chocolate-giving holiday went mainstream in Japan.[8]

Baseball's popularity in Japan survived the war years. When American troops retook the Philippines in 1945 they found baseball bats and mitts that Japanese soldiers left behind (from The National Museum of the U.S. Navy, photograph by U.S. Navy photographer Lt. C.F. Waterman).

When Yuzo enters the club and asks to see the manager, the staff mistake him for a member of the *yakuza*, one of Japan's longstanding organized crime gangs. Like men from any other walk of life, gangsters served in Japan's imperial forces during World War II, though some of them resisted conforming to military discipline. In the early postwar years, when even law-abiding citizens found it necessary to engage in illegal trade to stay alive, *yakuza* gangs operated black markets and grew wealthy from the desperation of others. In *One Wonderful Sunday*, a solicitous cabaret employee respectfully guides Yuzo to a back room while Masako waits out front. The employee seats Yuzo next to a gangster in an army cap who eats and drinks at the club for free in exchange for leaving the manager alone. One of the cabaret's "hostesses"—a woman paid to drink with the male patrons, a job that still exists in

Japanese bars and karaoke parlors—stumbles drunkenly past them. Without irony, the *yakuza* remarks that it's a shame what young women do to earn a living.[9]

Yuzo and Masako know that "black marketeering counts as lawful employment these days," but they scrupulously resist ill-gotten goods. Yuzo rejects the food, beer, and money that cabaret employees offer him, and he and Masako search for more wholesome entertainment. The movie couple is unrealistically upright in their adherence to moral ideals. What little they have they share with others, like the *onigiri* (rice balls) they eat for lunch after leaving the cabaret. The law-abiding lovers give one of their few *onigiri* to a homeless orphan.

In the lightest part of the movie, Kurosawa shows footage of zoo animals while his lead actors offer sardonic commentary. Paying a yen apiece to visit the Ueno Park Zoo, the oldest zoo in Japan, Yuzo and Masako observe that the animals live better than many humans. They have comfortable enclosures and regular meals, plus, "animals don't have to deal with inflation."

Animals also mate when and where they please, Yuzo might have added. His one vice is his desire to sleep with Masako despite the fact that they are unmarried, and after they leave the zoo he pressures her to go to his one-room apartment while his roommate is away. Masako again demurs. She convinces her fiancé to attend a nearby concert instead, a performance of Schubert's "Unfinished Symphony." Before they can purchase tickets, scalpers grab the last of them and begin reselling them for a higher price. Yuzo angrily confronts the opportunists, who give him a beating. After this indignity Masako agrees to go to Yuzo's apartment, where pictures of pin-up girls decorate the walls.

Feeling more miserable than ever, Yuzo says that he is as low as "stray dog." He grabs Masako, but she still does not want to sleep with him, and she flees the apartment. The camera lingers for several minutes as Yuzo paces his room and gazes at a toy animal. The scene plays out in real time with none of the montages or time lapses that Kurosawa used in his earlier films. Neorealist movies purposefully eschewed such editorial tricks in favor of raw, unblinking depictions of life's struggles. At the end of this lonely interlude Masako returns to the apartment, seemingly resigned to having sex, but she breaks down crying as she removes her coat. Ashamed, Yuzo consoles her and no longer attempts to pressure her into physical intimacy.

One of the most experimental moments in Kurosawa's career occurs at the climax of *One Wonderful Sunday*. After leaving the apartment, Yuzo and Masako spend the last of their yen at a coffee shop that overcharges them, so for the rest of their date they must find free entertainment. As night falls they come to an empty amphitheater, and on its stage Yuzo "conducts" an invisible orchestra in an imaginary "Unfinished Symphony." At one point he falters, and Masako turns to face the camera and implores the movie audience to show their support for Yuzo.

"Breaking the fourth wall" is the logical conclusion of the neorealist effort to narrow the gap between art and life. Italian directors often achieved this by working with non-professional actors, but in *One Wonderful Sunday* Kurosawa does it by asking the audience to participate in the movie. After waiting for applause, Yuzo and Masako smile, bow, and finish the "symphony." At the end of the pantomimed performance, Yuzo and Masako kiss, something movie characters could not do under wartime Japanese censorship but that American censors actively promoted.[10]

Japanese audiences did not cooperate with Kurosawa's plan, sitting silently as Masako pleaded with them for applause. Their apparent indifference extended outside the movie theater, where most people passed by homeless veterans and families without offering more than token assistance, if any. Aversion to human suffering is found in all cultures and time periods, but a leading American historian of the occupation notes that in Japan there is "no strong tradition of responsibility toward strangers, or of unrequited philanthropy." During the occupation, one Japanese writer suggested that the absence of a collective response to humanitarian crises stemmed from a widespread deficiency of love. In the case of *One Wonderful Sunday*, audiences may have stayed silent because of the Japanese cultural aversion to public displays of emotion. Yet these big-picture explanations obscure a simpler, more practical one: in the early occupation, the daily struggle to survive left people with precious little to give others either materially or emotionally.[11]

Despite the failure of his audience participation experiment, Kurosawa had reason to consider his sixth film a success. *One Wonderful Sunday* earned him the Best Director prize at the influential *Mainichi* newspaper's second annual film awards. Kurosawa had previously received prizes for screenplays, but this was the first time he won honors for his directing efforts. And he was only just getting started.

CHAPTER 7

Drunken Angel

More than being the first postwar movie with a *yakuza* protagonist, more than the *Mainichi* Best Film award it won, more even than its commentary on the failures of the occupation government, *Drunken Angel* (*Yoidore tenshi*) is significant as the first film to unite Kurosawa with his most remarkable star. Beginning with this feature, Mifune Toshirō would appear in 16 of the director's 30 films.

Mifune's life so far had been both unusual and illustrative of the era. Before his birth in 1920, his parents emigrated from Japan to the northern Chinese city of Qingdao, which the Japanese seized at the end of World War I. Most of the people Mifune interacted with as a youth belonged to the growing community of Japanese settlers in northern China, but he did not actually see Japan until he was twenty years old. Mifune served in the Japanese military during World War II, but his assignment was unusually fortuitous; he observed the war from above, taking reconnaissance pictures from airplanes. After the war he tried to use his photography know-how to get a job as an assistant cameraman at the Tōhō studio, but Tōhō put him in front of the camera instead. In 1947 Kurosawa watched Mifune audition and was "completely overwhelmed" by the young man's animalistic fervor. It was "as frightening as watching a wounded beast trying to break loose," Kurosawa wrote.[1]

In *Drunken Angel* Kurosawa cast Mifune as the raging, reeling gangster Matsunaga. Like Mifune himself, whose early life was both uncharacteristic of the Japanese experience and deeply entwined with it, Matsunaga is both an outlier and an everyman. He is a violent criminal, but his antisocial actions take place in the context of the occupation that influenced all Japanese lives. The movie revisits the idea behind the Takigawa Incident of 1933, which Kurosawa dramatized in *No Regrets for Our Youth* (see Chapter 5), that wretched environments can contribute to people's fall from grace. The title of the movie captures this uneasy duality with its imagery of a heavenly creature corrupted by an earthly vice.

Drunken Angel's environment is as wretched as it gets. The opening credits play over a shot of a fetid, bubbling, garbage-choked pool. Tilting the camera upwards, Kurosawa reveals that this unnatural marsh is the centerpiece of an unhappy community of shiftless men and fallen women. A trio of *pan-pan* girls with permed hair and form-fitting dresses sit by the pond smoking cigarettes. *Pan-pan*, signifying prostitute, is not a Japanese word, but a term that both American and Japanese

American troops outside the Yasuura House, a brothel on Tokyo Bay, 1945 (from Yokosuka City Council).

soldiers picked up in the southern Pacific and brought to occupied Japan where new brothels and prophylactic stations catered to American troops. As the number of prostitutes rose with the support of American and Japanese officials, the word *pan-pan* became part of occupation-era vernacular. Filmmakers, cartoonists, and radio producers popularized a quasi-romantic image of the *pan-pan* girl, which distilled so much about the material and social world of the occupation into a single, recognizable figure. In *Drunken Angel*, the noxious pond and the dolled-up *pan-pan* beside it are two symptoms of the same diseased environment.

The office of Dr. Sanada (Shimura Takashi) backs up against the putrid pool, and inside its walls the doctor delivers bad news to the *yakuza* Morinaga. The bespectacled, righteous Sanada was Shimura's his first starring role for Kurosawa after playing small parts in four of the director's earlier movies. With around 80 movies under his belt and two decades of acting experience stretching back to his youth in theater companies that toured Japan and China, Shimura brings a seasoned professionalism to the screen. When Sanada diagnoses Morinaga with tuberculosis, Morinaga reacts with violent anger than showcases Mifune's intensity, and Sawada responds with the grim rectitude typical of Shimura's parts. The yin-and-yang interplay between these two actors was electric, and Kurosawa would pair them together 15 times over the next 15 years.[2]

The good doctor is fighting a losing battle against his very surroundings. Mosquitoes invade his office from their breeding ground in the unhealthy water outside, and his examining room door will not stay open unless he props it in place with a trash bin. American censors tolerated these depictions of infrastructural decay, but they did not allow Kurosawa to show burned buildings at the edge of the cesspool in exterior shots. To imply a relationship between wartime bomb damage and postwar squalor came too close to criticizing the occupation, something movies could not explicitly do. Censors' attentiveness to such criticism was inconsistent. Just months earlier they allowed a shot of a ruined building next to an empty lot in *One Wonderful Sunday* to remain in the film (see Chapter 6). A relatively small number of censors examined tens of thousands of print, radio, and film submissions per month, and some questionable content slipped through the cracks. Yet it also made sense for the Americans to grow more sensitive to perceived criticism as time went on. At first they could blame the defeated militarist government for Japan's condition, but by the third year of the occupation the Americans owned at least some of the responsibility for the nation's problems. To adopt one of President Truman's favorite phrases, the buck stopped with them, but Japanese media could not say so.[3]

In *Drunken Angel* Kurosawa could depict gangsters and prostitutes and have his characters contract preventable diseases, but he could not suggest that American governance contributed to these phenomena. He could not point out, for example, that 90 percent of prostitutes who worked in government-sanctioned brothels tested positive for sexually-transmitted diseases in the spring of 1947. He also could not talk about "radiation sickness," the condition affecting people who survived the atomic blasts in Hiroshima and Nagasaki. He could talk about diseases whose causes were harder to pinpoint, like "cholera, dysentery, typhoid fever, paratyphoid fever, smallpox, epidemic typhus (spotted fever), diphtheria, epidemic meningitis, polio, and encephalitis," which over 650,000 people contracted during the first three years of the occupation. Many such cases were, in part, consequences of poor hygiene and poor nutrition. Of all the diseases ravaging defeated Japan, Kurosawa selected tuberculosis for Morinaga's diagnosis. Tuberculosis was a particularly feared disease, claiming over 100,000 lives in Japan in each year of the occupation between 1945 and 1950. Tuberculosis is highly contagious, so having it meant quarantining oneself from others or exposing friends and loved ones. Morinaga, already living at the fringes of society among gangsters and prostitutes, is likely to lose even these unwholesome associates when they learn that he is sick.[4]

The only person Morinaga can count on is the nigh-saintly Sanada, who never abandons a patient. The doctor is an alcoholic—the title of the film applies to Sanada as well as the barfly Morinaga—but he is committed to his profession and to serving the downtrodden. Even Sanada's nurse Miyo (Nakakita Chieko) is one of his hard-luck cases. She was a gang leader's abused wife but escaped that life when her husband Okada (Yamamoto Reisaburō) went to prison.

With its gangsters and *femme fatales*, its window-blind shadows and dirty streets, its deep-focus cinematography and morally-compromised anti-heroes, *Drunken Angel* is as much a film noir as a neorealist work. By copying a popular style that Hollywood perfected over the course of the 1940s, Kurosawa's critique of occupation-era society becomes a kind of Trojan horse: an American-looking movie that highlights the ways American governance was failing in Japan. Its commentary on American power is censorship-proof because it communicates that power through its style even more than through substance. A jubilant jazz number midway through is the most striking example. At a cabaret Morinaga operates on behalf of his boss Okada, palm trees and tropical motifs recall New York City's popular Copacabana nightclub. A real-life singer named Kasagi Shizuko, well-known in the postwar years, is on stage singing a song called "Jungle Boogie" that Kurosawa wrote for the film. Its refrain is a melodic imitation of the "Tarzan yell" from Hollywood movies. The way Kasagi writhes on the stage, the low-cut dress she wears, and her long, wavy hair all mirror American icon Rita Hayworth's appearance in *Gilda* two years earlier. The whole cabaret is swept up in this distinctly American form of entertainment, and disregarding Sanada's orders to take it easy, Morinaga quaffs his liquor and leaps onto the dance floor as the band swings and Kasagi sings.

Morinaga pays for his indulgence. The next morning at the doctor's office Sanada smells alcohol on the gangster's breath and angrily throws him out into the street. As he walks away, Morinaga passes a large sign advertising vitamins. He could choose a path back to health, but his lifestyle repeatedly causes him to stray from it, and that lifestyle is defined in American terms. It is significant that the vitamin sign is in Japanese while the cabaret's signs are in English, as foreign as its music.

Morinaga's *yakuza* career catches up to him as fast as his health problems. His boss Okada returns to reclaim his turf after three years in prison. He observes that the stinking pond at the center of the slum has not changed since he went away—a damning indictment of the slow pace of Japan's recovery. The *yakuza*, though, were stronger than ever. The gangs divided Japan into territories and managed the black markets and *pan-pan* girls within their respective zones. The gangsters were surprisingly open about their activities during the American occupation. Illegal buying and selling was not a matter of furtive, back-alley exchanges, but took place at semi-permanent bazaars that occupied whole city blocks. A popular euphemism for the bazaars was "blue-sky markets," because they operated in broad daylight. The *yakuza* there were easy to identify, often wearing Hawaiian shirts and two-toned shoes like the kind Morinaga wears in *Drunken Angel*. Japanese police and American military authorities tended to leave the *yakuza* alone, and in return the gangsters made payoffs and rounded up laborers for government construction jobs.

Okada and the other *yakuza* learn about Morinaga's tuberculosis when he coughs up blood at a dice game. They confine him to an apartment, but Morinaga escapes and heads for the slum. As he sits sadly at the edge of the pond, Dr. Sanada joins him and articulates the film's message: "It's not enough to treat your lungs. You're still surrounded by filth." Morinaga agrees to rest and recuperate at Sanada's home.

A dream sequence follows that uses the popular Japanese art motif of crashing

A black market in Tokyo, 1946 (photograph by U.S. military).

waves. It closely prefigures the dream sequence Kurosawa would stage for *Kagemusha* over 30 years later (see Chapter 26). In both dreams the protagonist encounters his own double, who rises from a coffin and chases him along a beach in slow motion. The tumultuous sea that fills the frame behind Morinaga and his dream-double recalls the early 19th-century woodblock print *The Great Wave off Kanagawa* (*Kanagawa-oki nami ura*), one of the most widely reproduced works of art in the world. In the print, three small boats float beneath a cresting wave that reaches out to the helpless crafts with foamy "fingers." The work invites viewers to contemplate human frailty against the power of nature, and Kurosawa taps into the same sense of impending doom in *Drunken Angel*'s macabre dream sequence beside a swelling sea. Morinaga is equally a victim of his own misbehavior and an overwhelming physical environment.

Danger looms not only for Morinaga, but for Sanada's nurse Miyo. Okada finds her at Sanada's home, where Sanada blasts the gangster for his "feudal" view of women. "Haven't you heard of equality?" he says to the dumbfounded Okada when the gangster tries to take Miyo by force. This adoption of American rhetoric checked a box that pleased the censors, but it also shows that Japanese liberals like Sanada did not find the occupation wholly without value. Rhetoric, however, only goes so far. Okada leaves for the moment, but he will return to claim his wife even if he has to kill Sanada.

Kurosawa sets up a quandary that has powerful implications for Japan's postwar situation. Sanada wants to call the police to protect Miyo from Okada, but Morinaga wants to handle Okada himself. Morinaga speaks of the *yakuza* code of honor. By putting his own life on the line, Morinaga will gain face in the underworld and maybe win back the friends he lost due to his illness. For Morinaga to let Sanada go to the police or risk his own life would make Morinaga look weak in the eyes of his peers. On the opposite end of the spectrum, the modern-minded Dr. Sanada ridicules the notions of face and self-sacrifice. When Miyo offers to go back to Okada willingly to keep the gangster away from Sanada, the doctor cuts her off and says "Japanese people commit too many sacrifices." Like the American authorities, he wants Japan to shed old ways of thinking and create a more peaceful and egalitarian society.

Morinaga chooses the path of violence, and in accordance with censorship policy the violence has tragic results. He goes after Okada with a knife, but a coughing fit causes him to lose the fight, and he bleeds to death on a landing overlooking the city. His clothes are covered in whitewash that the men spilled in the struggle: a new coat of paint on a man with an old worldview. When Sanada learns what happened, the doctor despairs because he could not save Morinaga. "You can't change anyone," he angrily concludes. Still, Miyo is once again safe, as Okada goes back to prison for the murder of Morinaga.

Kurosawa suggests that society can change for the better even when individuals do not. At the edge of the cesspool, Sanada meets two young women who had minor roles in the story. One, a bartender who loved Morinaga, intends to go to the countryside to bury the *yakuza*'s ashes in a healthier place. Another, a high school student whom Sanada mentors, shows Sanada her favorable grade report. Both of these women are leaving the slum for something better, making them both symbols and agents of positive change. Compared to the inspiring female leads of *No Regrets for Our Youth* and *One Wonderful Sunday*, the young women of *Drunken Angel* are barely visible, but they offer the best reasons for hope. Not surprisingly the American censors, with their great hopes for the emancipation of Japanese women, had a lot of influence on *Drunken Angel*'s ending; they required Kurosawa to rewrite an original, more "gruesome" one in which Sanada drives Morinaga's body around the slum for all to see. In both endings, though, the representatives of violent patriarchy are out of the picture and will not define Japan's future.[5]

Drunken Angel takes on the paradoxes of the occupation, a moment when women gained the right to vote but turned to prostitution in record numbers; when people enjoyed the pleasures of American entertainment but had to participate in the black market to survive; when those who lived through the deadliest war in history died by the thousands from preventable diseases. As a chronicler of this uncertain environment, Kurosawa was never more confident in his craft. He now had an angel and a demon to work with in Shimura and Mifune, and together the three would play out Japan's ongoing drama on a world stage.

CHAPTER 8

The Quiet Duel

While the American occupiers handed down edicts, Japanese elites pushed back. The new Japanese constitution that MacArthur's staff wrote went into effect in 1947, and it gave voters more power to select representatives to Japan's legislature, the National Diet. Once in office, though, politicians generally tried to protect their own interests. Yoshida Shigeru, a conservative member of the Diet who served two stints as prime minister between 1946 and 1954, tried to negotiate with MacArthur's headquarters over the finer points of policies like land reform; many politicians owned land and resisted American attempts to redistribute their wealth. The parallel governments, American and Japanese, went back and forth over the wording and the details of each new law, but the occupiers always had the final say. Yoshida once said to a high-ranking member of MacArthur's staff, "You think you can make Japan a democratic country? I don't think so." "We can try," the American official replied. It was a duel, but a one-sided one.[1]

One policy that particularly worried Japanese elites was the Americans' attempt to dismantle the nation's largest corporations. The new constitution declared war illegal, but it was the closure of Japan's factories that would make another war impossible. Accordingly, MacArthur's headquarters targeted the large "industrial and banking combines" that "played an important part in the Japanese war effort" and economy. These powerful corporate groups, the *zaibatsu*, were trusts with close ties to the Japanese government, and they used their influence to manipulate financial policy and foreign trade. Occupation authorities broke up some of the most powerful *zaibatsu*, like Mitsubishi and Mitsui, into several smaller companies. Around 1500 executives and managers from large *zaibatsu* resigned between 1945 and 1947, and the Americans destroyed or redistributed much of the industrial machinery that powered their factories. Quietly and illegally, some factory owners "disappeared" their equipment before the Americans could seize it, selling it or hiding it until conditions changed.[2]

The Americans did, in fact, change their minds about the *zaibatsu* when they began to fight a dangerous new duel in Asia: the Cold War. In October 1949, 1500 miles east of Japan, Chinese communists finally won a civil war that began over twenty years earlier. The American-allied, anti-communist Chinese forces retreated to the island of Taiwan. Most of mainland Asia was now under communist control, and Americans worried about what would happen next. A "Red Scare" poisoned politics in the United States, and American policymakers committed to standing firm against any further communist expansion. The "loss" of China, along with worsening tensions between the Western and Soviet sections of occupied Germany, kicked off a forty-year face-off between "the free world" and the communist world that sometimes turned bloody but mostly took place internally as each side built its strength and tried to silence dissenters in their ranks.

With Japan now on the front line of a new conflict, occupation authorities second-guessed their decision to break up the *zaibatsu*. A weak economy, they reasoned, meant increased risk of communist activity within Japan and decreased ability to resist communist aggression from outside. Furthermore, if the Cold War turned into a shooting war in any part of Asia, the United States would want to use Japan as a base from which to stage operations. Japanese industry could provide the Americans with useful supplies, transportation, and other logistical support. MacArthur's headquarters stopped dissolving Japan's large companies, and they began recovering their former strength and influence.

Historians describe this phase of the occupation as "the reverse course," and it also affected the Japanese labor movement and movie industry. Occupation officials believed that organized labor contributed to democracy and equality, but they never embraced strikes as a bargaining tool. In 1947 MacArthur personally intervened to stop a nationwide labor strike, which he described as a "deadly … social weapon." Workers at Tōhō studios went on strike several times during the occupation, including in 1948 when Kurosawa was working on his eighth film, *The Quiet Duel* (*Shizukanaru kettō*). In an early example of the reverse course in action, American soldiers in tanks supported Japanese police as they forcibly ended the longest Tōhō strike, which lasted 195 days. The environment had changed drastically in the two years since 1946, when Kurosawa worked on a Tōhō film about union organization in a movie studio; that movie, *Those Who Make Tomorrow* (*Asu o tsukuru hitobito*), has been screened very rarely since its original release, and it has never received home video distribution in any country.[3]

During the strike, Kurosawa and his actors kept working. Kurosawa adapted *Drunken Angel* for the stage and toured several major cities with the live theater version. The original stars, Mifune Toshirō and Shimura Takashi, reprised the parts of Morinaga and Dr. Sanada in front of live crowds night after night, receiving enthusiastic applause and deepening the chemistry that already existed between them. At the end of the play's run they resumed work on *The Quiet Duel*, but the unrest at Tōhō forced them to move production to the Daiei studio lot. It was the first time Kurosawa released a film through a studio other than Tōhō.[4]

In *The Quiet Duel* Shimura and Mifune play a father and son doctor team. A prologue shows how Dr. Fujisaki Kyōji (Mifune) contracted syphilis during the war. While operating on a wounded soldier named Nakada (Uemura Kenjirō) on an unnamed Pacific island, Kyōji cuts his finger and inadvertently comes into

American soldiers help break the Tōhō strike, 1948 (from *Mainichi Graph*, September 15, 1948).

contact with Nakada's blood. Afterward, Kyōji overhears Nakada confide to another recuperating patient that he has syphilis. Kyōji tests himself and confirms that he acquired Nakada's syphilis through the open wound.

Nakada got syphilis in the usual way: from a local woman, perhaps one of the "comfort women" (*ianfu*) the Japanese empire forced into sexual slavery for its soldiers. By creating military-run brothels, Japanese military leaders aimed to reduce

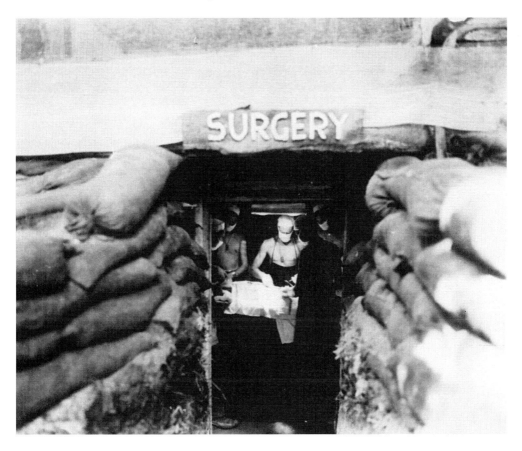

An American field hospital on Bougainville in the southern Pacific, 1943. During the war, both American and Japanese field hospitals operated near the front lines in difficult conditions (National Archives).

the number of rapes that took place in public areas under their jurisdiction. The precise number of Chinese, Korean, Filipina, Southeast Asian, and Pacific Islander *ianfu* is incalculable, as is the number of unsanctioned rapes that occurred anyway, but estimates converge in the low hundreds of thousands. The Japanese military provided condoms, but venereal disease spread through the ranks, and many soldiers brought their infections back to Japan at the end of the war.

After the wartime prologue *The Quiet Duel* jumps forward to the occupation. Kyōji is now working as a surgeon at his father's medical clinic. His fiancée Misao (Sanjō Miki) brings him meals every day, but Kyōji keeps her at a distance. Before the war they were happy—she thumbs through a photo album that proves it—but now Kyōji wants to cancel their engagement and will not tell her why. He tells nobody that he has syphilis, not even his father. The disease can cause madness if left untreated, so Kyōji treats himself using drugs from the clinic's supply room. A nurse named Minegishi (Sengoku Noriko) learns Kyōji's secret when she sees him injecting the medicine.

Minegishi has a problem of her own: an unwanted pregnancy. When the father of her unborn child abandons her, she despairs at the thought of raising a child alone. She is considering an abortion, an option that was legal in Japan under American control despite being illegal in the United States until the 1970s. Abortion has long been commonplace in Japanese history, and during the worst ancient and medieval famines so was infanticide. The Japanese public exhibits a broad tolerance for abortion, having no major religious opposition to it. *The Quiet Duel* is based on a play called *The Abortion Doctor* (*Datai I*, by Kikuta Kazuo), and the Drs. Fujisaki are no strangers to terminating pregnancies, but in the movie they encourage Minegishi to keep her baby.

Kyōji is less direct with his fiancée than his coworker. He cannot tell Misao that he has syphilis because she would surely wait for him to cure it, even if it took years, and during that time she would miss out on the joys of marriage and the possibility of children. Kyōji therefore treats her coldly, hoping for her own sake that she will leave him and find another, healthier man to marry. Misao, however, suffers Kyōji's change of personality with undying patience and faithfulness, and she does not give up on him easily.

Kyōji and Misao's engagement illustrates the state of Japanese marriage in the middle of the 20th century. Up until the late Shōwa *jidai*, Japanese parents usually arranged marriages for their children, often employing professional go-betweens to help with introductions and negotiations. Social and economic class played an important role in matchmaking, so parents' professions could severely limit their children's options. In the postwar period "love matches," in which young adults selected their own partners, became increasingly common. In 1947 arranged marriages accounted for 60 percent of all marriages in Japan, a drop from nearly 70 percent in 1942. The death and maiming of so many young men during the war created a shortage of prospective husbands, so single women sought out new match-making methods. "Group marriage meetings"—large social mixers similar to the Western phenomenon of "speed dating"—were a novelty of the late 1940s that helped single people find compatible partners within the uprooted urban throng.[5]

Even when young women and men took the lead in deciding whom to marry, parents remained involved in the formal making and breaking of engagements. In *The Quiet Duel* Misao communicates her father's wishes to her fiancé and her would-be father-in-law. Misao's father is eager to see Misao and Kyōji marry, but if Kyōji continues to delay, then he must seek a new match for his daughter. By way of response, Kyōji finally tells his own father why he wants to break the engagement. The elder Dr. Fujisaki encourages Kyōji to be honest with Misao about his condition, but when Kyōji refuses, it falls to his father to visit Misao's parents and formally announce the end of the engagement. Misao's father finds another appropriate match, and Misao accepts the decision with as much hopefulness as she can muster.

Though Kyōji is less than communicative with Misao, he has an easy rapport with his patients, and this allows Kurosawa to work in a reference to one of occupation officials' favorite topics. When a young boy comes in for an appendectomy, Kyōji chats knowledgably with him about baseball. At the time of *The Quiet Duel*'s production the Daiei film studio owned a professional baseball team, the Daiei Stars, which formed during the occupation and had to share a stadium with three other teams. When players from the ball club visited the movie set, it was hard to say whether the actors or the athletes were the bigger celebrities.[6]

Kyōji once again crosses paths with the ex-soldier Nakada, the man whose blood infected him. In place of his old army fatigues Nakada now sports a gaudy, Western-style suit and tie combo. His sloppily-assembled outfit is a visible manifestation of his chaotic effect on the lives of others. Disregarding Kyōji's instruction to treat his syphilis and refrain from spreading it, Nakada conceives a child with his wife Takiko (Nakakita Chieko). Whether as a rapacious imperial soldier or a tacky symbol of occupation-era lawlessness, Nakada is a shameless vector for a dreaded social disease. The syphilis bacterium that he transmits to his wife also infects their baby, who dies at birth. Nakada's anger and creeping insanity lead him to smash up the Fujisaki clinic, an emotional breakdown that provides the film's climax.

The original ending of *The Quiet Duel* had Kyōji lose not only his fiancée and much of his clinic, but his mind as well. The American censors found this outcome too bleak, so Kurosawa's filmed ending leaves Kyōji's fate open-ended. He continues to treat his syphilis and hope for an eventual cure. Minegishi has her baby, and there are hints that she and Kyōji may become a family and raise the child together. In different ways, both Kyōji and Minegishi's bodies were compromised, but both of them try to adapt to their new realities.

The Quiet Duel took shape as Japan adapted to yet another new reality: the occupation's reverse course. Though the film does not tackle topical controversies like labor strikes and their suppression, it does speak to the idea of new beginnings. Kyōji and Nakada belong to the same generation, serve in the same war, and receive the same diagnosis, but after the war Nakada flounders while Kyōji finds a way forward by painfully dismantling his old life and slowly building a new one.

Kurosawa was fascinated by the mystery of this divergence. Once, while discussing the roots of crime with his childhood friend and *Drunken Angel* cowriter Uekusa Keinosuke, Kurosawa pointed out that not all people who grow up in poverty become criminals. If two people's environments are the same, he reasoned, then the explanation for their differences must lie elsewhere. Kurosawa would revisit this problem many times in different ways, but it was never closer to the surface than in his next movie, in which Mifune and Shimura swap their scrubs for detective badges.[7]

CHAPTER 9

Stray Dog

Life in Japan was by no means easy between 1945 and 1948, but 1949 made some people nostalgic for the early part of the occupation. The reverse course that Americans hoped would spur economic recovery benefited Japan's biggest businesses (see Chapter 8), but it did not improve the lives of most citizens. Workers felt its effects in the weakening of their unions and the breaking of their strikes, and there were frequent layoffs as companies restructured themselves for the second time in a decade. The American planners who charted Japan's course tried to promote Japanese exports by lowering prices, but the result of this deflation was a wave of small business failures, falling wages, and reduced spending. The already-weak economy headed toward depression. Even children sensed the change thanks to cuts in education budgets. One American official frankly described the reverse course as "ruthless."[1]

Though the Americans would still be in charge for a few more years, people were already beginning to think about the occupation with a degree of abstract detachment. A new buzzword circulated in Japan that helped people understand the occupation in historical terms: *apure*, from the French *aprés-guerre*, meaning "after the war." The *apure* period was like its own little *jidai*, and it was populated by distinctively *apure* people like *pan-pan* girls, black marketeers, homeless veterans, and ubiquitous American troops. It was a *jidai* that Japan was preparing to leave behind. The Japanese government, which before the reverse course existed mainly to rubber-stamp American programs, began to prepare for independence. In 1949 the government announced a new department called the Ministry of International Trade and Industry (MITI), which would play a critical role in revitalizing the Japanese economy after the occupation.[2]

In the middle of Kurosawa's 1949 movie *Stray Dog* (*Nora inu*), Shimura Takashi and Mifune Toshirō's characters discuss the idea of *apure* as they sit drinking cool beer in the warm night air. The rookie detective Murakami (Mifune) is consumed with guilt because a pickpocket stole his gun on a crowded bus and sold it to a poor ex-soldier named Yusa, who used it to commit robbery and murder. Murakami spends weary days searching for Yusa and the gun among the Tokyo slums, and while he pounds the pavement he thinks. The veteran detective Satō (Shimura) warns his young partner that thinking is dangerous:

MURAKAMI: They there's no such thing as a bad man, only bad situations. Yusa is pitiable, isn't he?

SATŌ: We police can't think that way. When you chase criminals all day long, it's easy to become confused. We can't forget the damage a lone wolf does to the sheep.... Leave psychoanalysis to the detective novels. A bad guy is a bad guy, and I hate them.

MURAKAMI: I can't bring myself to think that way yet. After long years of war men turn into beasts at the slightest provocation, over and over.

SATŌ: You and I are from different generations. Or rather, it's the times that are different. What do they call it? Ap-, *apure*....

MURAKAMI: *Aprés-guerre.*

SATŌ: That's it. You're part of the postwar generation, like Yusa. So you over-identify with him.

MURAKAMI: Probably. My belongings were also stolen on a train as I returned home from the war.

SATŌ: Oh?

MURAKAMI: I was so angry. After that, I probably could have robbed someone, too. But when I came to that crossroads, I chose the opposite course and found this job.

SATŌ: There are two kinds of *aprés-guerre* people—people like you and people like Yusa.

Satō believes that the good are good and the bad are bad, and it is the job of the good to resist the bad. Amid the confusion of war and occupation, he says, young people have lost sight of that simple truth. Murakami, on the other hand, feels that the cruelty of war and the poverty of the occupation make good people do bad things. When they reached a fork in the road Murakami went one way and Yusa went another, but they might just as easily have done the reverse. To ask why Yusa follows one path and Murakami another, or to ask the same about Kyōji and Nakada in *The Quiet Duel* and Noge and Itokawa in *No Regrets for Our Youth*, is to ask larger questions. Can Japan overcome the challenges of the postwar period, or will it never recover from the pain of war and defeat? Are people helpless amid the shifting currents of history, or do they define themselves and the eras they live in by their choices and actions?

As detectives, Murakami and Satō might at least agree on one thing: the occupation dramatically changed the nature of Japanese police work. One of the first acts of the occupation when it began in 1945 was to dismantle the Kempeitai, the special police force of the wartime government. The Kempeitai served as military police in war zones and as thought police in Japanese towns and villages where they monitored and arrested political dissidents. The elimination of the Kempeitai was the first step in demilitarizing and decentralizing the entire Japanese police system. In 1947 the Americans pushed a new law which required each municipality with a population over 5000 to finance its own police force independent of the central government. Large cities divvied up policing by neighborhoods; there were 23 independent police departments in Tokyo alone. Different police agencies could share forensic data with each other in order to solve crimes, but they did not answer to any centralized authority. The creation of so many new police departments caused the overall number of police to increase from 84,000 in 1941 to 125,000 by the end of the occupation. In keeping with the Americans' gender equality goals, there was also a substantial increase in the percentage of female police officers during the occupation.[3]

As they had since the Meiji *jidai*, police operated out of clearly-marked stations and "police boxes": tiny buildings on street corners from which a small number of uniformed officers kept an eye on their immediate vicinity. In the early postwar years cops rounded up homeless loiterers and unlicensed prostitutes (as opposed to the prostitutes who worked in government-run brothels in designated zones) and sometimes intervened in *yakuza* street fights. One officer died and another was wounded in a gang-related shootout in Tokyo's Shibuya neighborhood in the summer of 1946. Many police, though, chose to work with organized crime rather than against it, which resulted in localized networks of corruption.[4]

At the beginning of *Stray Dog* Murakami is a clean cop, eager to perform his duties well, but when he loses his gun he does not hesitate to use his coworkers' underworld connections. While looking through pictures of pickpockets, Muramaki recognizes the face of a woman who stood next to him on the bus. A fellow officer knows her well and takes Murakami to meet her. She does not want to help the naïve detective, but Murakami follows her through back alleys and streetcars until she directs him to the illegal gun merchants downtown.

The American occupiers never relaxed Japan's strict gun laws. Gun ownership was illegal for most civilians, and from the American perspective that longstanding policy suited the goal of demilitarizing Japan. The Japanese police could carry weapons, but most did not; in 1948 fewer than 1 in 10 officers wore a gun. The 1600 police departments in the country owned as many as 197 different gun models, a lack of standardization that made stocking the proper ammunition difficult. In *Stray Dog* it also makes Murakami's missing weapon more difficult to trace.[5]

While prowling the occupation-era underworld Murakami blends in with the other desperate men of his generation, but a lack of criminal instincts makes him a fish out of water. Though in reality police and black marketeers frequently worked together when they could (see Chapter 7), the rookie Murakami is clean to a fault. At last he meets a fence (Sengoku Noriko) who loans stolen guns in exchange for rice ration cards. She admits that she loaned Murakami's gun, but she won't tell him where to find the borrower's ration card. In a move that presages many a buddy cop film, Murakami's boss assigns him to work with the more experienced detective Satō, whose methods are shady but effective. Satō is friendly with several black marketeers, and he knows how to get answers. He plies the fence with cigarettes and popsicles and teases her about her *yakuza* boyfriend. She then tells Satō the name of the man who has the ration card and where to find him: at an upcoming baseball game.

Murakami and Satō head to the baseball stadium for a capacity-crowd match

A Japanese policeman issues a citation to a black marketeer while a member of the American Military Police looks on, 1949 (photograph by U.S. military).

between Tokyo's Yomiuri Giants and Fukuoka's Nankai Hawks. Kurosawa uses footage from an actual meeting of the two teams and lingers on the roughly 50,000 enthusiastic fans in attendance. Baseball tickets were a luxury during the occupation, especially during the economic downturn of 1949, and the people who attended this game made every minute count. They cheered enthusiastically even for easily-fielded groundballs. It helped that they were watching the two most successful clubs of the late 1940s; the Hawks won the Japanese Baseball League in 1948 and the Giants followed in 1949.

As large and energetic as this crowd was, it paled next to the estimated one million people who turned out for the biggest baseball event of the occupation: the 1949 goodwill tour of retired Major League slugger Lefty O'Doul. A natural showman on and off the field, O'Doul gained a following among Japanese baseball fans in the mid–1930s when he and other legends of the game like Babe Ruth and Lou Gehrig visited Japan to play exhibition games and promote international friendship.

The Tokyo Giants took their name from O'Doul's team, the New York Giants, at O'Doul's suggestion. Over a decade later, when the reverse course caused new hardships in Japan and the Cold War made it critical for the United States to maintain a strong relationship with the country, MacArthur called in O'Doul. The aging hero toured Japan with his minor league team and entertained crowds that at one game included 14,000 war orphans who attended for free. He also met with Emperor Hirohito, who thanked him for his visit. The tour was a public relations success, and MacArthur, who often spoke in superlatives, called it "the greatest piece of diplomacy ever."[6]

At *Stray Dog*'s baseball game Murakami and Satō arrest the fence's associate and finally learn the identity of the man who has Murakami's gun. They visit Yusa's home, which is just a leaky shack attached to his sister and brother-in-law's dilapidated house. Yusa is not home, but his sister explains the detectives that he lost everything on his way home after the war.

It took years for Japanese citizens who were overseas at the end of World War II to come home. There were about three million soldiers and an equal number of civilians in the empire's former colonies, and throughout the occupation American ships traveled back and forth to China, the southern Pacific, and Southeast Asia to carry them back, one boat load at a time. The most difficult to repatriate were the prisoners of war. In 1949 the Soviet Union still held an unknown number of Japanese citizens—perhaps over a million—that they captured in their takeover of Manchuria, North Korea, and the Kuril Islands in 1945 (see Chapter 4). Many of these prisoners died in Siberian labor camps, and many more disappeared from the historical record forever. Other countries also used Japanese prisoners as laborers after the war. The Chinese retained a large number of their ex-occupiers, the United States used tens of thousands of them to rebuild infrastructure in liberated areas, and the British kept thousands in Malaysia and Burma. As their captors slowly released them, ex-soldiers and civilians trickled back into Japan, a steady stream of them every month until the early 1950s.[7]

While Murakami and Satō continue to search for the rogue ex-soldier, Yusa uses the gun to kill again. The detectives have only one gun between them, and Satō takes it when they split up to chase different leads. The censors who reviewed *Stray Dog*'s script instructed Kurosawa to check all gun-related scenes against actual police procedure to make sure the characters' handling of pistols was "technically correct." They wanted Japanese law officers to appear competent on screen. They also required movie criminals to be brought to justice. This requirement was not unique to occupied Japan; it was also part of the censorship code that Hollywood studios abided by from the 1930s through the 1950s. Yusa's fate was therefore sealed from the beginning, but he does not go down without a fight, and he shoots Satō during a narrow escape. Murakami soon catches up to him, and at the end of a chase the two *apure* men lay panting side by side in the dirt with Yusa in handcuffs.[8]

This image of the winded young men bookends the film's opening shot, a

Japanese soldiers at a train station in September 1945, shortly after the surrender (photograph by U.S. Navy photographer Lt. Wayne F. Miller).

close-up of a dog panting in the heat. The dog caused a minor controversy that Kurosawa would never forget. An American woman from the Society for the Prevention of Cruelty to Animals saw the movie and became convinced, without evidence, that the filmmakers had abused it. Kurosawa had to formally deny the allegation in a letter to occupation authorities, a task he found deeply irritating. "I never at any other moment experienced a stronger sense of regret over Japan's losing the war," he wrote years later.[9]

As the painful decade of the 1940s came to a close, it left virtually everybody in Japan with an agonizing number of regrets and what-ifs. When 1950 dawned, neither the Japanese nor the Americans knew that war was once again about to alter their shared destiny.

CHAPTER 10

Scandal

The only time Kurosawa used an English word as the title of a film was in 1950's *Sukyandaru*, the Japanese phonetic spelling of "scandal." On the movie's title card it is written in *katakana*, the alphabet used to spell foreign words. The Japanese word *shūbun*, meaning scandal, appears alongside it. The Japanese vocabulary is replete with loan words from the languages of other countries—Chinese words from antiquity, Portuguese and Dutch words from 16th-century European missions to the East, a host of English terms acquired during the Meiji and Taishō *jidai*—but the word "scandal" gained currency toward the end of the American occupation.

The biggest scandals of the era involved collusion between businesses and government. In 1946 between one and three hundred billion yen's worth of industrial goods that the *zaibatsu* were supposed to turn over to authorities simply vanished (see Chapter 8). Business leaders, likely with the help of Japanese or American officials who looked the other way, sold some of the material on the black market and stashed the rest away. Japanese politicians denounced those responsible but named no names, and none of the literal robber barons ever faced charges for the crime. Later in the occupation, Japanese companies regularly bribed officials in exchange for government contracts and occupation recovery funds. The "Shōwa Denkō scandal" of 1948, named for a fertilizer company that got caught engaging in this illegal *quid pro quo*, led to the resignation and prosecution of a prime minister but did not put a stop to the practice. These kinds of scandals would become a recurring feature of Japanese business and politics in the decades ahead (see Chapter 19).[1]

An event becomes a scandal not when somebody does something wrong, but when the public learns about it. Accordingly, Kurosawa's tenth movie focuses not on a scandal *per se*, but on the way scandals are reported, the fights that proceed from those reports, and the responsibilities that reporters and legal experts have when informing the public about a potential scandal.

The war was bad for Japan's newspapers. In 1937 there were around 1700 newspapers in the country, but by 1942 there were just 55. The decrease was due in large part to the government's strict control over mass communication. The postwar American censors were strict too, but by 1947 the number of daily newspapers in Japan was up to 69, with many thousands of new, smaller publications that ran less frequently. In July 1948 the Americans stopped reviewing Japanese news articles before publication, but they reserved the right to pull an issue from circulation after it hit newsstands. This post-publication censorship could cause serious financial losses for a newspaper, so editors exercised a high degree of self-censorship for the remainder of the occupation.[2]

There was also the risk that someone—the government, a business, an individual—could sue a newspaper if it reported on a scandal without sufficient proof. Japan's new civil and criminal codes put great emphasis on protecting freedom of speech and the press, censorship restrictions aside, but people could and did take publishers to court for libel. In 1946 when the conservative government of Prime Minister Yoshida Shigeru wanted to sue a Japanese Communist Party newspaper that insulted the Shōwa emperor, occupation authorities intervened to stop the lawsuit. In another case, though, the Americans allowed the Yoshida government to prosecute an individual protestor who criticized Hirohito. Japan is not a particularly litigious country—a character in *Scandal* accurately says that in 1949 there were only about 5900 lawyers in Japan compared to 170,000 in the United States—but publishers still had to consider the risk of retaliation when reporting on controversial topics.[3]

In *Scandal*, two celebrities sue a gossip magazine that falsely accuses them of having an affair. This is a lighter sort of *sukyandaru* than the financial and political crimes of the era, but Kurosawa's story reveals much about the postwar legal system and the kinds of publications that people wrote and read towards the end of the occupation.

An artist named Aoe Ichirō (Mifune Toshirō) takes a motorcycle trip into the mountains to do landscape paintings. At an overlook he talks with a trio of rustic local men who are excited to meet an artist. Soon a woman comes by to ask for directions to a nearby hot spring resort, a popular kind of tourist destination in Japanese mountain towns. Ichirō is staying there too, so he gives the woman a ride on his motorbike. A pair of photographers recognize the woman as Saijō Miyako, a famous singer, and take her picture.

The actress who plays Miyako is Yamaguchi Yoshiko, and she had one of the most remarkable lives of any film star of her generation. Like her co-star Mifune she was born in Japanese-occupied China. As a child she learned Mandarin well enough to pass as Chinese, which later caused problems for her in both China and Japan. Under the Chinese name Li Xianglan, Yamaguchi starred in propaganda films like *Song of the White Orchid* (*Byakuran no uta*, 1939) that painted a positive image of Manchuria's Japanese invaders. Once when Yamaguchi traveled to Japan to promote a film, a Japanese customs officer berated her for adopting the dress and language of an inferior culture. At the end of the war Chinese officials arrested her because they thought she was a Chinese woman who had collaborated with the Japanese occupiers rather than a Japanese woman who pretended to be Chinese on screen. After she proved her Japanese citizenship they released and deported her. Yamaguchi went on to have a successful film and music career in Japan, and she even appeared in a handful of Hollywood films as "Shirley" Yamaguchi, including 1952's *Japanese War Bride*. Later in life she served in the Japanese legislature and advocated for reparations to victims of Japanese war crimes in her native Manchuria and elsewhere.[4]

The shutterbugs who take Miyako and Ichirō's pictures are employees of a tabloid magazine called *Amour*. The *Amour* publishers are eager to find a *sukyandaru* to drive up sales. Out of context the photograph looks like evidence of a tryst, and the fact that Ichirō is a minor celebrity in his own right makes the image doubly valuable. When the photographers take their scoop back to the rag, the *Amour* team toasts their success with high-quality alcohol, not their usual *kasutori* moonshine.

The word *kasutori*, like the word *sukyandaru*, was a suggestive bit of occupation-era slang. Literally it referred to low-grade alcohol made from the leftover dregs of *sake* production. As a metaphor it referred to low-quality goods in general, including cheap tabloid magazines. *Kasutori* magazines flourished in the postwar years by celebrating as many forms of vice, degeneracy, and grotesqueness as their writers and illustrators could conceive. Beyond magazines, the term "*kasutori* culture" encompassed a whole panoply of pulp literature, erotic art, bawdy jokes, and other unwholesome forms of entertainment. Consuming *kasutori* culture meant imbibing the worst sort of filth, like a drunk downing cheap booze, but it was an alluring way to retreat from the grim realities of early postwar Japan. To emphasize that *Amour* trades in *kasutori* sleaze, Kurosawa's set decorators covered the walls and windows of the publishing house with illustrations of nude women.[5]

Titillating art had always existed in Japan, but the *kasutori* version of it felt new. Back home in his painting studio, Ichirō tells his female model that he no longer wishes to paint nudes as he did before the war. "We Japanese lack … the healthy spirit to accept the naked body," he muses. To Ichirō's model, though, such philosophical objections ring false. She believes that Ichirō no longer wishes to paint her nude because she is no longer as attractive as she used to be. Western or not, unhealthy or not, the proliferation of sexually-explicit art in postwar Japan had a profound effect on Japanese beauty standards. From the occupation onward, writes a leading historian of the period, "the idealized Western female figure, long limbed and amply proportioned, became … an ideal for young Japanese women to emulate." Kurosawa subtly links the *sukyandaru* to foreign influence in another way as well: the tabloid photographer takes the problematic picture with a European Leica camera rather than a Japanese brand like Canon or Nikon, two companies that pivoted from military goods to consumer products during the occupation.[6]

When the *Amour* issue featuring Ichirō and Miyako hits newsstands, Ichirō decides to fight back. The *kasutori* magazine's implication is an assault on decency and affront to his personal reputation. Ichirō pays a visit to Miyako at her home and tells her that since they live "in a modern nation with modern institutions" they should sue the tabloid for libel. Miyako hesitates, afraid of worsening the *sukyandaru* with a protracted legal battle. Ichirō meets with a fast-talking lawyer named Hiruta Otokichi (Shimura Takashi) who is willing to take the case for free. The

Kasutori **referred to low-grade alcohol as well as a culture of vice. This 1947 picture captures the flavor of the term (from** *Asahi Shimbunsha***).**

painter is initially skeptical of Hiruta's offer, but after he visits the lawyer's home and meets Hirtua's bedridden daughter Masako, he lets Hiruta take the case. A man who takes good care of his ill daughter must be on the up-and-up, Ichirō reasons.

Ichirō's moral appraisal of the lawyer fails to take into account the harsh economic realities of the late occupation. Hiruta needs money, all the more so because he has a sick daughter. His swindle is to take a bribe from *Amour*'s editor, a man named Hori (Ozawa Eitarō), in exchange for losing Ichirō's case on purpose. Hiruta is not thoroughly corrupt; he is, after all, not charging Ichirō. He tearfully confesses to Masako that he cheats his clients, but the shame of it weighs on him, and he drowns his guilty conscience in *kasutori* alcohol.

Hiruta is determined to give his daughter a happy Christmas, a holiday that Japan's non–Christian majority began observing in a secular way during the Meiji *jidai*. Christmas in Japan, as in the West, is a heavily commercialized event. Japanese department stores began capitalizing on Christmas's marketing potential in the late 1800s, and by the Taishō *jidai* their consumers were decorating Christmas trees, festooning homes with tinsel and Santa Claus figurines, and preparing special meals including "Christmas cake," a sugary invention unique to Japan. After the war a new generation took advantage of Christmas as an excuse for celebration, and the holiday soon acquired an association with lovers. Young couples began to reserve Christmas for intimate time together in advance of the more family-oriented New Year celebrations.[7]

Christmas in the occupation was a time for fun and romance, but it also imposed costs on Japan's strapped consumers. In *Scandal*, Hiruta brings home arm-fuls of presents for Masako that he can scarcely afford. Ichirō's model mentions having to buy Christmas gifts for her son. In a scene set to the tune of "Jingle Bells," Ichirō ferries a Christmas tree on his motorcycle while a group of street children crowd around him begging for presents. Miyako, having decided to participate in the lawsuit after all, joins Ichirō at the Hiruta household for Christmas and sings a Japanese-language version of "Silent Night." Afterwards, Hiruta and Ichirō go to a bar where they order a Christmas turkey, though the lawyer observes that "in this place there's no difference between the turkey and the chicken except the price." Framed by tinsel that crisscrosses the bar, Hiruta drunkenly resolves that in the coming year he will become a better person, and he leads the barflies in a chorus of "Auld Lang Syne." As 1949 gave way to 1950, these imported signs of the season reminded movie audiences of just how much Japan had changed during the last few years, and that a fresh year and fresh decade brought new opportunities to change with it.

The libel trial begins, and at first Hiruta does nothing to help his clients' case. *Amour*'s witnesses testify that, yes, the two celebrities arrived together by motor-cycle and spent time together on Miyako's balcony. Ichirō and Miyako bring wit-nesses as well: the three bumpkins who were at the overlook where Ichirō set up his easel. These men, who speak plainly and do not understand courtroom jargon, draw laughs from the trial's audience and even from the judge. Hori's defense attor-ney cleverly nullifies their testimony on technical grounds, and Ichirō's case seems doomed to fail.

At home in his studio the night before the verdict, Ichirō sits on his motorcycle and revs the engine. "Love on a motorbike" is how *Amour* described their made-up *sukyandaru*, but for Ichirō the motorcycle stands for something else entirely. Early in the film he explains to Miyako that when he rides his bike he feels carefree and rebellious. Now, facing defeat in court, hearing its engine gives him courage. In 1950 motorcycles also provided much-needed signs of life in the Japanese economy; the company Honda started in 1949 as a low-cost motorbike brand and soon began to export its stylish one-man machines around the world.[8]

The trial's last-minute reversal comes at a steep price. Hiruta's ailing daugh-ter Masako passes away near the end of the proceedings, and in order to be the man she wanted him to be he confesses his corruption before the court, exposes the tab-loid editor as a crook, and clears Ichirō and Miyako's good names. This unlikely tri-umph of truth is difficult to believe, but that is the point: *Scandal*'s pessimism about the free press and what Kurosawa called "its habitual confusion of freedom with license" is paired with a deep cynicism about the ability of Japan's legal institutions to discern between right and wrong. The director who in *No Regrets for Our Youth* looked forward to a more liberal, democratic, egalitarian Japan here articulates a kind of moral fundamentalism, a call for old-fashioned honor and decency to com-bat the anything-goes mentality of *kasutori* culture. The popular media will not do

The Honda Cub motorcycle is among the most-produced vehicles in history. This one delivered newspapers during the mid–Shōwa *jidai* (photograph by Rikita, Wikimedia Commons).

it, the courts fail to do it, so the job falls to courageous individuals. Kurosawa's fictional heroes and antiheroes merely provide the call to action.[9]

Unlikely though it may have seemed, everything did change for Japan in the new year, and very abruptly. On June 25, 1950, came the event that Prime Minister Yoshida called "a gift of the gods": North Korean communist forces invaded American-occupied South Korea.[10]

CHAPTER 11

Rashōmon

The outbreak of the Korean War in the summer of 1950 took American and Japanese observers by surprise. When Japan surrendered in 1945 it withdrew from the Korean peninsula, which it had occupied since 1910. To govern the 27 million liberated Koreans and take custody of the material the Japanese left behind, the American military occupied the southern half of Korea while the Soviet Union occupied the upper half. A few years later both powers delegated their halves of the country to local leaders. The north invaded the south on June 25, 1950, aiming to unify Korea by force. The few American troops still in the south retreated to a small corner of the peninsula, their backs against the Sea of Japan.

The 70-year-old General MacArthur had never been to Korea, even though he was technically in charge of its occupation as well as Japan's and it was only a 600-mile flight from his Tokyo headquarters. Suddenly he had to take quick action to prevent another communist takeover on Japan's doorstep. He was also responsible for the safety of the U.S. troops in Korea, and he needed to get them out or reinforce them with American troops from Japan as quickly as possible. Eight years earlier MacArthur had retreated during the Japanese invasion of the Philippines, and he did not intend to oversee another retreat now. But he needed Japan's help.

At the end of June there were around 126,000 American troops in Japan, and MacArthur would move 65,000 of them to Korea by the end of July. This required more ships and supplies than he had on hand. Furthermore, moving half of his force out of the country meant that Japan would be dangerously undefended in the event of a communist attack or uprising. The only way to relocate a large number of troops and replace them with new ones on short notice was to allow Japan to participate in the new war.[1]

Article IX of the postwar Japanese constitution that MacArthur's staff wrote expressly prohibited Japan from making war or maintaining armed forces. However, even before the document went into effect in 1947 Japanese politicians and American officials came up with creative ways to interpret—and ultimately ignore—Article IX. The Japanese bureaucrat who translated it from English to Japanese reordered clauses and inserted qualifiers so that the Japanese government could argue it had the right to maintain troops if their purpose was strictly self-defense. The American staffer who approved the Japanese translation understood the implications of this loophole but did not inform MacArthur of the changes. At first MacArthur strongly resisted Japanese remilitarization even when his superiors in Washington suggested that he allow it.[2]

Now that there was a war to fight, the occupation leader changed his mind. At the general's request, Prime Minister Yoshida's government created a new army under the misleading name "National Police Reserve." Its recruits did not deploy to Korea, but they took over American bases in Japan when American troops shipped out. The Japanese government also provided the Americans with thousands of specialist advisers who were familiar with Korea from Japan's 35-year occupation of the country.[3]

The benefits of the Korean war quickly spread through the Japanese economy. Japanese companies signed contracts with the American military to ferry goods on Japanese ships and employ workers in vital "support services." Japanese factories produced items for the war effort like metal, rubber, vehicles, and even weapons, including napalm bombs like the ones the Americans first used against Japanese soldiers six years earlier. The nation's industrial output for the year 1950 was higher than any year since the surrender, prompting a leading Japanese economist to describe the war as a tragedy for Korea but "a windfall boon" for Japan.[4]

At the very moment that Japan's economy returned to a state of war, movie characters became free to take up swords again. American movie censors curtailed their activities in June 1949, a year after they stopped pre-censoring newspapers (see Chapter 10). Censorship of Japanese newsreel footage continued, and censors still reviewed imported American and European films before releasing them to Japanese theaters; Soviet films had particular difficulty receiving distribution in occupied Japan. Nevertheless, occupation officials increasingly felt that it was "democratic" for Japanese films to have the right to entertain audiences as well as educate them, even if that meant putting more "questionable" content on screen. Like newspapers, movie studios censored themselves, avoiding explicit sexual content and anything that might make the Americans crack down again. As MacArthur's staff loosened the reigns, though, "feudal" content—including *jidaigeki* set in the time of samurai—was once again on the table. Filmmakers were free to exploit Japanese history's rich storytelling opportunities, and Kurosawa wasted no time in returning to the world of samurai.[5]

The 1950s film *Rashōmon* dived headlong into Japan's violent past. Kurosawa and co-screenwriter Hashimoto Shinobu combined two short stories from Taishō *jidai* writer Akutagawa Ryūnosuke, "Rashōmon" and "In a Grove" (*Yabu no naka*). Most of the film's plot comes from the latter story, but the framing device and title come from the former. Akutagawa died young in 1927, but in 1949 his fame found renewal when the Akutagawa Literature Prize was awarded for the first time since the end of World War II. Kurosawa's film *Rashōmon* did even more to bring Akutagawa back to the spotlight when it won the top prize at the prestigious Venice Film Festival and the Oscar for Best Foreign Language Film. Decades later Akutagawa remains one of the most well-known Japanese authors inside and outside of Japan, and *Rashōmon* is still one of the country's most famous movies.

Historically, the Rashōmon was a large gate that stood in a southern portion of Kyoto's city walls. Like many great gates, the Rashōmon was wide (106 feet), tall (75 feet), deep (26 feet), and had enclosed interior spaces that made it as much a building as a portal. Few signs of the gate remain today; built in the 8th century, it fell into disrepair in the 1100s when Japan's capital moved from Kyoto to Kamakura. Kyoto's growth moved away from the old Suzaku avenue that formerly fed traffic through the Rashōmon, and the neglected gate stood for a while as a reminder of old times and a refuge for criminals. According to old tales, people dumped dead bodies and left abandoned babies near the gate and on its second floor. In the 15th-century Noh play *Rashōmon* a demon lives on top of the gate. The edifice's macabre associations inspired Akutagawa's short story even though the gate was only a memory by the time he lived.

Kurosawa's movie opens with a shot of the half-crumbled gate (a convincing reconstruction) in pouring rain. A Buddhist monk (Chiaki Minoru) and woodcutter in tattered clothes (Shimura Takashi) sit beneath the gate's imperfect shelter, lost in thought. Another itinerant man (Ueda Kichijirō) arrives looking for conversation, and the first two tell him a shocking story that they heard that day at a nearby courthouse—or rather three stories, collectively perhaps more unsettling than all the famines, earthquakes, typhoons, fires, and highway robberies of daily life in 11th-century Kyoto.

The movie flashes back several days to when the woodcutter ventured into a nearby forest to gather kindling. In the woods he came across a woman's veil, a samurai's hat, a tangled length of rope, and a dead body. He informed the police and submitted an official report at the courthouse. There he met the Buddhist monk, who testified that a few days earlier he saw a samurai (Mori Masayuki) and a veiled woman (Kyō Machiko) traveling through the forest. The dead body the woodcutter found was the body of the samurai.

Also at the courthouse in the flashbacks is a notorious bandit named Tajomaru (Mifune Toshirō). Tajomaru is in custody for the murder of the samurai, and he alternates between detached, trance-like silences and fits of manic energy. Tajomaru confesses that he killed the samurai and forcibly kissed the veiled woman. At that point, Tajomaru claims, she willingly gave herself to him and afterward demanded that Tajomaru fight her samurai husband to the death. "To have my shame known to two men is worse than dying," she reportedly told the bandit. Yet during the fight, Tajomaru tells the court, the woman ran away.

This violent, sexualized opening of *Rashōmon* has complicated connections to the legacy of the occupation. It depicts a woman as property to be won and lost, something that American censors explicitly forbade between 1945 and 1949 (see Chapter 4). Yet its handling of the subject does not necessarily undermine the censors' agenda. The woman in *Rashōmon* speaks in "feudal" terms about her shame,

People pass beneath the Kaminarimon, a large gate in Tokyo similar to Kyoto's historic Rashōmon, in 1918 (from www.kinouya.com).

but she exhibits a high degree of agency. In Tajomaru's telling, the nameless woman chooses to have sex with the bandit, manipulates him into fighting for her, then escapes both of the men who would seek to claim her. The movie also engages with the Americans' promotion of kissing on screen, but in an unexpected way. The bandit intended the kiss to be the beginning of a rape, not at all what American film inspectors wanted Japanese audiences to associate with the so-called "modern" way of showing affection. However, in Tajormaru's version of events, the kiss is the trigger for the woman's change of heart.

Rain continues to fall on the Rashōmon as the monk and woodcutter tell their listener how the woman herself appeared at the courthouse to contradict Tajomaru's story. The kiss plays no role in her version of the murder in the grove. According to her, Tajomaru raped her and left without killing the samurai. She begged her husband to kill her because of the shame she felt, and when he refused she killed him with her dagger in a fit of madness.

Rape, always a charged topic, was an especially sensitive one during the occupation. Before Japan surrendered, as American troops invaded the nation's southernmost islands, individual women and entire families there committed suicide because they believed that American troops would rape and kill them. Such suicides were particularly prevalent on Okinawa, where the Japanese army sometimes made civilians, often indigenous Ryukyuans, take their own lives before the Americans landed in April 1945. Japan's soldiers used rape as a tool of war in China and elsewhere, and they reasoned that the Americans would do the same. During the occupation

American and Japanese officials sanctioned brothels in Japan in an attempt to minimize rapes (see Chapter 7). There were few reports of sexual assaults involving Americans while the occupation lasted, but American soldiers did commit rapes that went unreported. When American censorship ended, belated accounts of these crimes began to appear in Japanese media. *Rashōmon*'s use of rape as a plot point therefore came at a time when public discussion of sexual assault was on the rise. When Kyo's character reacts to her rape by contemplating death, she not only enacts a feudal concept of feminine honor consistent with a *jidaigeki*, she gives voice to an experience that too many Japanese women of the war generation knew firsthand.[6]

A more arcane subject for movie audiences in 1950 was *Rashōmon*'s points of contact with spiritual tradition. After the woman's account comes the testimony of her dead husband, delivered through a professional medium. Akutagawa's short story does not describe the medium or the ceremony she uses to summon the murdered man, but Kurosawa's film shows both. The medium's white robe, theatrical makeup, untidy black hair, and ceremonial use of bamboo branches recalls the archetypically insane character of Higaki Genzaburō in *Sanshirō Sugata Part II* (see Chapter 3). The medium is not insane, however, but a shaman. Shamanism in Japan dates to antiquity, and for centuries its folk practices existed in partnership with the more formalized religious practices of Shinto and Buddhism. The nation's classical and medieval courts employed diviners who practiced a kind of magic called *onmyōdō*, which coexisted with Japan's other tools for understanding the world and the divine. From the Meiji *jidai* onward, however, new legal definitions of Shinto and Buddhism excluded shamans and their rituals. Shamans continued to practice, especially in rural areas, but the services they provided became more esoteric and localized to the villages and neighborhoods in which they lived and worked. The inclusion of a shaman in *Rashōmon* reinforces the film's premodern setting and locates its mystical plot points outside the purview of typical 20th-century religious practice.[7]

The Buddhist monk at the Rashōmon gate represents a more familiar religious tradition, but the role of Buddhism in public life had also changed during moviegoers' lifetimes. Buddhism and Shinto were closely interwoven by the 19th century, sharing gods and sometimes combining places of worship. Yet the Meiji government, in an attempt to "modernize" and regulate them, declared the two religions separate and increased support for the nation's largest Shinto shrines. Politicians and textbooks spoke of Japan as a divine nation following a Great Divine Way (kannagara no daidō, "the great way of the gods") and emphasized the emperor's descent from the gods. Even under this regime that occupation authorities later called "State Shinto," however, nearly all Japanese people continued to practice Buddhism and esoteric faith traditions alongside Shinto. Buddhist temples and priests held rites associated with death, funerals, and remembrance, while Shinto's purview included births, weddings, and a diversity of festivals for harvests, purification, and the appeasement of gods. After the war, American occupation policy forbade the

Image from Percival Lowell's *Occult Japan* (1895) depicting a spiritual possession.

Japanese government from favoring one religion over another—though the Americans defined "religion" in ways that excluded much informal and historical religious practice—and new laws prohibited Japanese schools from displaying religious symbols or carrying out religious instruction. Buddhism and Shinto existed in an official state of parity, but religion's role in daily life tended to grow smaller in the postwar era. The Buddhist priests who used to travel the country delivering public sermons—not very theological ones, but rather lectures on honesty and clean living—no longer did so. Most simply waited for people to come to them for specific purposes like funerals.[8]

Availing himself of the appropriate spiritual interpreter for the occasion, *Rashōmon*'s dead samurai gives the court yet another version of his death: whatever happened between his wife and Tajomaru, when they left the grove together the samurai took his own life in humiliation. Each of the three people who were in the grove therefore insists that he or she was the one who did the deed.

Akutagawa's "In a Grove" ends there, but Kurosawa's film returns to the men sheltering beneath the Rashōmon for one last twist. The three men at the gate—the woodcutter, the monk, and the man to whom they tell the tale—fall to fighting when the third man picks up on an inconsistency. He accuses the woodcutter of stealing the woman's dagger from the crime scene where he found the dead samurai; the dagger played a role in each version of the story, but none of the people in the grove took it with them and the woodcutter did not report finding it. The monk is aghast to realize that the seemingly innocent woodcutter, whom he regarded as a friend, is both a liar and a thief. He despairs that all humans are untrustworthy and the world is as rotten as the crumbling Rashōmon, but just then a ray of hope appears. An abandoned baby squalls from a corner of the gate, and the woodcutter, full of pity, adopts it. He has six other children, he says, so one more won't make a difference. The monk tells the woodcutter that his generosity has restored his faith in humanity. Even flawed people, he realizes, can do good, and nobody is defined by their worst actions. What the bandit, the woman, and the samurai did in the grove remains unknowable, but each of them had the capacity to do either right or wrong, and all three probably did a bit of both.

Rashōmon's message was timely as Japan embarked on a new war five years after the last one ended in destruction and subjugation. War was a collective act of evil that inflated individual acts of evil like murder and rape to international proportions, and the Americans insisted that Japan renounce it forever. When they needed help in Korea, though, Japanese politicians and businesses eagerly obliged. Could Japan really go back to war without betraying its official anti-war stance? If *Rashōmon*'s woodcutter could lie and steal but move a monk to tears with his goodness, if Tajomaru could rape and kill but hold his head high in court, if the woman could manipulate and murder but appear guiltless in the eyes of the law, if the samurai could die and then tell the world about it, then why not?

CHAPTER 12

The Idiot

In the director's own opinion, 1951's *The Idiot* (*Hakuchi*) was nearly ruinous for Kurosawa. The studio through which he produced it, Shōchiku, destroyed much of his original four-and-a-half-hour cut, leaving under three hours extant and releasing only 100 minutes to theaters. Despite a major role for Shōchiku's star Hara Setsuko, *The Idiot* was not successful with audiences or critics. Had *Rashōmon* not won major international awards at the very moment that *The Idiot* flopped, Kurosawa's career might have stalled. Instead he moved quickly past it and *The Idiot* was just as quickly forgotten.

For years Kurosawa had wanted to adapt works of Russian literature. In fact, he had done so once already, staging a theatrical adaptation of Anton Chekov's play *A Marriage Proposal* during one of Tōhō's labor strikes. As far back as the late 1930s Kurosawa considered a film treatment of *Dersu Uzala*, a travel memoir by a turn-of-the-century Russian frontiersman; he finally did it in 1975 (see Chapter 25). Kurosawa read Leo Tolstoy's *War and Peace* "countless" times and eventually adapted a play by Tolstoy's colleague Maxim Gorky (see Chapter 17). Long-held ambitions notwithstanding, 1951 was a strange time for Kurosawa to release his first movie based on a Russian text. The proxy war in Korea between the Soviet Union and the United States was at its height, and Japan was deeply involved on the side of the Americans.

The Idiot's story came from 19th-century psychological realist writer Fyodor Dostoevsky, whom Kurosawa cited as his favorite author. Kurosawa's screenplay uses a postwar Japanese setting, but it retains the novel's Russian flavor by situating the action in Hokkaido, the broad, flat, snowy island at the northern end of Japan. Because of its low elevation, huge farms and ranches, frequent use of European-style architecture, and indigenous population of Ainu, Japanese people often say that Hokkaido is more like a foreign country than a Japanese prefecture. It is also very near the island of Sakhalin, which the Russians seized from Japan at the end of World War II.

The movie begins when Kameda Kinji (Mori Masayuki), the titular "idiot," arrives home in Hokkaido after his release from a prisoner-of-war camp. In 1951 the Soviet Union held far more Japanese prisoners of war than any other former Allied country, and family members of the thousands of missing men and women still gathered regularly to pray for their release. Kameda's POW camp, however, was run by Americans. While awaiting execution for war crimes, Kameda suffered epileptic seizures. The Americans diagnosed him with "idiocy" and released him. He is disarmingly honest about his condition, explaining it clearly and without shame to a gruff fellow repatriate named Akema Denkichi (Mifune Toshirō).

Unfortunately, real mental illness patients in early postwar Japan rarely had opportunities to discuss their conditions. Like many countries, "Japan was a harsh, inhospitable place for anyone who did not fall into a 'proper' social category." This was true for war veterans suffering from what is now called post-traumatic stress disorder as well as people with congenital afflictions or whose minds were ravaged by disease. Many such sufferers became homeless at the end of the war when family members could not or would not take them in, while others found reluctant support from relatives who tried to keep them out of sight. Too often, people with mental health problems concluded that suicide was their best option.[1]

A mentally-ill movie protagonist was a rarity in 1951, but *The Idiot*'s sympathetic portrayal of a former war criminal was typical. Most people condemned the war when they spoke of it at all, but at the same time they elected many former soldiers to high office, including some whom the Americans had imprisoned for wartime atrocities like future prime minister Kishi Nobosuke. After American media censorship eased, dozens of movies each year lamented the war but made heroes of Japanese soldiers. Published letters, autobiographies, and novels by still-imprisoned veterans struck a chord with readers, many of whom publicly called for the authors' early release. Accused war criminals usually expressed deep regrets about the war, but they detached themselves from their crimes by saying that they had only followed orders. *The Idiot*'s lead character suffers from amnesia and cannot remember what war crimes he committed, a decision that allows Kurosawa to sidestep Kameda's past and focus on the spotless life he lives after his release.[2]

Kameda's closest relative is a Mr. Ono (Shimura Takashi), who lives in Hokkaido's capital city, Sapporo. By Japanese standards, Ono is a large landowner. The American-designed land reform program of 1947 weakened the power of Japanese landlords by redistributing their land to tenant farmers (see Chapter 5), but the law was more generous to Hokkaido's landlords than to those in other prefectures. Farms and ranches in Hokkaido were, on average, much bigger than in the rest of Japan, which made it easier for farmers to use modern machines that achieved more efficient production, and the Americans did not want to jeopardize Hokkaido's agricultural output with excessive fragmentation of farmland. In *The Idiot*, Ono's daughter Ayako (Kuga Yoshiko) gives Kameda a tour of the property, which includes a herd of cattle, stands of tall pine trees, and fields that stretch to the horizon.[3]

With the help of his wealthy relative, Kameda finds a room in the home of a young man named Kayama (Chiaki Minoru). Kayama is not a veteran, but his father is "a former soldier, dishonorably discharged." The drunken patriarch is unable to provide for his family, so his son seeks financial security through less-than-ideal

Japanese prisoners of war in American custody on Okinawa, 1945 (Library of Congress).

means; the younger Kayama is in love with Ono's daughter Ayako, but he intends to marry a woman of ill repute named Taeko (Hara Setsuko) because of her even larger dowry. Ono plays matchmaker, which will earn him a percentage of Taeko's dowry. The wedding plot hits a snag when "the idiot" meets Taeko. The former prisoner-of-war and the bartered woman have an instant connection, and Kameda remarks that Taeko's eyes remind him of a prisoner facing a firing squad.

The execution of Japanese war criminals was a grim but alluring subject. During the occupation the Americans killed around 150 "Class A" war criminals, those guilty of the worst offenses. Japanese magazine, newspaper, and book publishers generated a huge amount of material about the war crimes trials and the lives and deaths of defendants. When Kameda tells Taeko about a prisoner he saw put to death, his tone and the movie's is hushed and sympathetic.[4]

The reason Taeko has a large dowry but few marriage options is that she is another kind of prisoner: the "kept woman" of a much older man. She became his mistress when she was 14 years old, but now he wants to release her, so he offers 600,000 yen to anyone who will take her off his hands. Long-term extramarital affairs were common in Japan, and in many cases people did not try very hard to keep them secret. Historically the most powerful men in the country—the *shō-gun*, the emperor, feudal lords in their regional fiefdoms, and even some wealthy commoners—kept harems of concubines. The Taishō emperor himself, Hirohito's father, was the son of one of the Meiji emperor's concubines rather than the empress. Concubinage officially ended during the Meiji *jidai*, but the status of "mistress" actually achieved legal recognition as part of the government's overhaul of family law. Between 1870 and 1885, the law considered a mistress to be part of a man's family and accorded her rights similar to a wife; such protections, however, did not apply to the male paramours of married women. Men could easily legitimize children born to their mistresses in order to make them eligible for inheritance. Still, Japanese culture valued female virginity, so single men concerned with social standing were reluctant to marry women known to have been mistresses.[5]

In *The Idiot* Kameda falls in love with Taeko, and she with him, but she worries that her reputation will ruin the ex-soldier's second chance at life. At Kameda's encouragement she escapes her own imprisonment by leaving her old lover and declining to marry Kayama, but she soon falls into the orbit of the brutish veteran Akama whom Kameda met on the ferry to Hokkaido. Mifune, who plays Akama, married and welcomed the first of two sons shortly before *The Idiot* began production, but later in life he also had a daughter by a mistress.

Kameda's return to Hokkaido disrupts not only his relative Ono's matchmaking plot, but Ono's status as a large landowner. Much of the 120 acres he claims to own actually belongs to Kameda by right of inheritance. During Kameda's absence, his father died and Ono seized his property. The question of inheritance creates a great deal of tension between Ono, his wife, their daughter Ayako, and Kameda, though Kameda remains largely aloof due to his "idiocy." Ono's solution to the problem is to have Ayako marry her cousin Kameda and keep the land in the family.

The Sapporo Snow Festival, which began in 1950 and quickly became Hokkaido's most famous cultural attraction, is the setting for Kameda and Ayako's tentative courtship. The huge celebration was evidence of Japan's economic recovery during the Korean War and people's increased ability to spend time and money on recreational activities. Within a few years the Snow Festival made Sapporo a major winter tourism destination. Amid its huge snow sculptures and revelers on ice skates, Kameda and Ayako awkwardly flirt. Or rather, Ayako flirts for both of them; the simpleminded Kameda lacks the social subtleties to do so, and moreover he still loves Taeko.

Despite so much focus on the question of marriage, *The Idiot* ends not with a wedding but with death. The foreshadowing of Taeko's "execution" pays off, not metaphorically through an arranged marriage but literally when Akama kills her in a jealous rage. He knew that she loved Kameda, not him. The ex-soldiers Akama and Kameda, united in grief and unable or unwilling to find new places in postwar society, purposefully freeze to death in Akama's snowbound home.

This macabre ending was out of step with the increasingly optimistic public mood of 1951, when the economy was booming and the end of the occupation was

The Sapporo Snow Festival, now in its eighth decade, has grown into one of Japan's largest public events (photograph by t-konno, Wikimedia Commons).

just around the corner. Unlike Kurosawa's last several films, *The Idiot* was a flop, and not only because the studio left so much of it on the cutting room floor. Like his tragic characters, the director of dark occupation-era stories like *Drunken Angel* and *Rashōmon* seemed unable or unwilling to adapt to the new, brighter era. Luckily for Kurosawa's career, his next film closed out the occupation with a life-affirming masterpiece that put any such doubts to rest.

CHAPTER 13

Ikiru

Throughout the seven-year American occupation, the Japanese government continued to convene in the same place it had met since 1936: a large, European-style edifice of concrete, granite, and steel in central Tokyo called the National Diet Building. From its creation in the Meiji *jidai*, the elected and appointed members of the bicameral Diet functioned in close partnership with a sprawling government bureaucracy that had close ties to the *zaibatsu* and the military. After the war, the American rulers of Japan dismantled the *zaibatsu* and the military and restructured the Diet to make it more democratic. Yet they hardly touched the sub-layer of Japanese government—the bureaucrats who made it run day to day.

For Japanese citizens, the most relevant government officials were not prime ministers and Diet representatives, but the men and women who worked in the nation's 47 prefectural governments, tens of thousands of village offices, and 1.3 million neighborhood councils. Before the occupation, the highest-ranking officials at each of these levels of government held office through appointment or elections in which wealthy landowners had virtually exclusive voting power. American authorities broadened the electorate by extending the franchise to women, lowering the voting age from 25 to 20, weakening the power of landlords, and making more government positions subject to election. They also gave Japanese voters the right of recall and weakened ties between each level of government so that local officials were responsible mainly to their constituents, not to the central government in Tokyo. However, in the latter half of the occupation and beyond, Japan's central government reclaimed a great deal of oversight authority and worked to standardize laws and administrative practices throughout the country. A stable network of career bureaucrats provided continuity as Japan navigated the occupation and embarked on the post-occupation era.[1]

Careers in government are prestigious in Japan and in East Asian cultures generally. Chinese constellations that spread to Japan in ancient times include figures like The Investigator, The First Minister, and Law Administrators. Under American leadership, over six million professional functionaries and technocrats worked in Japan's ministries and local government offices, and they played crucial roles in implementing occupation-era laws and administering public services. They also served as channels of communication between the Japanese government and

The National Diet Building, home of the Japanese legislature since 1936 (photograph by Kakidai, Wikimedia Commons).

MacArthur's headquarters and between Japanese politicians and corporate interests. The Americans purged bureaucrats who had clear militarist sympathies, and during the occupation's reverse course they denied government workers the right to strike, but ultimately they could not administer the country without the support of a large and effective bureaucracy. It was through these national and local administrators that the Americans achieved their ambitious goals in Japan, establishing public welfare programs like unemployment insurance and a universal healthcare system that surpassed anything available in the United States.[2]

In April 1951 MacArthur suddenly left Japan after nearly six years as its "blue-eyed *shōgun*." The general had publicly criticized President Truman's handling of the Korean War, so Truman relieved him of duty. The Diet passed a resolution thanking MacArthur for his leadership during the occupation, and the government announced a plan to build a large statue of the general in Tokyo Bay; it abandoned the statue idea when MacArthur told the American Congress that Japan was like "a boy of 12" learning the ways of "civilization" and modernity. The occupation lasted another year under new leadership, but the departure of MacArthur was a sign that Japanese sovereignty was nearly at hand.[3]

Representatives from Japan and the United States met in San Francisco to sign the formal peace treaty that brought the occupation to an end. The Americans would not really be leaving; the treaty gave them the right to maintain military bases throughout Japan. The United States, fighting a global Cold War, was unwilling to give up such an important strategic position in Asia. Still, the closure of occupation headquarters in April 1952 marked the end of an era. For the first time since 1945 the Japanese government was free to design and enact its own policies.

The nature and capability of Japanese government is a central concern of Kurosawa's 13th feature, *Ikiru*, which Tōhō released just months after the occupation ended. Like *The Idiot*, *Ikiru* takes inspiration from a 19th-century Russian novel, Tolstoy's *The Death of Ivan Ilyich*, but its translation to a Japanese setting is much more successful than Kurosawa's previous effort. *Ikiru* received a slew of foreign and domestic awards and became the most well-known of Kurosawa's *gendaigeki*, present-day stories.

Ikiru's protagonist is an aging bureaucrat named Watanabe Kanji (Shimura Takashi). As Chief of Public Affairs in a local government office, his days consist of stamping documents and moving them from one never-ending stack to another. When a group of mothers from the community comes to the office to complain about unsanitary water, Kanji's staff directs them to other offices like Public Works and the Parks Department, which in turn direct them to other offices and back to Public Affairs in a Kafkaesque caricature of bureaucratic runaround. "You call this democracy?" the women ask after a day of fruitless petitioning.

When Kanji misses a day of work for the first time in nearly 30 years, his coworkers react not with concern but with undisguised ambition. "Bureaucrats always wonder who will take the boss's place," says one. The younger clerks start calculating how many people have to die before one of them becomes section chief. Unbeknownst to them, Kanji took off work to see a doctor, who diagnoses him with advanced stomach cancer. Stomach cancer is a perennial contender for the most common type of cancer in Japan, where due to a combination of genetic, environmental, and dietary reasons it occurs far more often than in America or Europe. Yet the doctor who diagnoses Kanji lies to him about his condition, minimizing its severity so as not to cause panic and despair. Author Pico Iyer, a longtime foreign resident of Japan whose step-daughter developed Hodgkin's lymphoma, wrote in 2015 that "even now ... doctors in Japan try not to tell patients, or their families, that they have cancer." A cultural preference for giving bad news obliquely rather than directly extends even to life-and-death medical matters. Kanji clarifies the truth about his prognosis by talking to another patient who knows the pattern of stomach cancer symptoms.[4]

The Japanese healthcare system was in transition when Kurosawa made *Ikiru*. A series of laws between 1922 and 1944 required employers to provide health insurance to their workers, but the quality of coverage varied greatly from industry to industry. When the war ended, the issue of public health became urgent as communicable ailments spread through the country, and the Americans instructed the Japanese government to revise and standardize the nation's healthcare policies. For guidance, American and Japanese officials looked not to the underdeveloped American system, but to Britain, whose postwar centralization of healthcare culminated in the creation of the National Health Service in 1948. The creation of a similar universal healthcare system in Japan proceeded slowly, but by 1952 80 percent of Japan's citizens had health insurance. The Japanese government demonstrated its commitment to 100 percent coverage with the popular National Health Insurance Law of 1958.[5]

In addition to inefficient bureaucrats and unreliable doctors, *Ikiru* addresses the generational conflicts that marked postwar family life. Kanji's son and daughter-in-law (Kaneko Nobuo and Seki Kyōko) live with him but hope to use his pension money to buy their own home when the old man retires. They want a "modern," Western-style house, and they expect to pay a total of 500,000 yen for it—the equivalent of about $1300 in 1952. Over half of Japanese households at the time consisted of one or more elderly parent, one or more of their adult children plus spouses, and their children's children. Multiple generations living under the same roof was the historical norm, but in the postwar years more and more young Japanese people lived apart from their parents. New industrial jobs took them to cities far from the hometowns where their parents lived, and many gained the financial independence to live alone if they wished. In *Ikiru* Kurosawa sides with tradition by characterizing Kanji's son and daughter-in-law as selfish. When Kanji overhears them talking about moving out, he becomes depressed at the prospect of living out his final days alone.[6]

The pension that Kanji will receive when he retires is Japan's form of social security. The National Pension system began before the war, and in its earliest form it provided retirement income to military veterans and bureaucrats. In the 1950s and 1960s the pension system expanded to cover all residents of Japan, and its assets grew until it became the world's largest public pension system. By the early 21st century it was serving the needs of the world's oldest population. Kanji's pension income after a lifetime of public service amounts to 13,000 yen per month, or about $34 per month in 1952 terms. Like many Japanese people then and now, Kanji has private savings to augment his retirement income, but the monthly pension is an important source of security for him and an attractive opportunity for his son and daughter-in-law.[7]

After Kanji's cancer diagnosis, planning for his future seems futile. He stops going to work, avoids going home, and tries to enjoy life to the fullest on the streets of postwar Tokyo. While in a bar he meets a young writer (Itō Yūnosuke) who leads Kanji on a nighttime tour of the latest in urban entertainment. They visit a *pachinko* parlor, a kind of gambling arcade whose flashy machines combine elements of slots and pinball. *Pachinko* was illegal during the war but became a popular form of recreation in the late 1940s and early '50s. The parlors are especially popular with older people looking to supplement their retirement incomes with a lucky win. After playing *pachinko*, Kanji and his friend visit a beer hall selling Nippon Beer, a new company that split off from the Dai Nippon brewery conglomerate when the Americans temporarily broke up Japanese monopolies. Nippon Beer stood alone for a few years before recombining with another large brewery after the end of the occupation. When they leave the beer hall, Kanji and the writer continue to drink and dance the night away at a series of bars bearing modern English names and offering jazz and stripteases.[8]

"Golden Gai," a Tokyo nightlife hub that has changed little since the early Shōwa *jidai* (photograph by Mike Kniec, Wikimedia Commons).

Contemporary pleasures give Kanji a brief respite from his illness, but the nightlife's delights soon turn sour. In the early morning hours Kanji and his friend become nauseated and exhausted when their hired female escorts break into a drunken rendition of an American pop song. The one song that Kanji actually requests during his bar-hopping bacchanal is not a contemporary one, but a soulful, 30-year-old Japanese ballad from the Taishō *jidai*. Though he tries to enjoy himself in the cosmopolitan, hedonistic world of new Tokyo, Kanji's sensibilities belong to an older and arguably more wholesome era.

Wholesome is not how Kanji's son would describe his father. He sees Kanji's sudden change of behavior—skipping work, staying out all night—as evidence of an affair. Indeed, Kanji does spend time with a young, female employee from his office named Toyo (Odagiri Miki), who tracks the truant down to sign her letter of resignation. Kanji takes Toyo to an amusement park and even buys her a pair of nylon stockings from a department store. She eventually distances herself from Kanji, not wanting to become the mistress of an aged widower, but Kanji probably does not have romantic intentions toward her. He enjoys being with Toyo for her youth and liveliness; she is a psychological antidote to his terminal disease. Yet for Kanji's son, who remains ignorant of his father's cancer, the young woman represents a threat to his inheritance.

It is Toyo who gives Kanji the idea that changes the rest of his life. She explains to Kanji that she is leaving the bureaucracy to take a job on a toy company's assembly line. Making something tangible that brings people joy gives her more satisfaction than stretching "an hour's worth of work into a day" as a government drone. Kanji has too little time left to start a new career, but in an epiphanic moment he realizes that he can still create something substantive, and he can do it from within the bureaucracy. He finally returns to work, determined to solve one real problem before he dies: the unsanitary water crisis that the group of mothers complained about at the beginning of the film. Kanji encounters the same procedural roadblocks that frustrated the mothers, but he persists, visiting the site himself and shepherding a plan through the labyrinthine system in which he spent his life.

At this point Kurosawa suddenly truncates *Ikiru*'s linear narrative and jumps ahead five months to Kanji's funeral. A framed picture of the deceased bureaucrat sits at the head of a hall. Kanji's coworkers and relatives sit *seiza*-style, formally resting on their knees, on the *tatami* floor in black suits and ties. A typical Japanese funeral like Kanji's includes a wake, a meal, and then interment of the deceased's ashes. Kanji's funeral, though, has an extra feature: a gaggle of press that converges to report on the death of a beloved civil servant who created a beautiful new park where once there was only stagnant water.

Having traced Kanji's path right up to the moment when he discovers his purpose, Kurosawa sidesteps the hero's actual achievement and asks the audience to reckon with its troubling aftermath. The purpose of *Ikiru* is not only to celebrate a bureaucrat's triumph over the system, but to condemn the system that made that triumph so difficult in the first place. In this the movie has much in common with *Scandal*, Kurosawa's movie about a crooked lawyer's path to redemption in a corrupt system (see Chapter 10). Once Kanji is gone, his coworkers minimize his role in creating the park. They mock the press and the public for attributing it to the work of one man. The whole bureaucracy must share the credit, they say, and one of them plans to leverage the park's popularity into a run for higher office. Such opportunism is all the more tactless because it takes place at Kanji's wake.

As the bureaucrats congratulate themselves on the job they did not do, the mothers of the community arrive to pay their respects. They enter the room in tears and light sticks of incense on the altar. After the mothers leave, the other bureaucrats fall silent, shamed in the knowledge that no constituents would have come to mourn them if they had died instead of Kanji.

For Kurosawa it is not enough that one good official brings about one belated change for one community. The bureaucracy, the people, and the press must all work in tandem to achieve lasting transparency, accountability, and progress. *Ikiru*'s call to action coincided perfectly with the restoration of Japan's independence after seven years of occupation. Whether the country's public officials would use their power for the benefit of the people remained to be seen.

PART THREE

The Miracle Years

CHAPTER 14

Seven Samurai

Jidaigeki imitate the past but tell us about their present. For Kurosawa, the basic nature of Japan did not change when samurai became bureaucrats, *kimono* gave way to shirts and slacks, and capitalism replaced feudalism. The thirteen movies Kurosawa wrote and directed during war and occupation showed how dramatically conditions in Japan changed in just a few years, but they also dealt with human experiences—life and death, pride and shame, sacrifice and suffering—that remained constant across eras. In 1954 his epic adventure *Seven Samurai* (*Shichinin no samurai*) reconstructed a stratified medieval society and held it up as a mirror for midcentury audiences who knew the meaning of change but whose lives exhibited remarkable continuities with the past.

Among the movie's heroes are farmers. In Kurosawa's earlier *jidaigeki The Men Who Tread on the Tiger's Tail* (see Chapter 4) and *Rashōmon* (see Chapter 11), the commoner characters of a porter and a woodcutter guide modern audiences through esoteric medieval worlds. The farmers of *Seven Samurai* make even better audience surrogates; the odds of a Japanese moviegoer being a farmer or having a farmer in their family were high in 1954, when over 40 percent of Japan's population worked in agriculture. Samurai, as popularly conceived, existed for only a few centuries, but farmers were eternal.[1]

Within a few years, Japanese farmers would enjoy the same cutting-edge conveniences and comforts as urban workers, but in the early 1950s rural people's lives were not yet outrageously different from their medieval forebears. Farm families still lived in rustic houses with few modern amenities, most village roads were unpaved, people used human waste for fertilizer, and field workers did their planting and harvesting by hand rather than with machines. The sight of stoop-backed farmers shin-deep in mud, planting rice seedlings one at a time, was as common in postwar Japan as in descriptions from the 1500s, the century in which *Seven Samurai* takes place. To be sure, there were important differences. The American land reform program of 1947 empowered the poorest farm families with new legal protections and created an accessible path from tenancy to landownership (see Chapter 5). This meant that postwar farmers had more freedom to choose what to do with their land—whether to plant new crops or to sell it and pursue other sources of income—than their ancestors who served in perpetuity to the wealthiest villagers and feudal lords. And unlike the farmers of the distant past, modern ones could easily travel by train to enjoy urban recreations like movie theaters. Nevertheless, before rural standards of living grew exponentially in the 1960s and '70s, people who worked the land could readily identify with *Seven Samurai*'s depiction of medieval farm life.[2]

Farm incomes, however, were already in the midst of a long-term rise. They began to climb at the end of the war when food shortages and a booming black market drove up crop prices. City folk envied country people, who not only had easier access to food but could charge what they liked for it. Farmers generally stayed ahead of the inflation that constantly weakened urban consumers' purchasing power during the 1940s. Rural incomes climbed even further during the Korean War when members of farm households who did not farm full-time found employment in other industries, often in factories. Like the farmers in *Seven Samurai*, 1954's rural people were not as impoverished as their rustic villages and time-honored farming methods might suggest.[3]

The movie's farmers are similarly complicated, and they articulate a range of viewpoints and attitudes. They are not always heroic and sympathetic; some are downright comical, and some are inscrutable. Even after spending nearly four hours among them and their fields, we cannot claim to know them. They are too multifaceted and have too many secrets to let the samurai or urban movie audiences in completely.

What we do know is that the farmers need help to maintain their way of life. When dozens of bandits on horseback raid the village to steal crops and women, the village elder (Kōdō Kokuten) hits upon an idea: hire *rōnin*, masterless samurai, to defend the village. Movies often portray *rōnin* as lone wolf heroes and honorable mercenaries. In *Seven Samurai*, though, most *rōnin* are untrustworthy, and only a few are great fighters.

Illustration touting *nōchi kaikaku* (land reform), the American-backed farmland redistribution program of the late 1940s (from National Archives of Japan).

Many of them probably lack masters due to personal disgraces or battlefield defeats. The village elder knows better than to hope for heroes, but he expects that some hungry *rōnin* will be desperate enough to protect the village in exchange for food. He sends a group of villagers including Yohei (Hidari Bokuzen), Manzō (Fujiwara Kamatari), and Rikichi (Tsuchiya Yoshio) to a nearby town to hire as many warriors as the village can feed.

Samurai were supposed to serve feudal lords called *daimyō*, the most esteemed members of their own caste, not lower categories of people like farmers or merchants. Even lacking masters, most *rōnin* the villagers meet are too proud to consider the farmers' proposal. Others are too weak or undisciplined to be of use. Just as the villagers prepare to abandon their quest, they witness a samurai named Kanbei (Shimura Takashi) humble himself to help the local townsfolk. When a thief takes a child hostage, Kanbei cuts off his topknot and shaves his head to disguise himself as a monk. He then approaches the kidnapper under the pretense of offering food and uses his incredible speed and swordsmanship to rescue the child. A samurai's topknot is one of the outward signs of his membership in the warrior caste, and to remove it is nearly unthinkable except as an act of extreme contrition. For Kanbei to remove his as part of a ploy to help townsfolk in distress, accepting no reward afterward, shows a selfless devotion to service and a willingness to use non-traditional strategies to achieve victory. He is the perfect answer to the villagers' problem, and after hearing their plight Kanbei agrees to help them.

Two other samurai—youthful, eager Katsushirō (Kimura Isao) and coarse, vulgar Kikuchiyo (Mifune Toshirō)—also see Kanbei's feat and ask to become his disciples. Kanbei reluctantly takes Katsushirō under his wing, so the villagers now have two samurai in their service. Kikuchiyo's undignified demeanor, though, causes Kanbei to reject him. Caste and propriety are important to Kanbei despite his unconventional methods, and he easily discerns that Kikuchiyo is not a trueborn samurai. The farmers need all the help they can get, but they say nothing and leave the recruitment of additional *rōnin* to Kanbei's discretion.

The interactions between the samurai, the farmers, and the pretender Kikuchiyo center on the question of class identity, a highly-charged topic in the mid–1950s. The film appeared as the U.S. and the Soviet Union advanced different notions of class mobility. American politicians and free-market theorists insisted that capitalism gave everybody the opportunity to gain wealth, effectively rendering class meaningless. Communism held that poor farmers and workers, as well as colonized people around the world, could only achieve social and economic advancement by seizing power from elites. Communist forces fought American troops to a stalemate in Korea in 1953 and defeated French colonial forces in Vietnam in 1954, proof that their side had global appeal as well as strength.

Seven Samurai brings a third perspective to the debate: what if class was beside the point? In feudal Japan it was caste rather than class that mattered, and caste was a matter of parentage. Though peasants might grow wealthy and samurai might fall into poverty, their social inequality was an inalterable reality, and the lower caste always owed deference to the higher. Despite years of intense Americanization and a profitable Cold War alliance with the United States, Japan in the 1950s continued to exhibit a firm commitment to the idea of social hierarchy. Samurai no longer existed (though many people, including Kurosawa, traced their lineage to old samurai families), but fixed notions of rank and identity still influenced how people interacted. Japanese businessmen bowed low to their bosses when they met on the street, and seniority-based promotions helped ensure that they would always do so. People spoke to their superiors using the Japanese language's special honorific mode instead of the more casual diction used between friends and equals. Despite new gender equality laws and more economic opportunities, women in the workplace often had to serve tea to their male coworkers in addition to their regular duties, and in the home they did more than an equal share of housework. In rural areas, the families of former tenants and the families of former landlords still played out old customs of *corvée* labor in which "child" (*kobun*) households did a certain amount of unpaid work for "parent" (*oyabun*) households, even in cases where the former surpassed the latter in wealth. Clearly it was not only class that determined one's place in the world, but also characteristics like age, sex, and ancestry. *Seven Samurai* repeatedly stresses the difficulty of transcending such categories.[4]

The farmers Yohei, Manzō, and Rikichi wait patiently while the samurai Kanbei and Katsushirō recruit four more of the best *rōnin* that food can buy. This brings the total number of samurai to six, one less than the number Kanbei considers minimally sufficient to protect a village, but they cannot wait for a seventh; the farmers' harvest and the return of the bandits are just days away. The team sets out for the village, but they soon discover another in tow—Kikuchiyo, undeterred by the mockery of the samurai, comes along uninvited, hopping on rocks, cavorting in rivers, and leaping from trees with animalistic zeal.

By not belonging to an identifiable social group, Kikuchiyo exists outside of human society as conceived in the 16th century. Kikuchiyo is not a samurai, a craftsman, a merchant, or a priest, and he says he hates peasants; he seems to belong to none of medieval Japan's recognized castes, nor to any of the stray categories like actor, musician, butcher, or criminal. While preparing to play this enigmatic figure, Mifune studied the movement of monkeys. Though monkeys are comical figures, they also represent wisdom in the Asian zodiac and are sometimes said to serve as intermediaries between gods and humans. The animals have a strong association with Japanese philosophy thanks to the famous iconography of the "see no evil, hear no evil, speak no evil" trio. Along the forest road that leads to the village, Kikuchiyo proves that he knows the lay of the land, and the samurai finally accept him as a kind of mascot. When the warriors create a banner for the coming battle, they represent themselves as six circles, the farmers as the Japanese symbol *ta* for "field," and Kikuchiyo as a triangle in between.

The villagers struggle to accept the presence of any samurai in their midst, even the ones they hired to defend them. They hide in their homes when the warriors arrive, lest the hungry *rōnin* prove as bad as bandits. The scene echoes the arrival of American soldiers on Japanese shores less than a decade before the release of the film, when civilians feared the worst from the foreign army. Kikuchiyo tricks the villagers out of hiding by falsely announcing a bandit raid, and the speed with which the frightened people emerge from their homes to beg the samurai for help can be taken as a satire of how quickly Japan went from dreading the Americans to relying on them for aid. Yet even after the farmers meet the samurai face to face, they take pains to hide their most valuable possessions from them. Manzō forces his teenage daughter Shino (Tsushima Keiko) to cut her hair and dress as a boy to keep any lustful samurai at bay.

Bringing the political parallel up to the present, the village defense plan recalls the birth of Japan's controversial Self Defense Force in the early 1950s. According to medieval policy farmers ought not have weapons of their own, but Kanbei arms the movie's farmers with bamboo spears and trains them for battle. Japan's American-authored postwar constitution stated that Japan could never again maintain its own army, and in postwar treaties the United States promised to defend Japan in the event of attack. Yet in the summer of 1950 the U.S. reacted to the shock of the Korean War by instructing Japan to raise something very much like an army for the defense of the nation (see Chapter 10). Four years later, when *Seven Samurai* arrived in theaters, the Japanese Self Defense Force was a large, multi-branched, well-equipped army in all but name.[5]

In *Seven Samurai* the issue of farmers and weapons becomes a point of passionate disagreement when the villagers prove more resourceful than the samurai expect. It is Kikuchiyo who notices the farmers are hiding something when he sees Yohei carrying a real spear, not a hand-carved bamboo one. He forces the farmers to reveal an entire horde of samurai weapons and armor that they stole from the bodies of fallen warriors who died in nearby battles. Sometimes the farmers went so far as to murder retreating samurai who were wounded or isolated. Kikuchiyo wants to use the weapons and armor in the coming battle, but the samurai are angry when they learn what the farmers have done, and they are unwilling to benefit from the deaths of their caste-mates.

It falls to Kikuchiyo, the only character who sees the problem objectively, to maintain the tenuous alliance between farmers and samurai. Shouting, pacing, and throwing spears against the wall while the other samurai sit silently, he turns the farmers' sins against the warrior caste:

> Kikuchiyo: What did you think these farmers were, Buddhas? Don't make me laugh. There's no creature on earth as wily as a farmer. Ask them for rice, barley, anything, and they say they don't have any. But they've got it. They've got everything. Dig under the floorboards. If it's not there, try the barn. You'll find plenty. Jars of rice, salt, beans, *sake*. Go up in the mountains, they have hidden fields. They lie and bow and play innocent, but they'll cheat you. After a battle, they hunt down the losers with their spears. Listen, farmers are misers.... They're mean, they're stupid, and they're murderers.... But who made them into such creatures? You did, you samurai, damn you! In war you burn their villages, trample their fields, steal their food, force them to work, rape their women, and kill them if they resist. What are they supposed to do? What are farmers supposed to do, damn it?

At the end of Kikuchiyo's speech, Kanbei has tears in his eyes, and quietly he asks, "You were born a farmer, weren't you?" *Seven Samurai* tolerates no romantic illusions about the nobility of rural life or the honor of warriors. Beneath caste and class are only people with moral failings.

Soon Katsushirō, the youngest samurai, commits a moral failing of his own. While wandering in the woods at the outskirts of the village, he encounters Shino, Manzō's daughter. He mistakes her for a boy but discovers the truth when he touches her chest. In a glade of flowers in the shadows of the forest the two young people from different walks of life give in to passion, and afterward they begin to spend time together in secret. One of the samurai, Kyūzō (Miyaguchi Seiji), sees the lovers together, but he agrees to keep their secret; if the village were to learn about the relationship, the peasants' initial suspicions about the samurai's intent would appear to be confirmed.

The importance of secrecy in matters of the heart was a relatable notion for 1950s audiences. Old concepts about chastity, especially feminine chastity, did not vanish with the fading of the samurai in the Meiji *jidai*, the emergence of the "New Woman" of the 1920s (see Chapter 2), or the promotion of gender equality after World War II (see Chapter 5). Even as Japan explored its new post-occupation identity, both men and women often preferred to keep their trysts secret in the interest of preserving their privacy and avoiding awkward public situations. Moreover, as long as arranged marriages remained the norm, fathers and mothers tried hard to preserve at least the illusion of virginal daughters and virtuous sons. Katsushirō and Shino's illicit affair is undoubtedly romantic, an enviable example of young love, but it is also doomed from the outset. For all of the usual reasons plus caste, the two are simply not free to follow their hearts.

The samurai decide to strike the bandits first to relieve the growing tension in the village, and when they do they observe a deeply troubling consequence of prevailing attitudes toward feminine honor. The farmer Rikichi guides the samurai to the bandit's lair in a large hut near a waterfall. There the outlaws live with several captive women from the village. The samurai set fire to the hut and cut the bandits down as they run out the door. Most of the captive women run out as well, escaping to safety behind the samurai, but one of them pauses at the door of the hut. Rikichi sees her and runs to her, but when she sees him her eyes grow wide with fear and she runs back into the hut to meet a fiery death. She was Rikichi's wife, and in choosing to die rather than return to her husband she enacts two ideas with deep roots in Japanese culture. First is the notion that one's value is closely tied to one's standing in the eyes of others. Despite Japan's broad tolerance for escort work and pornography, the appearance of sexual purity and fidelity remained a component of feminine honor into the modern era. The fact that Rikichi's wife was forced to have sex with bandits might affect how her husband and fellow villagers regard her. The second idea underlying this scene is the belief that suicide can restore or at least atone for lost honor. Suicide plays a key role in many samurai-era *jidaigeki*, but unfortunately is not confined to historical fiction; throughout the 20th century Japan's rate of suicide was among the highest in the world (see Chapter 19).

After the gruesome tragedy of Rikichi's wife's suicide comes an even more startling revelation, both for the samurai and for moviegoers: the bandits have rifles.

Members of Japan's *de facto* **army, the Self Defense Force, on parade in 1954 (from** *Mainichi Graph*, **July 14, 1954).**

Rifles were new to Japan in the late 1500s, having arrived in the middle of that century on Portuguese trading ships. Samurai embraced the new weapons and began to use them in battle in addition to swords and spears. Japanese manufacturers almost immediately began to design their own firearms, but gun ownership never became widespread in the country. Many young men became intimately familiar with guns while serving in World War II, but strict gun control laws kept the devices out of civilian hands. Even police use of guns was controversial. At a 1952 May Day demonstration where student and leftist groups denounced Japan's Cold War alliance with the United States, police shot lethal rounds into a crowd of activists that breached the imperial palace grounds and threw several guards into the moat. This "Bloody May Day" incident—coming just days after the end of the occupation—embarrassed the Japanese government, which condemned the protestors but also barred police from bringing guns to future demonstrations. When *Seven Samurai* came to theaters in 1954, Self Defense Force soldiers, a small number of licensed hunters and ranchers, and *yakuza* members carried guns, but it was exceedingly rare to see them in public.[6]

The samurai's raid reduces the bandits' numerical advantage, but the rifles pose a grave threat, and the warriors must eliminate them before the final battle. They eventually seize two of the three firearms, but unlike many historical samurai, the movie's protagonists do not use them. *Seven Samurai*'s heroes fight using only their wits and traditional weaponry, and Kurosawa's script suggests a moral contrast between cowardly foreign weapons and time-honored Japanese ones. This subtle critique of Westernization and modernity differentiates Kurosawa's post-occupation films from the ones he made under the American regime. The director's linkage of guns with villainy and swords with honor would be even more pronounced in 1961's *Yōjimbō*, where he would pair it with a profound Cold War metaphor (see Chapter 20).

Even with fewer guns and bandits to face, the decisive battle is costly for the samurai and the villagers. The bandits come in waves over the course of three days and two nights, and between assaults the defenders bury their dead on the slope of a hill. A bullet from the last bandit rifle fells Kyūzō, the best swordsman among the samurai, and another dies in hand-to-hand combat. Slain villagers repose in mounds beneath the fallen samurai. There is one poignant exception to the hierarchical structure of the mounds: the pretender Kikuchiyo dies after slaying the bandit leader in the final assault, and the three samurai who survive the battle inter him alongside their dead comrades on top of the hill, giving him in death the status he could never attain in life.

Young Katsushirō lives through the battle that saves the village, but there is another fight that he cannot win. On the samurai's last night in the village, the farmer Manzō learns that Katsushirō and Shino have been intimate together, and he denounces his daughter as damaged goods. The day after the battle, when the triumphant villagers return to their fields, a chastised Shino goes with them. She pauses for a last look at her samurai lover, then moves on to live the life into which she was born. Katsushirō, standing at his mentor Kanbei's side, must do the same.

Seven Samurai is pessimistic about the ability of individuals to reshape the social structures that define their lives. When Kikuchiyo and Katsushirō push against the hierarchy, one for respect and one for love, the hierarchy pushes back harder. At the end of the film there is no change in the uneasy relationship between the castes, and the individual bonds forged between samurai and farmers do not last beyond the unusual circumstance that created them. Death was the only possible reward for the *rōnin*. As for the three survivors, Kanbei can only conclude, "We lost."

Seven Samurai's fatalism had disquieting implications for 1950s Japan, which had to decide whether to expand or push back against the transformative policies of the occupation—everything from gender equality to farmers' liberation to enforced pacifism. Independent but firmly allied to the United States, Japan also had to navigate the Cold War, a fight in which there might be no winners. Kurosawa's next film focused specifically on the fear that modern weaponry might once again bring nuclear horror to Japan, and that this time there might be no recovery.

CHAPTER 15

Record of Living Things

The number of people who died in the atomic bomb attacks in Hiroshima and Nagasaki in August 1945 has never been known precisely—it is no fewer than 200,000 and may be nearly double that—but in 1954 the hydrogen bomb's worldwide death toll was known with perfect accuracy. One man, Kuboyama Aikichi, died in a hospital on September 23 of that year several months after a cloud of radiation from the American H-bomb test at Bikini Atoll enveloped his fishing boat, the *Dai Go Fukuryū Maru* (*Lucky Dragon #5*). Kuboyama, a 40-year-old husband and father, was the first victim of the second generation of nuclear bombs, a category of weapons far more destructive than the two relatively small devices the Americans used against Japan at the end of World War II.

The Japanese media covered the H-bomb tragedy in detail, and the event raised alarm about the risk of global nuclear war. Before the *Fukuryū Maru*'s crew fell sick and Kuboyama died of complications during treatment, the fishermen unknowingly delivered their irradiated catch to market. There was a nationwide panic in Japan about the potentially radioactive fish that made their way to seafood processing facilities and grocery stores before anyone realized what had happened.[1]

A short time after the *Fukuryū Maru* incident, Kurosawa's favorite film score composer, Hayasaka Fumio, walked into a meeting with the director and announced that he could not work that day. Hayasaka had scored seven of Kurosawa's movies, starting with *Drunken Angel* in 1948, and the two were close friends. On this day Hayasaka was despondent, and not only because he was suffering from the tuberculosis that would soon end his life at the age of 41. He confessed that the reason he could not work was that he was crippled with anxiety about nuclear weapons. Kurosawa, moved to see his friend in such a state, soon began to work on a script inspired by the conversation.[2]

The result was *Ikimono no kiroku*, Kurosawa's fifteenth film and Hayasaka's last. It has been released under the English title *I Live in Fear*, but this is not literal. *Record of Living Things* is more accurate and better captures the movie's apocalyptic stakes. While the story centers on one man and his obsession with nuclear bombs, the movie's concerns extend beyond any specific individual. The opening credits play over long shots of urban commuters crossing busy intersections and boarding streetcars, conveying the sense that all of human civilization, and indeed every living thing on the planet, is in jeopardy.

When the film arrived in theaters in 1955, more and more people in Japan were voicing their opposition to nuclear weapons. Public discussion of the atomic bombings of Hiroshima and Nagasaki was difficult during the occupation because American censors discouraged it, but when the occupation ended in 1952 activism about past and present nuclear issues flourished. The Japanese government began to issue financial assistance to *hibakusha*, the term for atomic bomb victims who survived the blasts but later experienced a variety of related health problems. Doctors published studies about their *hibakusha* patients, survivors published their own memories, and in 1955 the city of Hiroshima opened a museum and memorial that became a focal point for atomic bomb remembrance. Movies began to tell bomb stories for the first time, both directly as in 1952's *Children of the Atomic Bomb* (*Genbaku no ko*) and more or less metaphorically as in 1954's *Godzilla*. After the *Fukuryū Maru* incident a group of Tokyo housewives started an anti-nuclear petition that 30 million people signed. The tragedy also prompted the creation of a grassroots organization called the Movement Against Atomic and Hydrogen Bombs (*Gensuibaku kinshi undō*). Both the petition and the organization called for the worldwide elimination of nuclear weapons, since it was no longer just the Americans who had the power to destroy the world in a flash; the Soviet Union successfully tested its first nuclear bomb in 1953. The Japanese public as well as scientists and government officials were skeptical of the new idea of "deterrence," the notion that more nuclear powers made war less likely because of the threat of mutual annihilation.[3]

Record of Living Things is not about the bombs themselves, but about the fear that they create, and how individuals and societies process that fear. The protagonist, Nakajima Kiichi (Mifune Toshirō), allows his fear of nuclear weapons to control every aspect of his life. Kiichi takes drastic measures to protect himself and his family from the disaster that he believes is inevitable. In his mind, his fear is appropriate given the scale of the threat, but his family is at odds over how to respond to his increasingly outrageous proposals. A doctor named Harada (Shimura Takashi) is called upon to help determine whether Kiichi is sane—whether he is responding logically to a very real danger, or whether the intensity of his reaction betrays an unsound mind. The question has direct bearing on the Japanese anti-nuclear movement of the mid–1950s. It asks how much conscientious people should do to protect themselves during the nuclear era, and whether it is possible to do enough or too much when the survival of life itself is at stake.

Dr. Harada first sees Kiichi and the Nakajima family at a family court mediation. While Kiichi scowls in irritation, his adult children and their spouses explain why they are bringing legal proceedings against him. "All Japanese people share your concerns," one of them tells the patriarch, but most people don't let their fear rule them. "You think I'm insane," snaps Kiichi. After this unpromising exchange, Dr. Harada learns the reason for the dispute: Kiichi recently purchased 1.6 square kilometers of land in remote Akita prefecture (the birthplace of Kurosawa's father as well as Mifune's) and began building an underground bunker to protect his family

Checking for radiation in an Osaka fish market after the Fukuryū Maru incident of 1954 (Wikimedia Commons).

from nuclear fallout. The children saw this as a waste of the family's money, but it was only the beginning. Kiichi soon decided that even rural Akita was not safe enough, and he began preparations to move the family out of Japan altogether, to the part of the world he deems safest: Brazil.

Japanese citizens had two good reasons to consider their country unsafe in the nuclear age. One was the special relationship between Japan and the United States. The Americans maintained a strong military presence in Japan even after the occupation and the Korean War ended, and this could have made the country an early target in a war between the United States and the Soviet Union. Moreover, the Americans stored nuclear weapons at their Japanese bases and on nuclear submarines in Japanese waters. Just a few years earlier, General MacArthur advocated dropping multiple atomic bombs on the Chinese-Korean border, an action which could have sent clouds of radiation and toxic rain drifting over Japan. It didn't happen, but if fighting broke out again in Korea or somewhere else in Asia, either the U.S. or the U.S.S.R. might choose to end it with a nuclear salvo that could affect Japan. The second reason Japanese people felt particularly concerned about their safety was that in 1954 their government began exploring the idea of using nuclear power plants for electricity. In 1955 the Diet passed a law declaring that Japan could develop nuclear power for "peaceful purposes." The country's lack of conventional energy resources, especially oil, meant that nuclear power was an economically-sensible way to keep the lights on, but it was a deeply unpopular one. Nuclear power plants posed a frightful risk to their immediate surroundings and to the entire nation, and voters' feelings on the matter meant that Japanese politicians had to tread carefully. Government officials publicly condemned nuclear weapons, but their simultaneous support for nuclear energy made their words ring hollow.[4]

In this environment it was not unusual to feel afraid, but not everybody was afraid in equal measure, as *Record of Living Things* illustrates. While considering the Nakajima case over dinner, Dr. Hanada asks his eldest son how he feels about the bombs. His son replies, casually and matter-of-factly, that he is afraid of them just like everyone else. "If you're afraid, then why are you so calm?" Hanada inquires. "Well, there's nothing we can do about it," the son replies. Signing petitions, joining mass movements, and voting for anti-nuclear politicians offered ways to express one's opinion, but they could not will the world's growing nuclear arsenal out of existence. American and Soviet nuclear weapons tests continued even after the *Fukuryū Maru* tragedy, and Japan had no choice but to live with its fear.

Kiichi's alternative solution, immigrating to Brazil, is not quite as absurd as it sounds. Brazil was a great distance from the world's nuclear powers, and Kiichi believes that global wind patterns would keep fallout away from it, but there is demographic appeal as well; Brazil has more people of Japanese descent than any country outside Japan. During the Meiji *jidai*, as Japan forged new ties with the West, people who could not find work in Japan often found it on farms in California and all along America's Pacific coast. Then, in the 1910s and '20s, racist laws in the United States blocked Asian immigration. After the closure of the United States and before the Japanese military seized Manchuria for large-scale settlement in the 1930s, Japanese people looking for work abroad turned to Brazil. Coffee planters there needed more laborers, and tens of thousands of Japanese citizens provided it. Entire families moved to the South American jungle to work on plantations, and although conditions and pay were poor, over the decades Japanese immigrants in Brazil acquired their own farms. Emigration from Japan declined in the 1950s as the domestic economy boomed, but the Japanese enclaves in Brazil continued to attract families by the hundreds for the next several years. By the early 21st century there were over 1 million Japanese-Brazilians living in Brazil.

Kiichi contacts a wealthy Japanese-Brazilian (Tōno Eijirō) who wants to sell his farm, and he invites him to Japan to convince the skeptical Nakajima clan to move to South America. The man has Japanese features but a deep tan and a white tropical suit that makes him look exotic to Kiichi's dumbstruck relatives. He also behaves like a foreigner, engaging in few of the standardized niceties of polite Japanese conversation. Kurosawa's depiction of the man as less-than-fully Japanese, and the Nakajima family's cold reception of him, reflects the discrimination that often greeted Japanese-Brazilians when they visited their ancestral country.[5]

Kiichi's family does not relish a self-imposed exile in a foreign land, and they pursue a legal injunction against the patriarch. Only Kiichi's wife and youngest daughter are not openly hostile to his plan. Mrs. Nakajima, who dresses traditionally and seldom speaks, is more comfortable in the role of obedient spouse than litigant, while the youngest daughter exhibits great filial piety by submitting to her father's authority without complaint. If either of these woman have their own opinions on the bombs and the move to Brazil, they do not express them.

Kiichi extends his invitation even to his illegitimate children and mistresses, whose chief concern is not nuclear weapons but securing a place in the Nakajima family registry. Every Japanese family maintains a *koseki*, a registry, that lists its members' births, deaths, and relations to each other. Adding illegitimate children to the registry makes it easier for those children to claim inheritance and to apply for jobs and loans, since employers and lenders can request copies of applicants' *koseki* to learn more about them. Kiichi tries to make his family—or, rather, his families— see that their safety is more valuable than money, but none of them are moved by his appeal.[6]

The source of the Nakajima family wealth is a foundry that Kiichi owns and operates. He needs to sell it to finance the move to Brazil, but his children are determined to retain ownership of the facility, and his illegitimate children want a piece of it as well. One of the foundry's most important clients is the power company Tokyo Gas, a business that would suffer if Japan switched *en masse* from fossil fuels to nuclear energy. Even if nuclear bombs vanished from the face of the earth, the existence of nuclear technology poses a threat to the Nakajima family business. Selling the factory, like moving to Brazil, is therefore not as irrational as Kiichi's children assert.

Nevertheless, Hanada and the family court arbiters reluctantly side with Kiichi's children and forbid the patriarch from selling the factory or accessing the family's funds. They stress that Kiichi's fears are valid, but they conclude that he cannot force his family to go along with his unusual plans or deprive them of their livelihoods by doing so himself. Yet Hanada remains troubled by the case. If extreme fear is justified, he wonders, then why should society not tolerate extreme reactions to that fear?

Kiichi provides a persuasive answer to that question when he takes his most drastic action yet: burning his own foundry to the ground. The frustrated patriarch believes that without the foundry and its income, his children will have no choice but to flee Japan with him. On the morning after the fire Dr. Hanada visits the ruined foundry just in time to witness the old man's final breakdown. Too late Kiichi realizes that he has not only destroyed his family's future, but the wellbeing of dozens of employees as well. As the factory workers stand around him demanding to know what is to become of them, Kiichi finally understands that he has gone too far, and something in him breaks.

Japanese businesses have a paternalistic relationship with their employees. The same Confucian philosophy that encourages reciprocal loyalty between children

Kyoto's Kinkakuji pavilion as it appeared before the arson (photograph by E.G. Stillman).

and parents and between citizens and the state also applies to ties between businesses and workers. Throughout most of the 20th century it was commonplace for large businesses to provide room and board for their employees, who in return spent most of their waking hours at or near the workplace. In hard times companies were supposed to avoid layoffs at all costs, and workers in return were supposed to stay with their companies for life rather than move from job to job in search of better pay or conditions. This system, sometimes called "familistic management," eroded in the post-occupation period, but aspects of it remain in effect in the 21st century. Toyota, for example, still houses much of its workforce in dorms and company-owned apartment blocks near its factories. It operates company stores where workers shop for their daily necessities, and it offers schools and technical colleges for employees and their families. Nearly every company in Japan continues to expect long hours and long terms of service from employees.[7]

In *Record of Living Things* Kiichi fails to balance the responsibilities that come with being the head of a family and the head of a business, and his failure has serious repercussions for the Nakajima family, the employees of the foundry, and ultimately Kiichi himself. After weakly offering to take all of his employees with him to Brazil—something he patently lacks the funds to do without the foundry, even if the workers wanted to leave Japan—Kiichi's children commit him to a mental institution. The movie sympathizes with Kiichi's fear, but it also shows how his unrestrained reactions to that fear damage his relationships with others.

The burning of the foundry has similarities to the most infamous arson in Japanese history, which occurred just five years before the release of the movie. In 1950 a young Buddhist monk suffering from mental illness burned down Kinkakuji, the famous "Golden Pavilion" that had stood in Kyoto for over 550 years and was widely considered one of the most beautiful buildings in Japan. Its senseless destruction after surviving so many fires, earthquakes, and wars over the centuries was an inconceivable indecency. The young monk, like the fictional Kiichi, was obsessed with the idea of American bombs, and during World War II he became certain that Kinkakuji would perish in an air raid. He could not stop imagining its destruction even after it survived the war, so he eventually did the deed himself. A 1956 novelization of the arsonist's life, based on interviews he gave in prison, explores this and other aspects of his troubled psychology. A replica of Kinkakuji opened on the original site a few years after the destruction of the original.

Despite the flurry of popular activity after the *Fukuryū Maru* scare, *Record of Living Things'* tale of nuclear paranoia did not translate to box office success. Kurosawa blamed its failure on Japanese people who "did not want to look at reality," but this was unfair. Moviegoers saw enough reality in their daily lives and wanted something different when it came to entertainment. Kurosawa's next effort, an action-packed *jidaigeki*, would fare far better.[8]

CHAPTER 16

Spiderweb Castle

In the wake of the hydrogen bomb scare of 1954, Japan experienced not fire and fury but an era of unprecedented prosperity. Between 1955 and the early 1970s the Japanese economy grew by around 10 percent each year, an incredible rate under any circumstances but all the more shocking because of how abysmal conditions were just a decade earlier. During this period of rapid growth, Japan became one of world's most robust international traders, its economy became the world's second largest, and its people found themselves among the world's most comfortable and well-provisioned. This transformation is remembered as Japan's "economic miracle" (kōdokeizaiseichō, "rapid economic development").

The miracle took place within what some Japanese historians call the "Pax Americana," a supposed period of peace that lasted from the end of World War II through the end of the Cold War and even beyond. During this time the United States guaranteed Japan's security, and with few defensive obligations of its own Japan channeled its resources into domestic growth and technological innovation. In other words, thanks to the special patronage of the United States, to whom Japan deferred on international issues, Japan was able to build cars and electronics instead of bombs and then sell those goods on the global market until the rest of the world began to fret about their costly addiction to Japanese goods. Under "Pax Americana," the empire that Japan lost on the battlefield it won back in the market.[1]

Yet "Pax Americana" is a poor name for what Japan and the world experienced in those years. Rather than an era of tranquility, the 1950s-60s was a period of unending conflict. During this time people in Japan worried greatly about nuclear weapons and often protested American actions that they believed put Japan at risk. The American military used Japan as a staging area, encouraged Japan to spend more on its Self Defense Force, and harnessed Japanese factories and shipping to support its wars in Asia from Korea to Vietnam to the Middle East. This arrangement had some economic benefits for Japan, but it also came with costs, including frequent public unrest over issues of security (see Chapter 19). Japan's tense relationship with the other Cold War superpower, the Soviet Union, cast a shadow on the miracle years as well. Prime Minister Hatoyama Ichirō traveled to Moscow in 1956 to secure permission for Japan to join the United Nations after the Soviets blocked Japan's initial application. Even as Japanese businesses entered a new golden age,

Cold War politics prevented them from realizing their full potential. China's large population of potential consumers was tantalizingly nearby, but since China was a communist nation, the United States declared it off-limits for Japanese exports. In some ways the Japanese miracle occurred in spite of Japan's relationship with the United States, not because of it.

International trade played a role in the economic miracle. Before the war, silk and other textiles were Japan's most common exports, but in the late 1950s "heavy" manufactured goods far surpassed them. Exports of Japanese automobiles first exceeded imports of foreign ones in 1958, and motorcycles, machine tools, plastics, watches, and television parts soon followed. Through agencies like MITI (see Chapter 9), the Japanese government encouraged the production of these "strategic" goods. The government encouraged cooperation between the nation's businesses, between business owners and their employees, and between businesses and the Bank of Japan which provided loans and a safety net. The government also strictly limited foreign investment in Japan so that domestic officials and business leaders could exercise complete control over economic matters. Japanese leaders also tried, as much as their obligations to the United States allowed, to limit the import of foreign products that might compete with Japanese industries.[2]

At the same time, imports created sweeping changes in Japanese society. A 1954 security treaty between Japan and the United States included a clause in which Japan agreed to buy $50 million worth of American food, notably wheat and milk. These products were rare in Japan before the war, but from the mid–1950s their availability and popularity increased steadily. Milk and bread eventually became staples of Japanese school lunches and essential parts of modern, well-stocked kitchens. Rising imports of American beef further contributed to the Westernization of the Japanese diet. As people ate less and less of the old staple food, rice, the government introduced subsidies and tariffs to protect Japanese agriculture.[3]

Kurosawa's movies, even the action-packed *jidaigeki* that dominated his output during the economic miracle, reflected the pattern of international give-and-take. As exports they brought attention to Japanese art and culture by winning major foreign film awards, and two of them (*Seven Samurai* and *Yōjimbō*) would be remade as westerns. They were also imports of a sort, drawing inspiration from foreign books and plays. In 1957 Kurosawa's sixteenth feature, *Spiderweb Castle* (*Kumonosujō*, often retitled *Throne of Blood* in English), blended Japanese and Western inspirations more seamlessly than anything the director had yet achieved.

Spiderweb Castle translates Shakespeare's Macbeth into a medieval Japanese setting. Kurosawa conceived the project a decade earlier but delayed it due to the release of American director Orson Welles' *Macbeth* in 1948. Now he, his crew, and his cast including regulars Shimura Takashi and Mifune Toshirō hiked up the slopes of Mt. Fuji to film the supernatural drama in the mountain's misty air. A nearby American military base assigned personnel to help clear and level the ground for the construction of a replica castle.[4]

Spiderweb Castle's dreamy, minimalist aesthetic is reminiscent of *sumi-e*, a centuries-old painting technique that also went international in the 1950s. Cinematographer Nakai Asakazu, who worked with Kurosawa on more than half a dozen films, used Mt. Fuji's natural conditions to make the edges of the dark castle walls appear to melt effortlessly into the surrounding clouds. Similarly, *sumi-e* paintings by artists from Sesshū Tōyō in the 15th century to Nakahara Nantenbō in the 20th use splashes of black ink on pale backgrounds to create simple, colorless scenes characterized by silhouettes and outlines. By the time *Spiderweb Castle* appeared in theaters it was no longer only Japanese viewers who might notice its debt to *sumi-e*; in the 1940s and '50s American modernist painters like Mark Toby, Franz Kline, and Ad Reinhardt studied the Japanese technique while pursuing their own experiments with ink blots, blank spaces, monochrome fields, and abstract sketches.[5]

Kurosawa transforms the Scottish general Macbeth into Washizu (Mifune), a Japanese general in service to a feudal lord. Shakespeare's play opens with three witches who set Macbeth on his path to treason, and these figures also adapt to suit the Japanese setting. Washizu and his fellow general Miki travel into the titular forest and encounter a *yamanba*, a ghoulish mountain hag that is a stock character in folk legends and supernatural Noh plays dating back to the medieval period. *Yamanba* appear as old women who sometimes offer sage advice to mountain travelers, but sometimes eat them as well. They are similar to *yaseonna*, lovelorn women who waste away until they become demons, and *Spiderweb Castle*'s spirit has often been identified as such, but there are separate Noh masks for these creatures and they appear in different plays. The movie's spirit sits in a clearing spinning on a loom—an image that Kurosawa took from the *yamanba* in the Noh play *Kurozuka*—and she prophecies to the dumbstruck generals that Washizu will soon become lord of the domain and Miki's sons will rule after him.[6]

The *yamanba* in *Spiderweb Castle* is among the earliest and most influential big-screen *yōkai*, the term for a panoply of folklore creatures that gained new popularity thanks to 20th-century media. *Yōkai* and the related categories of *yūrei* (ghosts) and *kaijū* (giant monsters) range from the grotesque, like monstrous skeletons and bug-eyed devils, to the almost cute, like living umbrellas and cucumber-loving imps known as *kappa*. Japan's post-occupation generation became familiar with these medieval characters through mass-produced paperback *manga* (comic books) like the enormously successful *GeGeGe no Kitarō* by Mizuki Shigeru, which debuted in 1960. *Yōkai* also figured in television *anime* (a shortening of the English word "animation") and in horror movies that became major earners for Japanese studios with the success of films like *The Ghost of Yotsuya* (*Tōkaidō Yotsuya kaidan*, 1959), and *Onibaba* (1964). By the end of the century *yōkai* also appeared in videogames, a lucrative new global industry that Japan dominated beginning in the late 1980s. The resurgent popularity of *yōkai* in the modern era ensured that Japanese people remained knowledgeable about their traditional stories during a period of rapid globalization and cultural change.[7]

Cast and crew of *Spiderweb Castle*, 1956. From left to right: Akiike Shinjin, Yanoguchi Fumio, Kishida Kuichirō, Nonagase Samaji, Saitō Takao, Mifune Toshirō, Chiaki Minoru, Shimura Takashi, Saitō Teruyo, Muraki Yoshirō, Kurosawa Akira, Nezu Hiroshi, Nakai Asakazu, and Motoki Sōjirō (from *Kinema Junpō* no. 155, 1956).

Supernatural beings overshadow the events of *Spiderweb Castle* and *Macbeth*, but it is characters' worldly ambitions that lead them to their destinies. When they emerge from the confusing fog of the forest, Washizu and Miki receive new land and titles for their loyal service to the lord of the domain. Yet Washizu's wife Asaji (Yamada Isuzu) wants more. She encourages Washizu to fulfill the *yamanba*'s prophecy before the lord learns of it, and Washizu becomes a reluctant traitor in a game of political intrigue.

An 1834 illustration of *yōkai*, by the renowned artist Hokusai.

Shakespeare scholars view *Macbeth* as an allegory for the reign of James I, who traced his lineage, erroneously, to a legendary Scottish hero named Banquo. Banquo appears in the play as Macbeth's fellow general, the character Kurosawa named Miki. *Macbeth* is deeply concerned with questions of legitimacy, masculinity, and civil war, all of which reverberated in England in the early years of the 17th century. Washizu and Miki do not represent specific Japanese politicians past or present, but they do resonate with debates about governmental legitimacy in 1950s Japan. Prime Minister Kishi, who served from 1957 to 1960, was a formerly-imprisoned war criminal whose stance on international security triggered some of the largest political protests in Japanese history. Beneath him, the unelected bureaucrats of agencies like MITI shaped economic policy behind closed doors. Elected members of the legislature rubber-stamped bureaucrats' recommendations about foreign trade and other issues without serious public debate, causing some Japanese commentators to refer to the Diet as a "puppet," an "ornament," a "gimmick," and "a magic invisibility cloak" (*kakuremino*) that shrouded the machinations of a deeper, more obscure level of government. The lack of transparency and accountability in postwar Japanese government caused grumbling not only among journalists and leftists, but also among businessmen who had to follow industrial policy set by clerks "not much older than their own grandchildren."[8]

Nevertheless, businessmen benefited from behind-the-scenes relationships with bureaucrats during the economic miracle of the 1950s and '60s. Many industry leaders had relatives in government, such as the MITI director who was the nephew-in-law of the president of Fuji Steel. Business owners and bureaucrats both tended to come from the country's most prestigious high schools and universities, a commonality that fostered a powerful "old boy" network. Bureaucrats gave privileged treatment to the most well-connected business leaders, for example by granting them preferential access to imported raw materials. Scandals occurred frequently when the press uncovered back-room deals, such as the rigged bidding for railroad, bus, and boat contracts in the "Hakone railroad war" of the late 1950s. Whether or not Kurosawa intended his *Macbeth* adaptation to speak to these issues, its exploration of political conspiracies made it an appropriate story for a period in which there was cynicism about political leaders and the powers behind them.[9]

Suspicion falls on Washizu as soon as he assassinates the lord of *Spiderweb Castle*, but the murderer himself is not the most blameworthy culprit. Asaji and Washizu work together to carry out the bloody deed and then move into Spiderweb Castle, where Asaji immediately begins plotting against Miki. In keeping with the *yamanba*'s prediction, the childless Washizu names Miki's adult son his heir, but Asaji has other plans. She becomes pregnant and convinces her husband to order the assassination of Miki and his son. The assassination attempt in which Miki dies but his son escapes occurs offscreen, and Washizu has a nervous breakdown when Miki's ghost appears to him that night at a feast. Mifune's paranoid and panicked performance in this scene conveys Washizu's strong feelings of guilt about his role in Asaji's conspiracies. Shakespeare's Macbeth, by contrast, takes a more active role in the death of his friend Banquo. By eliding this plot point, Kurosawa places the responsibility for Washizu's rise and fall squarely on his wife, the secret power behind the throne, the manipulator who herself is an unwitting agent of the *yamanba*.

Spiderweb Castle shows that real power does not reside in high office, but in networks of relationships over which no individual exercises full control. That point is crucial to understanding the entwined nature of Japanese government and industry, which scholar Haitani Kanji describes as "a spiderless cobweb": a network that functions because its closely-connected parts pursue a shared goal with no central oversight.[10]

Searching for a way out of the trap, Washizu reenters Spiderweb Forest to confront the *yamanba*. He is alone and beset by enemies; Asaji lies near death after giving birth to their stillborn son, and Miki's son marches with an army to end Washizu's reign. The spirit of the forest assures Washizu that he will rule the domain until the trees themselves march against him. Believing such a thing to be impossible, Washizu returns to his castle in a spirit of confidence. Banners bearing a centipede, a symbol of both war and poison, ripple in the wind over Washizu's stronghold, declaring his readiness to fight but also hinting at his guilt. As in *Macbeth*, the forest "moves" because the approaching army cuts down tree branches for cover, and upon seeing this omen Washizu's own archers riddle him with arrows in one of Kurosawa's most violent and iconic scenes. Spiderweb Castle fades back into the mist, and an unseen chorus chants a warning about the dangers of excessive ambition.

Kurosawa's ambitious production, on the other hand, was rewarded when the British Film Institute selected *Spiderweb Castle* to screen at the opening night of its new National Film Theater on the Thames, not far from the former location of Shakespeare's Globe Theater where the original *Macbeth* ran three and a half centuries earlier. Japanese audiences also rewarded Kurosawa's Shakespeare adaptation by making it one of the most successful Japanese films of 1957. Its themes of ambition and conspiracy spoke to the dark side of post-occupation governance in Japan, which grew more difficult for ordinary citizens to influence as career bureaucrats worked with strategic industries on long-term political and commercial priorities. Japan was becoming an economic powerhouse and resuming its participation in global affairs, but the trade-off was the emergence of a governmental-bureaucratic-industrial complex that operated by its own secretive set of rules. Kurosawa's next feature would implicitly question the durability of this new reality.

CHAPTER 17

The Lower Depths

The late 1950s was not Japan's first experience with miraculous prosperity. In the nation's collective historical memory, the most famous example of abundance and luxury is the Genroku *jidai* (1688–1704). The Genroku era, part of the overarching Tokugawa *jidai* (1603–1868), was a mostly peaceful period in which merchants and artists flourished, Japanese cities grew larger, and consumers could afford to pay higher prices for essentials as well as for indulgences like theater. Unlike the 1950s, foreign trade played very little role in the economic landscape of the Genroku *jidai* because the *shōgun* imposed strict limits on foreign goods entering the country and rarely allowed Japanese people or products to leave. Yet even without an export sector helping to encourage growth, the people of the Genroku generation enjoyed a golden age of material satisfaction and cultural vitality.

The good times did not last long. The Genroku *jidai* was the high-water mark of the Tokugawa period, but by the 1710s there were signs of trouble that soon grew to outright crisis. In the 1730s the nation suffered from deadly famine, the population stopped growing, and jobless people concentrated in urban slums. Samurai, merchants, and peasant households alike fell into dire poverty. There were many more ups and downs to come, and the pattern suggested an unpleasant truth: after a period of great prosperity might come an equally great collapse. Just as the famous Genroku *jidai* had come and gone, the sudden prosperity of the late 1950s would not last forever, and poverty was not a thing of the past but a perennial reality of human existence.[1]

1957's *The Lower Depths* (*Donzoko*) marked the first time that Kurosawa used the Tokugawa *jidai* for a setting. Notably he did not choose its comfortable Genroku years, but one of its inequality-ridden slumps. Whereas as his peer, director Ozu Yasujirō, spent the late 1950s making gentle, colorful movies like *Good Morning* (*Ohayō*, 1959) and *An Autumn Afternoon* (*Sanma no aji,* "The Taste of Sanma," 1962) about young families acquiring new household appliances and fun accessories, Kurosawa responded to Japan's economic miracle with a black-and-white portrait of despair that was strikingly out of step with the prevailing mood of the day. Yet *The Lower Depths* was, in its way, a timely reminder about eternal truths that should not be forgotten amid the comforts of the moment.

Kurosawa's source material was a 1902 Russian play by Maxim Gorky that had already received two major film adaptations. The first, a 1921 Japanese silent version (*Souls on the Road, Rojō no Reikon*), highlights the duty of children to parents and parents to children. Kurosawa was an admirer of silent films and remembered seeing several in his youth, but his *The Lower Depths* has far more in common with a French talkie version from 1937. That movie, by director Jean Renoir, focuses on friendships and romantic relationships between downtrodden boarders at a flophouse. Kurosawa's adaptation uses the flophouse setting but focuses less on relationships and more on the social problems that the boarders experience. Kurosawa also injects the story with Buddhist content as his characters turn to religion to make sense of their unhappy lives.

The decaying wooden huts where *The Lower Depths* takes place are at the bottom of a large pit whose stone and earth walls are the foundations of a Buddhist temple. The pit is a dumping ground for the garbage of those who live nearby, including Buddhist monks who either do not know or do not care that they are pouring their trash on the homes of a ragtag assortment of social misfits. Inside the larger of the two huts live a masterless samurai (Chiaki Minoru), a dying woman and her husband (Miyoshi Eiko and Tōno Eijirō), a prostitute (Akemi Negishi), a street food vendor (Kiyokawa Nijiko), a gambler (Mitsui Kōji), a drunken kabuki actor (Fujiwara Kamatari), a woodworker (Tanaka Haruo), a musically-inclined cobbler (Fujiki Yū), and a thief (Mifune Toshirō). Almost all of these actors had worked with Kurosawa before, but one newcomer was the sumo wrestler Fujitayama, who plays a porter; the first televised sumo broadcast happened in 1953, and Kurosawa's casting of Fujitayama capitalized on the sport's growing popularity as more and more households acquired television sets during the economic boom.

In past and present alike one of the government's most important tasks was to put the right amount of money into circulation—sometimes officials triggered price and wage drops by reducing coinage, and sometimes they boosted commerce and inflation by increasing it. Events like famines and natural disasters could overtake and drive policy changes, sometimes augmenting their effects or rendering them moot. The protagonists of *The Lower Depths* live in a period when money is scarce, but some of them remember boom years when currency was easier to come by. Their poverty is not the result of unemployment or laziness, but simply low wages. Nearly all of the characters have jobs, and their jobs define them. None are idle except for the dying woman, and she gives her scraps of food to her husband so that he can continue his work cleaning iron pots and pans.

The economy's ebb and flow was something over which common people had little control, a truth that was illustrated again in the 1950s. At the beginning of that decade the Japanese economy was in recession thanks to deflationary policies that American occupation authorities introduced in 1949 to lower the price of goods (see Chapter 9). The recession could have lasted through the 1950s and made the post-occupation period very different, but instead it was short-lived. The Korean War increased production and wages, and Japan's post-occupation leaders promoted

Thanks to television, the ancient sport of sumo was growing in popularity when Kurosawa cast wrestler Fujitayama in *The Lower Depths*. The wrestlers pictured here in a 1955 bout are Wakanohana on the left and Chiyonoyama on the right (Wikimedia Commons).

economic growth by lending heavily to key industries even at the risk of inflation. By the end of the decade Japanese workers and their families had enough money to save, spend, and even splurge. Washing machines, vacuum cleaners, TVs, and other consumer goods evolved from luxuries and conveniences to must-haves. *The Lower Depths* reminded contemporary audiences that they had not earned their good fortune any more than their hardworking forebears had earned their deprivation; unpredictable historical events and shifting government priorities determined the sizes of paychecks and helped make the difference between boom and bust.[2]

The landlord (Nakamura Ganjirō) of *The Lower Depth*'s flophouse is a stooped old man who lives in the pit's smaller but marginally nicer wooden hut. He charges as much as he can from his tenants, who hate him for it, but his daily life is scarcely different from theirs. Down in the depths class and caste have little meaning, and landlord and samurai live side by side with thief, prostitute, and laborer in shared squalor. "Here we have no lords or noblemen," the woodworker says, putting a positive spin on the pit's miserable microcosm. The thief takes advantage of the weakness of social hierarchies—and social *mores*—by sleeping first with the landlord's wife Osugi (Yamada Isuzu) and later with Osugi's sister Okayo (Kagawa Kyōko), which causes a great deal of strife in the small community.

At the other end of the spectrum, shared comfort also made people think differently about traditional social distinctions. In his book *Shinohata*, an intimate, firsthand account of two decades of life in a Japanese village, sociologist Ronald Dore recounts how the economic miracle changed the way people saw themselves in relation to each other. Some families had been rich and powerful for generations while some had "a history of poverty and obscurity," but in the years of high-speed economic growth the differences between the two became almost trivial. Families who used to command and families who used to obey now lived on terms of "neighbourly equality." When it came time for Japanese communities to elect representatives to local government or delegate communal responsibilities, the decisive factor was no longer wealth or even ancestry, but personality. Years after the occupation ended, Dore observed Japanese people of all walks of life using occupation-era language to denounce the "feudal" habits of the past and praise the new, more "democratic" era—an era that came about not because of American rhetoric, but because of a rising economic tide that lifted all boats.[3]

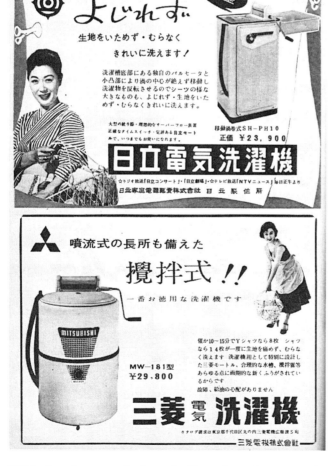

The fact that the economic miracle spread wealth so evenly was perhaps the most miraculous thing about it. Nearly everyone in Japan suffered during the tragic years of the 1940s, which meant that the prosperity of the 1950s eased virtually every life as well. The economic boom was "not socially divisive in the sense of benefitting one group or class at the expense of another," writes historian Chalmers Johnson, but elevated all groups: industrialists, factory workers, shopkeepers, farmers, "salarymen" in newly-built offices, and housewives in homes stocked with the latest appliances. As standards of living rose, people said that they no longer felt the need to "lower the head" to their supposed superiors. This figure of

1956 advertisements for household products from Hitachi and Mitsubishi (from *Sōen*, October 1956).

speech overstated the case; the hierarchy-based etiquette of bowing remains a familiar sight even in 21st-century Japan. The way people thought about wealth and status changed as the miracle transformed lives, but on a cultural level, Japan's unwritten rules about who sits where at community events, who pours whose drinks at after-work parties, and who gives what to whom on gift-giving occasions survived the miracle years and the ups and downs that came after it.[4]

When characters in *The Lower Depths* show any deference to each other, it is with heavy irony, as when the thief adds the honorific suffix *sama* to his rude nickname for a policeman. If most moviegoers in 1957 were too polite to emulate Mifune's gleeful rudeness, they did enjoy it vicariously; his irreverent performance in *The Lower Depths* earned him his first major domestic acting honor, the Mainichi Best Actor award.

Into the pit's flattened social microcosm comes a smiling pilgrim (Hidari Bokuzen), through whom the film engages with Buddhist attitudes about wealth. When the poor pilgrim says that money does not matter in the afterlife, the dying woman eagerly listens to his egalitarian vision of the world to come. Yet the drunken actor refers to a folk belief that "Five coins isn't even enough to get you across the Sanzu River," the Japanese equivalent of the River Styx. At Japanese funerals mourners often set six coins on the casket so that the deceased can pay the toll. Towards the end of the movie the characters sing a *bakabayashi*, a "fool's orchestra," whose lyrics include contradictory lines like "money buys your fate in hell" and "money buys Buddha's mercy." Like a coin, the moral significance of money is two-sided.

Typical religious sentiments in the 1950s and '60s included the likes of "Generally, I'm not one for praying," "I don't know whether there's anything in it," and "I still don't know what are the proper prayers to offer up." Yet most people still did pray, at least on occasion. They lit incense and made offerings of food, water, and *sake* to their ancestral shrines just "to be on the safe side." Religious observance still had a place in postwar society, but practitioners were quick to acknowledge how little they knew about the theory and history of their syncretic religions or about the literal existence of gods and an afterlife. Ahead of his time, the Buddhist pilgrim in *The Lower Depths* expresses the same kind of agnostic piety. When the thief asks him if Buddha is real, the pilgrim replies with a smile, "I'm sure he is for those who want him to be," and counters by asking "who's to say a lie is always bad, or the truth always good?"[5]

Death comes twice to the pit, once to the boarders' hut and once to the landlord's. When the dying woman finally expires, only the pilgrim, who barely knew her, prays for her smooth passage to the next world. Her husband is drunk when it happens and afterwards seems at a loss, while the other characters are simply grateful to have heard the last of her hacking cough. Later, the landlord receives a fatal injury when his tenants stop him from beating his wife's sister. Nobody saw who struck the fatal blow, but both the thief and the landlord's wife go to jail for the crime. There is no solidarity among the people of the pit; the pilgrim scurries away rather than provide witness testimony, and the rest go back to cheating each other while gambling and mocking each other's ambitions. Their relative social and economic equality does not lead to peace, harmony, or happiness.

The Lower Depths told a cautionary tale in the era of high-speed growth, but Kurosawa followed it with a film that was far more uplifting. His eighteenth feature would be a pure adventure unencumbered by weighty philosophy, and its sunlit exteriors would stand in brilliant contrast to the dark enclosures of *The Lower Depths*.

CHAPTER 18

The Hidden Fortress

By the late 1950s a rising number of people wanted for little that could be manufactured or sold, so they began to desire things that had no price tag. The economic miracle meant that consumers could purchase comfortable lives in the present and still have plenty left over to save for the future, which they did at a rate that put American saving habits to shame. This left only the past to buy, but what Japan had lost during the first half of the 20th century could not simply be bought back.

The most obvious losses were physical structures. Whatever the Meiji and Taishō governments had not razed in the pursuit of progress, American bombs destroyed in the pursuit of peace. Among the hundreds of thousands of structures destroyed by wartime bombing were over 200 venerable buildings that had been specially designated as National Treasures. The beautiful wooden castles that dotted Japan for centuries were mostly gone, leaving behind only stone foundations or grassy fields. The same was true of many ancient Buddhist temples and Shinto shrines, not to mention the wood-and-paper houses that most people lived in before switching to modernized, prefabricated homes.

Though few people would have chosen to go back to the rougher, hungrier lifestyle of the past, Japan's visible changes contributed to a sense of cultural orphanhood. "By the mid–1950s there was a visible movement to preserve physical and cultural aspects of Japan that had survived the war, and a growing sense of alarm at the continued destruction of historic buildings through reconstruction and economic growth," writes architecture historian Cherie Wendelken. District preservation movements, in which neighbors banded together to protect buildings of local historical interest, were a product of the 1950s and '60s and possibly the first organizations of their kind in Asia.[1]

"New" was everywhere, but "old" was in demand. *Dentō ronsō*, meaning "traditional discourse," was a buzzword for the wellspring of interest in all things uniquely Japanese. In 1955 the government enacted the Law for the Protection of Cultural Properties, which redefined National Treasures to include not only ancient structures still standing but also newer buildings and replicas of ones that had been destroyed. Long-gone castles reappeared incongruously at the center of rebuilt cities, becoming symbols of local pride and beacons of tourism. Crumbling samurai residences and modest, formerly-overlooked farmhouses received official protection and refurbishment, as did the homes of recent and ancient Japanese artists. There was also a surge of interest in identifying and celebrating regional dialects, local festivals, traditional dances, and handmade craft techniques all across the Japanese archipelago. These "intangible cultural properties" could receive official protection as well, and prefectures and towns promoted their local traditions to attract visitors and encourage sales. In the era of high-speed economic growth as social relations and the physical landscapes took on new forms, symbols of the past provided a welcome sense of continuity and identity.

In this nostalgic context Kurosawa released his eighteenth film, *The Hidden Fortress* (*Kakushi toride no san akunin*, "The Three Outlaws of the Hidden Fortress"). The script by Kurosawa, Hashimoto Shinobu (*Rashōmon, Ikiru, Seven Samurai*), and Kikushima Ryūzō (*Scandal, Throne of Blood*) is uncharacteristically lighthearted. A sense of danger pervades the film, but there is little attention to the kind of social problems that usually drive Kurosawa's dramas. Instead *The Hidden Fortress* has strong comedic overtones and a romanticism about premodern life that borders on the fantastical. Japanese audiences who craved positive portrayals of Japanese history and culture made this exciting, upbeat *jidaigeki* Kurosawa's most financially-successful film to date.

To shoot the film Kurosawa returned to Mt. Fuji, where he had shot parts of *Throne of Blood* the year before. The iconic mountain itself was a protected national treasure, having been included in the Fuji-Hakone-Izu National Park in 1936. Kurosawa's decision to shoot on the isolated mountain, with its thin air and

Japanese cities touted their history during the economic boom. In 1957 Nagoya began rebuilding its castle, which was destroyed in the war, and in 1959 Japan Post issued anniversary stamps for the city (from *Japan Post*).

difficult-to-predict weather, was an extravagance that was only possible due to the Tōhō film company's comparatively easy access to money during the economic boom. Even still, the studio balked when Kurosawa stretched a planned 10-day shoot at Fuji's Myōjin Pass to around 100 days. The director was waiting for the weather to improve in order to get precisely the right shots, and in the meantime he passed the days in apparent idleness, for example by stacking smooth stones along a river-bank with members of his crew. Fuji's erratic weather pattern was exacerbated in late September 1958 by the landfall of the Kanogawa typhoon, at the time the strongest typhoon on record. Flooding and landslides in Tokyo, less than 100 miles from the filming location, killed over 1200 people, wounded a nearly equal number, and left over ten times as many homeless. Even in a country accustomed to dozens of typhoons each year, this was a huge blow in terms of lives and property lost.[2]

Despite the natural disaster, Tōhō executives considered the production delay on *The Hidden Fortress* excessive, and they told Kurosawa that he needed to compromise his vision or else set up his own production company to finance his future movies. He established Kurosawa Productions in 1959. Tōhō continued to act as Kurosawa's distributor, but for the foreseeable future the liability for any losses would fall primarily on Kurosawa himself. It was a risk worth taking for the director, who had long resented the oversight of money-minded studio executives.

In *The Hidden Fortress*'s long opening shot, the first widescreen shot of Kurosawa's career, two commoners stagger through a valley arguing about their past and future. Tahei (Chiaki Minoru) wants to go back home after their brief stint in a warlord's military ended in humiliation. Matashichi (Fujiwara Kamatari), on the other hand, refuses to return to their village until he strikes it rich. The two part ways at the corpse of a samurai; despite the dead samurai in the center of the shot, the tone of the scene is comical thanks to Tahei and Matashichi's exaggerated bickering. Their rapid-fire dialogue and slapstick physicality have roots in a two-man comedy genre called *manzai*, which was popular on stage before jumping to television in the postwar era.

The prospect of treasure looms before each of the protagonists in turn. A gang of samurai forces Tahei to join a work crew that is digging out a stash of gold under a recently-captured castle. Meanwhile, Matashichi learns about a large cash reward for a missing princess, but soon an army presses him into grunt work as well. The two friends meet again as their respective work groups clash with musket-wielding samurai overseers on a broad, outdoor stair, and in the confusion they escape together. There is a revealing juxtaposition between the grim, slave-driving, death-dealing samurai and the comical yet practical behavior of Tahei and Matashichi. The commoners' contorted facial expressions, crass language, and wild emotional swings mark them as figures of fun, but what they want—safety and prosperity—is far more sensible than whatever the samurai hope to achieve with their back-and-forth battle over a few square meters of a ruined castle town. In the comfortable, egalitarian, peace-loving Japan of 1958, the characters of Tahei and Matashichi made relatable heroes precisely because of their profit-minded, risk-averse nature, which the movie exaggerates for comic effect.

The two friends literally stumble into wealth while camping in a rocky valley alongside a small stream. They notice that some of the wood Tahei gathered for their fire does not burn, and upon inspection they find that they are trying to burn gold—the "sticks" are actually gold bars in disguise. Unfortunately for them, the valley's gold has a guardian: an imposing, bearded man (Mifune Toshirō) who watches them from higher up the valley.

For a small nation, Japan has many gold mines, and until the 20th century the metal made an attractive basis for currency. Between the world wars, however, the global economy suffered a wave of economic crises that made direct conversions between money and gold increasingly risky. When a nation lost gold due to a trade imbalance or too many people redeeming paper money for gold, it had to choose between unattractive alternatives. It could issue increasingly worthless paper money, which might cause inflation, or it could make less money available to its businesses and citizens, which might trigger recessions and depressions. In 1931 Japan's leaders, after much debate and a couple of reversals and counter-reversals, cut the nation's ties with the international economy by refusing to send gold abroad. Government officials who wanted to maintain the international "gold standard" sometimes suffered violent reprisals, as when banker and Finance Minister Junnosuke Inoue was assassinated in 1932. After World War II Japan did not return to the gold standard, but rather linked the value of the yen to the U.S. dollar, the currency of its protector and ally.[3]

Gold remained culturally significant even when it was no longer directly linked to monetary wealth. The first National Treasure designated under the 1951 Law for the Protection of Cultural Properties was Konjikidō, a small, 12th-century building covered entirely in gold leaf in the ancient town of Hiraizumi in northeastern Japan. The famous Golden Pavilion in Kyoto, Kinkakuji, was rebuilt and covered in gold leaf in 1955 (see Chapter 15). Later in the century some bathhouses and hotels created solid gold or gold-plated bathtubs to attract guests looking to immerse themselves in aureate gleam; one of these baths is reportedly the largest golden object in the world. Fancy confections and drinks using gold flakes as garnish became a common sight as the boutique food industry matured into one of Japan's most innovative sectors. Twenty-first-century Japan is one of the world's leading consumers and producers of gold, and gold is a component in many of the electronic devices that Japan exports to the world.[4]

While Tahei and Matashichi celebrate their discovery of the gold stash, the bearded man approaches and informs them that the gold belongs to the princess of the Akizuki domain—the missing princess whom Matashichi learned about earlier in the film. Princess Yuki is the last survivor of the Akizuki ruling family, which the rival Yamana domain recently wiped out. If the princess can avoid the Yamana forces and recover her family's hidden gold, she can mount a counteroffensive. If not, her dynasty will come to an end. The bearded man intends to help her, and he forces Tahei and Matashichi to assist him by carrying the gold out of the valley to a rendezvous with the princess.

The Akizuki princess bears a royal title because she is the daughter of a medieval warlord, but modern Japan had princesses, too. At the end of the 1950s there were over half a dozen of them. The American occupation government abolished most nobility titles in the mid–1940s, but terms like "prince" and "princess" still applied to members of the imperial family, and their doings attracted popular interest. Emperor Hirohito's aunt and two nieces used the title princess, as did Hirohito's four daughters who survived to adulthood. The eldest of the daughters married into a cadet branch of the royal family, but the other three gave up their titles when they married commoners; two married descendants of nobility in the early 1950s, and the third married a financial analyst in 1960. When *Hidden Fortress* came to theaters, the most important princess-to-be in the land was Shōda Michiko, the daughter of a flour miller who met Hirohito's son Akihito on a tennis court in 1957 and became his fiancée in 1958. Sporty and thoroughly "modern"—Michiko spoke English from childhood and practiced Catholicism before converting to Shinto for her marriage in 1959—Japan's newest princess would become Empress Michiko when her husband took the throne in 1989.

Hidden Fortress's Princess Yuki (Uehara Misa) is hiding out at the titular redoubt where the bearded man brings Matashichi and Tahei. There the bumbling pair learns that the bearded man calls himself Makabe Rokurōta, the name of a great samurai of the Akizuki domain. Absurdly, Matashichi and Tahei do not instantly realize that they are in the company of the missing princess and her loyal guardian. In their defense, Makabe and Princess Yuki go to great lengths to keep their identity secret. Since Yuki's educated diction could give her away, she pretends to be mute around Matashichi, Tahei, and other strangers. The script finds much humor in the fact that the commoners do not recognize the princess as their social superior. In their ignorance they occasionally make advances on her, but these are foiled either by Yuki herself, who is alert and always carries a riding crop, which she wields skillfully, or by others, including a young woman whom the travelers liberate from a Yamana brothel.

The movie's unlikely quartet leaves the hidden fortress and travels through a series of gorgeous landscapes that celebrate Japan's natural beauty. In addition to the punishing grandeur of Mt. Fuji, Kurosawa took his actors into the rocky Horai Gorge of western Japan, part of the Setonaikai National Park. As he did so memorably in *Rashōmon*, Kurosawa shoots scenes in the dappled half-light of groves and alongside sparkling streams that, with the help of mirrors, cast wavering reflections onto the actors' faces. Yet unlike *Rashōmon*, whose forest has a dark, claustrophobic feel appropriate to the evil events that take place there, *The Hidden Fortress*'s forests are bright and beautiful. So too are its granite cliffs and sloping river valleys. The new, wide film format that Kurosawa used for *The Hidden Fortress* conveys each location's breathtaking beauty.

Holiday excursions to the mountains and seaside had long been popular forms of recreation in Japan. Kurosawa depicted one such idyllic trek in *No Regrets for Our Youth* (see Chapter 5) and another in *Scandal* (see Chapter 10). During the postwar boom, as people found themselves with more time and money for leisure activities, visiting Japan's sites of natural beauty became an expression of cultural pride. Wartime bombing destroyed many man-made structures, but it left the mountains, valleys, and dense forests that covered over three-quarters of the Japanese archipelago intact, and the most impressive of them welcomed growing numbers of domestic tourists. In the first ten years after the war Japan expanded its number of national parks by 50 percent, adding over 1650 new acres of protected land and coastline. In 1957 a new law introduced Quasi-National Parks ("places of great natural scenic beauty next to the National Parks") and Prefectural Natural Parks, which caused the number of protected acres to grow exponentially. The nation's train agency, Japan National Railways, used slogans like "Discover Japan" to encourage urbanites to get away to *inaka*, the countryside. Weekend vacationers left the newly-acquired conveniences of their modern homes to walk in the woods, stay in traditional-style inns, visit old or reconstructed historical sites, and seek "authentic" local experiences that put them in touch with what travel brochures called the "womb of Japan," the "Japanese heart," and the "real Japan." Those too young to remember life before the economic boom were among those most entranced by the lure of *inaka*: a survey in the early 1990s found that 70 percent of adults under 40 had visited "the mountains, a forest, valley or other natural area for a non-work purpose during the past year." At the end of the century Japanese people visited their national parks at three times the rate Americans visited theirs.[5]

Matashichi, Tahei, Makabe, and Princess Yuki's romp through the Japanese wilderness takes them to a colossal waterfall (probably the Shiraito Falls near Mt. Fuji), jagged cliffs dotted with pines, and wide rivers flowing through bamboo forests and tall grasses. Makabe references one location, Mt. Suribachi, by name—not the Mt. Suribachi on remote Iwo Jima where American Marines famously planted a flag in 1945, but one of many other similarly-named mountains on the Japanese home islands. The protagonists do not simply pass through this eye-catching scenery, but actually use it to their advantage; the landscape provides them shelter from the weather and from enemy troops.

The Hidden Fortress, with all its humor and excitement, marks a change in Kurosawa's approach to violence. In his earlier medieval tales *Rashōmon* and *Seven Samurai*, combat was a physical extension of characters' moral struggles. Fighting in those movies was more grim than glamorous, and it was a means to an end rather than an end unto itself. In *The Hidden Fortress*, however, swordplay is pure spectacle. Audiences' nostalgia for the past translated to a willingness to believe in the noble ideals of the samurai and to admire cinematic warriors' strength for its own sake. In one long interlude in the film's second half, Makabe rides away from the rest of the quartet and engages in a friendly but potentially-deadly duel with an old comrade

The park now called Sanriku Fukkō is one of many National, Quasi-National, and Prefectural Natural Parks established in the 1950s and '60s (photograph by the author).

(Fujita Susumu). In this fight there is no right or wrong, only an exhibition of bravery and skill.

Near the end of their journey the travelers happen upon a large *himatsuri*, a fire festival where villagers dance, sing, and play *taiko* drums and *shakuhachi* flutes around a celebratory bonfire. Fire festivals take place in many parts of Japan, but the most famous ones occur near the old capital of Kyoto, a leading destination for travelers seeking echoes of old Japan. Kurosawa highlights the elemental beauty of the event, punctuating wide shots of the crowd and flames with closer ones of Princess Yuki smiling and dancing in the crowd. This is precisely the kind of "authentic" local encounter that tradition-seeking tourists of the late 1950s craved, and Princess Yuki is an attractive representation of the ideal tourist experience. First-time actress Uehara was a new face for audiences in 1958, as anonymous as the young female models in railroad advertisements who met with rustic locals and gazed happily at historic landmarks and scenic vistas.[6]

The Hidden Fortress has an upbeat ending, as optimistic as anything Kurosawa ever filmed. With the help of Makabe's dueling partner the protagonists escape enemy territory with their lives and most of Princess Yuki's gold. Reflecting on the value of travel, Yuki says, "The happiness of these days I would never have known living in a castle." Matashichi and Tahei, too, have seen the world, and they end their adventure little richer but with smiles on their faces.

The movie's nostalgia is inextricable from its sense of national pride. Some critics view the ending, in which Princess Yuki and Makabe plan to rebuild the destroyed Akizuki kingdom using the gold they smuggled through enemy territory, as an instance of "fairy tale logic." In the context of medieval Japanese warfare it does beggar belief, but in the context of 1958 and Japan's economic miracle it was no more implausible than the fact that Japan had gone from total collapse to astonishing plenty in the span of a decade. The flag of the Akizuki kingdom, a huge crescent moon on a plain background, has more than a passing resemblance to the modern Japanese flag's circular red sun on a field of white, and when Kurosawa superimposes it over Yuki's face it elicits what film scholar Catherine Russell calls "a nostalgic longing for an imaginary nation" that was readily transferable to the real nation. Expressions of patriotism were firmly discouraged during the American occupation, as were depictions of Japan's feudal past. It was now six years since the occupation ended, and a new kind of patriotism was taking root: a patriotism based on "social reconciliation and peaceful nation-building" powered by miraculous economic growth and adorned with Japan's celebrated natural treasures.[7]

The popular escapism of *The Hidden Fortress* paved the way for future action/adventure movies like *Yōjimbō* (1961) and *Tsubaki Sanjūrō* (1962), not to mention George Lucas's *Star Wars* (1977). Yet Kurosawa would never abandon his interest in the darker parts of postwar life, as his next feature, the independently-financed *The Bad Sleep Well*, would prove.

CHAPTER 19

The Bad Sleep Well

Prosperity does not always bring contentment, and security does not necessarily mean peace. If Japan appeared tranquil in 1960 with its thriving economy, its productive relationship with the United States, and a successful bid to host the 1964 Summer Olympics in Tokyo, that appearance was shattered when 300,000 protestors surrounded the Japanese legislature in a mass protest that would oust a prime minister but fail to achieve its larger goals.

At issue was Japan's renewal of a security treaty with the United States. The treaty extended the lease of military bases to the United States in return for the continuing American commitment to protect Japan in the event of an attack. Members of anti-war and anti-nuclear organizations like Gensuikyō, which formed after the *Fukuryū Maru* incident of 1954 (see Chapter 15), objected to the treaty on the grounds that nuclear weapons at U.S. bases in Japan put Japanese lives in danger. As the date of treaty ratification approached in the summer of 1960, protests grew in size and intensity. An estimated "5 million students, farmers, workers, housewives and highly diverse groups of citizens across the country" expressed their opposition to the treaty and, by extension, the entire strategic relationship between the two nations. Most protests were nonviolent, but on June 10 a group of demonstrators attacked the car of the American ambassador, Douglas MacArthur, Jr., son of the general who governed Japan from 1945 to 1951. Five days later a third of a million people surrounded the Diet building in Tokyo where the Japanese legislature convened to ratify the treaty. Prime Minister Kishi Nobusuke deployed the police to keep the protestors from entering the building, and in the ensuing violence and crush of people a 22-year-old university student died. American president Dwight Eisenhower was supposed to visit Japan on the occasion of the treaty renewal, but Kishi asked him to cancel the trip out of concern for the president's safety and to avoid additional publicity. The Diet ratified the treaty, but Kishi and his cabinet resigned shortly thereafter.[1]

The man who replaced Kishi as Prime Minister, Ikeda Hayato, was hardly less controversial. He played a key role in creating the security treaty in the first place, but few people knew that. Instead they remembered Ikeda from some of the biggest business scandals of the 1950s. In 1952 Ikeda resigned as head of MITI after newspapers quoted him saying "It makes no difference to me if five or ten small businessmen

Protestors crowded the streets near the Diet Building to oppose to the Japan-U.S. Security Treaty of 1960. One protestor, 22-year-old Kanba Michiko, lost her life (from Asahi Shimbunsha).

are forced to commit suicide" as long as Japan's big corporations thrived. His exile from high office was short-lived, and not long afterward he was one of several officials implicated in a scandal involving shipbuilding contracts. When he took over as Prime Minister in 1960 Ikeda continued the government's cozy relationship with the United States and with Japan's export-oriented businesses, and he secured a legacy "as the single most important individual architect of the Japanese economic miracle."[2]

The failure of the protestors to stop the security treaty and the ease with which Japanese politicians survived scandals contributed to a sense that Japan's leaders were beyond accountability. Japan's deferral to the United States on matters of defense was unpopular, but it was a cost-effective form of national security, so it continued. Behind-the-scenes collusion between bureaucrats and businesses existed alongside runaway economic growth, so it remained the norm even when the press uncovered serious legal and ethical breaches. Shortly after Ikeda's death in 1965 the newspapers popularized the term "black mist" to describe the cloud of scandal that tainted his hand-picked successor, Satō Eisaku. Satō's Minister of Transportation resigned when the press discovered his illegal financial dealings, but by the end of the decade he was back in a position of power as if nothing had happened. If there is a crime at the heart of every large fortune, then at the heart of Japan's postwar fortune were many crimes, as well as a disregard for the will of the people. There was little that citizens could do, either individually or collectively, to make the system cleaner, more transparent, or more responsive to public opinion.[3]

The Bad Sleep Well (*Warui yatsu hodo yoku nemuru*) is a cinematic protest against the cycle of corruption, scandal, and impotent outrage. With noir flourishes that hearken back to Kurosawa's occupation-era films *Drunken Angel* and *Stray Dog*, the movie invents a tortured hero who is willing to sacrifice everything to bring justice to a rotten system. *The Bad Sleep Well* came to theaters just weeks after the bloody security treaty protests and the resignation of the Kishi government, and Kurosawa's producer and production designer later remembered that "powerful people felt uneasy" about the movie. During filming, Tōhō executives pressured Kurosawa to avoid making any direct parallels between the corruption in his movie and real-life corporate or government scandals. The director used his new, personal production company to make the film, but Tōhō was still an important distribution partner for him, and Kurosawa resented the studio for not letting him dramatize the full extent of corruption in Japan. Years later he admitted that he envisioned Kishi himself as the ultimate villain of the film, though the final script only hints at this in its closing scene. Still, *The Bad Sleep Well*'s searing revenge fantasy is quite clear in its condemnation of the elites of the miracle era.[4]

The movie opens at a wedding reception that a group of journalists crash in order to report on the father of the bride. His name is Iwabuchi (Mori Masayuki), and he is one of the top executives of Dairyū, a business with close ties to the government-owned Public Corporation for Land Development. Prior to the events of the film, the police raided Dairyū's offices and arrested their top accountant for embezzlement. The journalists believe that Vice President Iwabuchi and the rest of Dairyū's executive staff, who are also at the wedding, will be next. They guess right; with dramatic timing, the police arrive and arrest a man whose work involves Public Corporation contracts.

The scandal is a kickback scheme in which Public Corporation awards construction contracts to Dairyū in exchange for a share of the funds. This was a common kind of illegal activity in Japan, where officials moved easily through the "revolving door" that linked the bureaucracy with key industries. The government's active support for certain sectors of the economy blurred the lines between public and private interests. The shipbuilding deal that temporarily halted future prime minister Ikeda's rise in the mid–1950s was just one of several scandals that exposed the misuse of public money in rigged contract negotiations.

The groom, a man named Nishi Koichi (Mifune Toshirō), is also closely associated with the scandal: he is the bride's father's secretary. Nishi acquired the cushy position after becoming engaged to his boss's daughter, adding nepotism to Dairyū's list of corporate sins. The bride and groom wear classic wedding attire, Nishi in a black *montsuki* and the bride in a white *shiromuku*. In the postwar period it became common for couples to change into Western attire like tuxedoes and evening gowns for their receptions, but the Nishi-Iwabuchi wedding is a highly-formal affair. The stoic, unsmiling faces of the bride and groom contribute to a sense of old-fashioned stiffness, but the fact that the bride (Kagawa Kyōko) stumbles as she enters the reception hall clues the audience in that something is amiss beneath the event's dispassionate surface.

More than the arrest of a guest, it is the arrival of the wedding cake that shatters the tension in the room and ushers in an atmosphere of shock and fear. Western-style wedding cakes entered Japan in the cosmopolitan 1920s, during the Taishō *jidai*, but they did not become wedding-day staples until the latter half of the Shōwa *jidai* in the 1960s, '70s, and '80s. Often, the cake the bride and groom "cut" is a rubbery, inedible facsimile; the couple inserts a knife or sword into a preexisting notch in the display cake while waiters serve slices of a real one to the guests. Japanese wedding cakes are therefore literally symbolic, but few ever symbolized anything as disturbing as the cake in *The Bad Sleep Well*. It appears toward the end of the reception in the shape of a rectangular, eight-story office building with a rose sticking out of a seventh-floor window. The assembled reporters recognize the cake as a model of a specific government office—an office from which a Dairyū employee jumped to his death five years earlier during an investigation into the bidding process for the building's construction. The rose marks the window from which the suicidal leap occurred. The sight of the cake sends the Dairyū executives into a panic while the reporters grin at the return of a juicy old scandal in the midst of a new one.[5]

Not long after the reception, Dairyū's accountant, temporarily out of jail but facing re-arrest, jumps in front of a truck rather than submit to a new round

Like many weddings in the Shōwa *jidai*, the 1959 wedding of Crown Prince Akihito and Princess Michiko featured both traditional and Western-style formalwear (from Imperial Household Agency).

of interrogation. Suicide in Japan reached a new peak between 1958 and 1960, and many suicides stemmed in part from victims' financial problems despite the nearly uninterrupted economic growth of the 1950s and '60s. Only a small subset of suicides involved financial crimes or public scandals, but these grabbed headlines and seemed to become more common as the century wore on. In a striking example from the late 1990s, four Japanese bankers and bureaucrats killed themselves during a five-month period amid a major corruption inquiry. *The Bad Sleep Well*'s two Dairyū suicides seem to presage the start of a similar wave until Nishi intervenes.[6]

When another Dairyū executive, Wada (Fujiwara Kamatari), prepares to jump to his death at a Public Corporation development site, Nishi suddenly appears and stops him. For reasons that Wada does not understand, Nishi convinces him to fake his death instead. It is all too believable that multiple Dairyū men would take their own lives during the ongoing investigation, so when Wada disappears nobody questions what happened to him. Sitting in a stylish black sedan, Nishi and Wada watch Wada's funeral from a distance. When Dairyū chiefs Moriyama (Shimura Takashi) and Shirai (Nishimura Kō) come to pay their respects, Nishi plays Wada a secret tape recording of the two men discussing their satisfaction about Wada's "suicide." His death, they said, removes another potential witness from the investigation. The conversation that Nishi recorded happened at a cabaret called Noir, and the upbeat American music that plays in the background creates an irreverent juxtaposition as the men watch Wada's funeral. Wada does not yet fully understand Nishi's reason for saving his life, but he agrees to help Nishi carry out a plot against Dairyū's leaders.

The macabre way that *The Bad Sleep Well* frames its suicides illustrates how the public's attitude toward suicide changed during the miracle years. Between 1950 and 1960 the leading Japanese newspapers *Asahi Shinbun* and *Yomiuri Shinbun* ran hundreds of death notices each year about suicide victims. Many of these notices struck a romantic tone when detailing the suicides of young lovers, authors, and artists. A contemporary novel about a lovelorn woman who takes her life in the beautiful Aokigahara Forest near Mt. Fuji contributed to that place's popularity as a suicide destination; by the end of the 20th century, the number of suicide attempts in Aokigahara regularly reached 100 to 200 per year. Outsiders often attributed Japan's high suicide rate to the old samurai practice of *seppuku*, also known as *harakiri*, but activists inside Japan did not accept the practice as a cultural inevitability. In the late 1950s and early 1960s Japanese sociologists, doctors, and government programs began to address the country's suicide problem, and one tactic they used was to reframe suicide as a consequence of social pressure rather than an individual act of will. Some of the most high-profile suicides in Japanese history, like those of defeated samurai or teenage kamikaze pilots at the end of World War II, involved victims who were not necessarily eager to die but felt compelled to do so because of social and political expectations. Anti-suicide researchers and activists seized on this fact in order to deglamorize suicide. In 1957 one scholar went so far as to write that "when [suicide] is only about social rules, it is like a homicide." Kurosawa's characters in *The Bad Sleep Well* express the same opinion. Journalists accuse Vice President Iwabuchi of killing the Dairyū accountant by instructing him to commit suicide, and Nishi tells Wada that the colleagues who celebrated his "death" are no better than murderers.[7]

Nishi and Wada's first act of revenge is to drive Shirai insane. They frame Shirai for embezzlement, after which Shirai grows nervous and paranoid. Nishi hastens Shirai's descent into madness by letting him catch a glimpse of Wada's "ghost" in a dark alleyway. As expected, Iwabuchi and Moriyama try to encourage Shirai to commit suicide. When he does not, Iwabuchi hires a *yakuza* gunman to do the job. The distinction between pressuring a subordinate to commit suicide and having him murdered him disappears entirely as Iwabuchi proves himself willing to do either.

Nishi finally reveals the reason for his revenge scheme. He rescues Shirai from the *yakuza* and takes him and Wada to the seventh floor of the building that inspired the ominous wedding cake. There Nishi reveals that he is the illegitimate son of the man who jumped from the building five years earlier. Since then, all of Nishi's actions, from joining the Dairyū company to marrying Iwabuchi's daughter, have been part of an elaborate plot to make Iwabuchi pay for the suicide. He knows that the legal system will never hold powerful men accountable for their underlings' suicides and that reports of scandal and corruption in the newspapers achieve little or nothing. Nishi sees himself as a warrior for justice, a man working for "all the helpless people who don't even know they've been had." As Iwabuchi's judge, jury, and perhaps executioner, Nishi will avenge his father's death and strike a blow against Japan's culture of corruption.

Like a vigilante superhero, Nishi has a secret hiding place that reveals more details about his personality. He lives underneath an abandoned munitions factory where he worked as a boy during World War II. This was Kurosawa's first explicit reference to the war since 1951's *The Idiot*, and it came at a time when the Japanese government considered the war and its aftermath distant history. In 1956 the government's Annual Economic Report proclaimed that contemporary events should no longer be referred to as "postwar" (*sengo*) events. Around the same time, a widely-discussed essay by writer Nakano Yoshio declared that "the 'postwar' has ended," and the phrase became so popular that in 1958 Nakano had to clarify what he meant by it. In the context of the economic miracle, it seemed ludicrous to use the word "postwar" to describe both the misery of the late 1940s and the comfort of the late 1950s. There were also political benefits to consigning the war and occupation to history; Prime Minister Kishi supported removing the anti-war clause from the Japanese constitution in order to "move out of the postwar era" and "eradicat[e] completely the consequences of Japan's defeat and the American occupation." Kurosawa, however, refused to whitewash the memory of the war from his films. In *The Bad Sleep Well* Nishi walks around his decaying wartime factory hideout, lost in his memories. Unlike most other wartime industrial sites, this one was never redeveloped by Public Corporation, Dairyū Construction, or their ilk. The place where

Nishi faced bombs and starvation as a youth remains untouched by the more subtle evils embedded in postwar reconstruction, and it is there that Nishi fantasizes about revenge for past and present injustices.[8]

The munitions factory is also the site of Nishi's downfall. His wife, whom he loves despite marrying her under false pretenses, learns about his plan to ruin her father and discovers the location of the hideout. She loves Nishi, but her father tricks her into revealing Nishi's location. Iwabuchi and his thugs kill Nishi and Wada, and destroy all the evidence of corruption and forced suicides that the heroes amassed over the course of the film. Corruption remains entrenched, and "now all Japan will be tricked the same way." Yet it was a close call for Dairyū and Public Corporation. As the newspapers' interest in the scandal runs its course, Iwabuchi admits that he has not slept well lately, and he shows some sadness that murdering Nishi has cost him his daughter's love. Nevertheless, he does not abandon the corporation or denounce its dirty dealings.

In 1960 Japanese citizens saw a young protestor die outside the parliament building, and they saw the treaty that she died protesting go into effect anyway. They saw a career bureaucrat tainted by multiple scandals ascend to the role of prime minister, and they saw stories about business malpractice in the papers. *The Bad Sleep Well* affirmed that they weren't imagining things; back-room deals and closed-door negotiations allowed government officials to ignore the feelings of the people, and corporate corruption remained entrenched even when its exposure led to resignations or suicides.

In his next two films Kurosawa would again cast Mifune as a lone hero fighting against overwhelming odds and corrupt authorities, but the *jidaigeki Yōjimbō* and its sequel *Tsubaki Sanjūrō* dare to imagine the possibility of victory.

CHAPTER 20

Yōjimbō

In *Yōjimbō*, a scruffy *rōnin* (Mifune Toshirō) in a worn-out *kimono* is caught between two powerful crime bosses who both try to use him to wipe out the other. The two villains control every business in their dusty little town, employ dozens of thugs, and even have access to guns, but the nearly-nameless hero uses cleverness and skill to beat them both. Squeezed between two evils, the hero finds a third way.

Yōjimbō came to theaters in April 1961, the same year that the first official summit of "non-aligned" countries opened a new front in the Cold War. Most of the 25 nations that formed the Non-Aligned Movement were Asian or African, belonging to what Americans referred to as "the third world" as opposed to the United States and its allies (the first world) and the Soviet Union and its allies (the second world). The non-aligned nations were determined not to become pawns of the Cold War superpowers; many of them had suffered under American, European, Russian, and Japanese imperialism before securing their independence after World War II, and they were wary of falling under foreign influence again. The Japanese government, a former occupier that reaffirmed its alliance to the United States with the 1960 security treaty, could not participate in the inaugural Non-Aligned Movement Summit that took place in Belgrade, Yugoslavia in September 1961. Yet the Japanese government was keenly interested in the movement, and perhaps a bit envious as well.

In 1955 Japan sent representatives to a meeting of Asian and African nations in Bandung, Indonesia, where participants worked to define the goals of non-alignment. The nations in attendance supported the sovereignty and equality of all nations, the pursuit of peaceful solutions to problems between nations, and rejected special defense agreements that strengthened the most powerful countries. In later meetings this bloc of non-aligned nations also expressed opposition to nuclear weapons, but some of them, like India, eventually developed their own nuclear programs. Japanese leaders, despite their subjugation to the United States in matters of international security, saw value and opportunity in a non-aligned approach to the Cold War. Greater cooperation between Asian nations made it easier and safer for Japan to invest in the region and encourage trade that benefited Japanese businesses. The non-aligned movement also created an avenue for Japan to resume trading with communist China; the Chinese government sent representatives to Bandung as well, and they spoke with their Japanese counterparts about ways to increase

Japan sent representatives to the 1955 Bandung Conference, an early step in the creation of the "non-aligned" movement (from Foreign Ministry of the Republic of Indonesia).

trade between the two countries. Trade organizations from China and Japan signed numerous agreements with each other signaling their desire to trade, but the United States continued to impose strict limits on the amount of goods that Japan could sell to China.[1]

Though Japan could not claim to belong to the "third world," Japanese politicians, businessmen, writers, and globally-minded citizens began to conceive of Japanese policy as belonging to a third way. Western economists use the phrase "third way" to describe economies that blend elements of free-market capitalism and state planning, and some of them cite Japan as an example. The bureaucratic planning that drove the Japanese economy did not fit the capitalist ideal of free markets, but corporate power and the crushing of strikes like one at the Miike coal mine meant Japan was hardly socialist; Japan's Socialist Party ebbed after its leader was assassinated on live TV in 1960. In the Japanese context, though, the idea of a third way goes deeper than questions of economic theory—it echoes the Buddhist philosophy of *nakadō*, "the middle way." Sometimes used as a synonym for Buddhism itself, this idea holds that the secret to enlightenment is not extreme self-indulgence or extreme self-denial, but rather moderation in all things. During the Meiji *jidai*, priests and government officials alike cited *nakadō* to encourage people to take "a neutral stand between labor and capital." As good Buddhists, they argued, labor activists should not resort to extreme measures like strikes or revolt, and business leaders should not thoughtlessly pursue profits at the expense of employees' well-being. During the Cold War the implications of a third way were much the same. Under the terms of its treaties with the United States Japan could not be truly neutral, but popular sentiment about nuclear weapons, military bases, and sovereignty meant that Japan was not unequivocally pro–American, either.[2]

Charting a narrow course between ideological lightning rods, Japanese leaders advocated "separating politics and economics" (*seikei bunri*). Treating those spheres separately could help justify seemingly contradictory policies like trading with communist nations while remaining politically anti-communist. In the wake of the demonstrations of 1960 Prime Minister Ikeda promoted the ideals of "tolerance and forbearance" (*kanyō to nintai*) and tried to keep a "low posture" on controversial matters of national security.[3]

Mifune's title character in *Yōjimbō* walks his own third way between two hostile camps, even adopting a literal "low posture." He shrugs one shoulder as he walks, giving him a hunched, lopsided, unprepossessing appearance accentuated by his old clothes and unkempt facial hair. As the opening credits fade away, he stops at a crossroads. Three dirt paths branch off in front of him, each one flanked by tall grass. The *rōnin* throws a stick in the air and walks in the direction it points.

He soon comes across a farmhouse where a father, mother, and son are bickering over money. As the samurai watches, the son threatens to go seek work as a mercenary while his father implores him to stay on the farm. Meanwhile, the mother spins silk, a task that many rural Japanese women still did in the 1960s despite the availability of cheaper imported silk. The farm family in *Yōjimbō* complains that tradesmen and their prices change too quickly; the local *sake* brewer pays more for homespun silk than the silk merchant, but only irregularly. They worry that increased competition over silk could bring unwanted opportunists to town, and the father scowls at the *rōnin* when he says this.[4]

Kurosawa's audiences were also cautious about money matters during the miracle years. Though they lived in a time of great prosperity, they saved more of their paychecks than the people of any other first-world nation. At the start of the 1960s the average Japanese household put away around 20 percent of its total annual income, whereas the rate of savings in the United States was only around 11 percent. For both moral and monetary reasons the Japanese government encouraged citizens to save and be thrifty. The government operated convenient savings accounts through the Postal Savings System, which started in the Meiji *jidai* and allowed people to access their bank accounts at any neighborhood post office. During war and occupation saving money was difficult and even unwise, since inflation wiped out the value of money faster than people could spend it, but when prices stabilized people began to store some of their rising incomes away for future use. By the 1960s the Postal Saving System was the largest consumer bank in Japan, and by the end of the 20th century it was "the largest financial institution in the world," with more assets than any other bank or credit company. The trillions of yen that Japanese customers deposited in interest-bearing postal accounts went to Japan's Ministry of Finance, which reinvested it, held on to it to slow inflation, and frequently caused scandals by mishandling it. Nevertheless, the perceived security of the Postal Savings System in comparison to corporate banks was an important factor in its popularity; people still remembered how many private banks went out of business during the global economic crisis of the 1930s. Throughout the economic miracle many Japanese households handled their money with caution and frugality, and the government encouraged them to plan for the future rather than commit too much to the present.[5]

Moving on from the wary farmers, the samurai enters a dusty town whose residents seem outright fearful. Men and women peek out of slatted windows and around the edges of their wood-and-paper sliding doors, retreating when the *rōnin* glances their way. Kurosawa often spoke of the influence of John Ford's westerns on his *jidaigeki*, but the better comparison to *Yōjimbō* is Fred Zinnemann's *High Noon* (1952), whose cowardly townspeople barricade themselves indoors while a lawman faces outlaws alone in the street. *Yōjimbō*, though, is far darker; one of the samurai's first sights is a dog with a detached human hand in its mouth, suggesting that people aren't even venturing out to bury bodies. For a masterless samurai, though, danger and violence mean opportunity. The town constable soon emerges from hiding to offer the *rōnin* a job as a bodyguard, a *yōjimbō*.

Yōjimbō's town is dangerous because two rival clans run illegal gambling games that attract drifters and criminals, and their soldiers fight each other for supremacy. One of the clan bosses, Seibei (Kawazu Seizaburō), keeps his headquarters at the town brothel, but his wife Orin (Yamada Isuzu) is the real mastermind. The other boss, Ushitora (Sazanka Kyū), operates out of the local inn. "Instead of buying silk, they're buying thugs" in a battle for control of the town. Like the Cold War arms race that showed no sign of abating, the two powerful factions hold everyone hostage in a war of brinksmanship.

An idea from *The Bad Sleep Well* (see Chapter 19) is repeated in *Yōjimbō*: "To make a fortune, you have to kill and steal." To prove his worth, the *rōnin* lops off the arm of a gambler and leaves three others bleeding to death in the street. The bosses then begin a bidding war for his services as a *yōjimbō*. Like Mifune's character in *The Bad Sleep Well*, the samurai hides his true identity from his prospective employers, giving his name as "Kuwabatake Sanjūrō" which means "thirty-year-old mulberry field." The bosses recognize this *nom de guerre* as a reference to the town's mulberry orchards, which feed the silkworms that supported the local economy before gambling and gang warfare eclipsed them. The samurai's identity and actions both point toward the same goal: purging the town of conflict and restoring its pastoral tranquility.

American crew load a bomb onto a fighter-bomber aircraft at Kadena Air Base, Okinawa, 1962 (photograph by U.S. Air Force photographer Staff Sgt. Robert J. Carr).

Like Mifune's character in *The Bad Sleep Well*, "Sanjūrō" dirties his hands while fighting for the greater good. He kidnaps two of Ushitora's men and blames it on Seibei, and Ushitora responds by kidnapping Seibei's beloved son. Seibei then kidnaps a woman of Ushitora's household, whose young son cries pitifully for her while Sanjūrō stands idly by. A man named Gonji (Tōno Eijirō) owns the restaurant where Sanjūrō makes his plans, and when he complains that he has no customers thanks to the worsening terror and violence, Sanjūrō becomes impatient. Like Nishi in *The Bad Sleep Well*, Sanjūrō is willing to sacrifice the people around him in the name of vanquishing evil. He kills gamblers and thugs without remorse, but what really angers the bosses is when he spills a storehouse full of grain, sets fire to the silk business, and floods a warehouse with vats of *sake*. The economy of the town collapses along with the fortunes of the gangs. Even the coffin-maker becomes destitute, because "when the fighting gets this bad, they don't bother with coffins." The townspeople remain in limbo waiting for the bloody stalemate to end. Rather than treat the spheres of economics and politics separately like the Japanese policymakers of the 1960s who tried to conduct business on both sides of the Cold War, Sanjūrō exploits the connection between economic and political power in order to goad the rival gangs into all-out conflict.

The samurai has skill and cunning, but he falls behind in the arms race when Ushitora's brother Unosuke (Nakadai Tatsuya) comes to town toting a six-shooter pistol. Like nuclear weapons during the Cold War, a modern gun is a trump card in the world of *Yōjimbō*, and Unosuke wields his with confidence. He captures Sanjūrō at gunpoint and gives the *rōnin* a beating.

It is tempting to describe Sanjūrō's final triumph in mythic terms as the archetypical underdog defeats a stronger, better-equipped enemy. The sight of the scrappy *rōnin* striding toward Unosuke, whose shot goes wild, is one of the most enduring images of Kurosawa's career. Yet Sanjūrō does not win by himself. When the injured samurai escapes Unosuke's clutches, Gonji the restaurateur smuggles the samurai to safety in one of the coffin-maker's barrel-shaped ossuaries. From the coffin Sanjūrō watches Unosuke lead an assault that destroys Seibei's gang. Then, when the time is right, he rises like an avenging ghost and cuts down Unosuke and the rest of Ushitora's men. Unosuke's pistol lies empty and useless, the gangsters are gone, and peace returns to the town along with a more wholesome economy.

When Japan rose from the dead to become a leading economic power in the 1950s and '60s, it "saw and presented itself as a peacemaker in a post-war world threatened by the ambitions of belligerent superpowers." The country's leaders tried to be modern Sanjūrōs by charting a middle course, partnering with neutral nations, and advocating for peace and prosperity. A nameless samurai who defended people caught between warring giants and tried to restore normalcy to a world gone mad was the right myth at the right time. Yet Japan was not neutral; it all but belonged to a mighty nuclear superpower, and it played an important if unequal role in the United States' Cold War strategy. If Sanjūrō could not navigate a small, fictional Cold War without getting blood on his hands and getting bloodied himself, could Japan expect to fare any better in the real one?[6]

CHAPTER 21

Tsubaki Sanjūrō

By 1962 it was common for samurai movies to cast a critical eye on the bygone warrior caste. In the miracle era, frequent scandals in government and industry made people question whether the elites of yesteryear had behaved any better. Movie directors increasingly selected lower-caste protagonists for their *jidaigeki*, and anti-samurai movies like Kobayashi Masaki's *Harakiri* dominated the film landscape. Written by frequent Kurosawa collaborator Hashimoto Shinobu, *Harakiri*'s story about the hypocrisy of feudal elites won the 1963 Cannes Special Jury Prize. That same year the movie *Bushido: The Cruel Code of the Samurai* (*Bushidō zankoku monogatari*, "Bushido, a Story of Cruelty") took aim at the infamous samurai code of honor, arguably more of an invention of Meiji *jidai* propagandists than a true medieval ideology. Samurai also appear as villains in the long-running *Zatoichi* film series that began in 1962. Its titular hero is an expert swordsman but not a samurai; he belongs to a masseuse's guild whose members are blind beggars.[1]

Kurosawa's samurai movies did not quite fit the trend. Bad samurai crop up in his *jidaigeki*, but usually as foils for good samurai. His characters sometimes comment on the evils that samurai can do, but heroic samurai are far more common in Kurosawa's work. They exhibit loyalty and cleverness in *The Men Who Tread on the Tiger's Tail*, they defeat outlaws in *Seven Samurai*, and the samurai of *Hidden Fortress* is resourceful and honorable. Even the Macbeth-inspired samurai protagonist of *Spiderweb Castle* is less a villain than a victim of fate.

The samurai known by the pseudonym "Sanjūrō" (Mifune Toshirō) is clearly a hero, but he nods to the spirit of the moment by identifying more with the lower castes than with his own. In his first appearance in *Yōjimbō* he serves as a bodyguard, but not for the rich and powerful leaders who usually employed samurai in that capacity. Instead, like his forerunners in *Seven Samurai*, he acts as protector for local peasants and shopkeepers who cannot or dare not defend themselves. Furthermore, whereas most samurai names derived from their lineage or the noble houses in which they served, Sanjūrō takes his adopted surnames from the agricultural products of the places where he sojourns. In *Yōjimbō* it was "Kuwabatake," a reference to the mulberry trees whose leaves the townsfolk harvested to feed their silkworms. In the sequel *Tsubaki Sanjūrō* (simply *Sanjuro* in the English release), the *rōnin* gives his family name as "Tsubaki," or camellia, after the flowering tree whose leaves are used in green tea. By naming himself after cultivated plants instead of the elite houses that profit from the labor of farmers and foresters, Sanjūrō elevates the land and those who work it to the level of nobility.

The name "Tsubaki" also speaks to a major shift in what Japanese people imbibed for leisure in the late Shōwa *jidai*. Tea, brought to Japan from China, was the caffeinated drink of choice from antiquity until the 20th century. The Japanese tea ceremony whose deceptively simple elegance took shape between the 13th and 15th centuries eventually became one of the most internationally-recognized examples of Japanese aesthetics. Yet from the 1950s onward tea rapidly lost ground to coffee. Like most things Western, coffee entered Japan in a noticeable way during the Meiji *jidai* when the country's first two coffeehouses opened in Tokyo in 1888. In the Taishō *jidai* of the 1910s and '20s, as more Japanese people traveled abroad and acquired Western tastes, coffeehouses proliferated, and some teahouses replaced their entire stock with coffee. There were so many coffeehouses by the 1930s that the ultranationalist government felt the need to crack down on them, closing those they believed catered to "liberals" and "Marxists." During the occupation coffee came back into official favor, and its appearance in movies impressed American censors as an indication of Japan's embrace of Western habits. It is no accident that the protagonists of Kurosawa's *One Wonderful Sunday* spend some of their hard-earned yen on a date at a coffee shop and dream about opening their own (see Chapter 6). During the economic boom of the 1950s and '60s, coffee shops cropped up in virtually every town and village in Japan. Amid heavy competition they set themselves apart by adopting various themes, some family-friendly like jazz or rustic Americana, and some more salacious like Tokyo's infamous "maid cafes" whose waitresses wear erotic uniforms. Whether ordinary or outlandish, postwar Japanese coffee shops provided popular meeting places for young lovers, retreats for businessmen blowing off steam, and casual brunch options for families. Rows of coffee vending machines dispensing hot and cold cans of ready-to-drink java also became ubiquitous in late Shōwa Japan, and the country's coffee industry reached an estimated $10 billion per year by the end of the century.[2]

In order to keep up, tea vendors diversified and emphasized their drink's connection to tradition. Instead of just plain green tea, teahouses and shops began to offer thicker, sweeter, more caffeinated varieties like sweetened *matcha*. The Japanese government promoted locally-grown teas as export goods, and later it designated the techniques of the tea ceremony as Important Intangible Cultural Properties. The cultivation of camellia trees remained an important part of the economies of certain Japanese prefectures, especially Shizuoka in central Japan and Kagoshima in the far southwest, even as domestic consumption declined. Sanjūrō's embrace of the camellia in his eponymous 1962 film was only a minor footnote in Japan's beverage wars, but the association of tea with a popular movie hero was a point in the native drink's favor.[3]

The way Sanjūrō chooses his surnames—by looking at his surroundings—recalls

Japanese photographers in a coffee shop, 1950. From left to right: Nagai Kaichi, Domon Ken, Inamura Takamasa, Miki Jun (from Asahi Shimbunsha).

the way many Japanese families chose their names at the end of the 19th century. With some exceptions, prior to the Meiji *jidai* only samurai houses used surnames. Family names were status symbols and it was illegal for people of the lower castes to use them, but artists could acquire them due to great esteem, and wealthy commoners sometimes purchased the "right" to use them from elites who did not enforce the law. In 1875 the Meiji government, as part of its sweeping legal and social reforms, required all citizens to choose and register a surname. Those who did not already have strong claims to family names had to invent them, often with the help of their local, literate priests. Names based on general or specific places were popular choices, like "Tanaka" meaning "in the field" and "Yamaguchi" after the name of a prefecture. Many people watching *Tsubaki Sanjūrō* in theaters could trace their own surnames to nearly arbitrary choices made by their grandparents and great-grandparents less than a century earlier.[4]

Sanjūrō's new adventure begins when, from his room in a darkened inn, he overhears a group of young samurai plotting to purge their lord's household of corruption. The samurai are humorously naïve. When their leader announces that the lord's superintendent has agreed to a private meeting to discuss their plans for reform, they all rejoice, but it is clear to Sanjūrō that the young warriors have walked into a trap. The superintendent's men surround the inn, trapping Sanjūrō and the good-hearted but feckless young samurai. Sanjūrō offers to protect the youths and exchanges words with Muroto Hanbei (Nakadai Tatsuya), the superintendent's dangerous-looking mercenary. Muroto recognizes Sanjūrō's quality and orders his men to withdraw.

Sanjūrō and Muroto share a connection as outsiders. Other characters talk about their clan and their well-connected relatives, but Sanjūrō and Muroto lack these things. Sanjūrō wears a familial crest on his clothes, but whatever connections it signifies to lord and family have long been severed. By contrast, the youngsters Sanjūrō helps and the elders Muroto protects all belong to the same lineage group. Medieval clans were networks of people related by blood, marriage, and fealty. Echoes of feudal lineage networks persisted into the 20th century, especially in rural areas where "parent" households headed entire villages' worth of "child" households bound to them through blood, marriage, adoption, or simple tradition (see Chapter 14). The child families paid their respects to parent families on significant dates and provided extra hands at planting and harvest time, and in return parent households made monetary gifts on important occasions, issued loans at preferential rates, and helped find spouses for child household members of marriageable age. These habits slowly died out as economic growth put rural households on more equal footing, younger generations moved away from the countryside, and attitudes about social hierarchy softened, but some of the old arrangements lingered for decades, at least as polite gestures.[5]

The film *Tsubaki Sanjūrō* focuses especially on the women of its fictional clan. Two in particular, the wife (Irie Takako) and daughter (Dan Reiko) of the chamberlain, become prisoners of the superintendent when he tries to frame the chamberlain. They are not typical damsels in distress. The movie treats them with dignity befitting their samurai status, and their quiet competence stands in contrast to the overeager young male samurai. When the daughter escapes her captors on her own and rendezvouses with Sanjūrō and his young followers, Sanjūrō remarks to them that she is a great samurai and "more reliable than all of you."

While not as patriarchal as the historical clans, miracle-era institutions from government to business to family had room for improvement in the eyes of many women. By the 1960s women's legal equality was constitutional law, but that did not mean that there was nothing left for women to achieve. Japanese women of the miracle years took advantage of new and more accessible forms of contraception that allowed them to have fewer children and seek more opportunities outside the spheres of home and family. During the occupation American authorities responsible for feeding the impoverished nation worried that Japan's birthrate was too high, but by the end of the 1950s the birthrate was barely above replacement level, and it continued to drop during and after the economic miracle. In addition to exploring new career paths, many women organized to help their fellow citizens. Women activists were instrumental in postwar political movements like the anti-nuclear movement and the security treaty protests; the one fatality when police clashed with protestors outside the Diet building in June 1960 was a woman, 22-year-old university student Kanba Michiko, who in her short life was active in a variety of causes. Michiko's death and the publication of her life story galvanized Japanese activists, particularly women activists. The Japanese media often described women activists of the 1960s

The Group of Fighting Women and other activists march in Tokyo in 1972 to protest restrictions on women's bodily autonomy, such as a law that banned the "abortion pill" and that allowed doctors to sterilize women with some heredity conditions without their consent (photograph © Matsumoto Michiko).

as "housewives and young mothers," labels that emphasized their gender, but like the martyred Michiko they did not limit themselves to "women's issues." Beginning in 1970 the nationwide Group of Fighting Women (*Gurūpu tatakau onna*), whose members often gathered in coffee shops, advocated greater support for single mothers, defended female and male workers from corporate attempts to weaken workplace regulations, and protested American military bases in Japan. The samurai women of the past might have been proud of these 20th-century warriors for social justice.[6]

While the movie's strong women, helpless young men, and unconventional *rōnin* plot to save the lord's household, the corrupt conspirators try to draw them out of hiding. A farcical series of moves and countermoves results in some narrow escapes for the good guys and bad guys alike, but nothing changes until Sanjūrō offers to switch sides—the same tactic he used in *Yōjimbō*. Sanjūrō causes chaos inside the clan, cutting down many of Muroto's men in secret. Meanwhile the samurai women learn the location of the framed chamberlain when he sends bits of paper down the camellia-lined stream that flows from his prison to their hiding place. Sanjūrō's team finally captures the villains and places the honorable chamberlain in command of the clan. On his way out of town Sanjūrō slays the now-masterless Moroto in a duel and walks on in search of the next adventure. Mifune would play roles nearly identical to Sanjūrō in the films *Zatoichi Meets Yōjimbō* (*Zatoichi to yojimbō*) and *Machibuse*, both from 1970, but neither of these were Kurosawa movies and they changed the character's name from Sanjūrō to avoid copyright problems.

Kurosawa was finished with sequels, but he was not yet through with his charismatic star Mifune. Their next film would return to the world of contemporary Japanese business for a crime story every bit as stylish and fast-paced as their recent *jidaigeki*.

CHAPTER 22

Heaven and Hell

While filming *The Lower Depths* in 1957, Kurosawa made the memorable decision to walk on the set in his indoor shoes. Although the flophouse set was technically an indoor space, the set decorators made it so filthy with muck, clutter, and dust that most of the crew wore their street shoes when they walked on it. Yet it was a point of pride for Kurosawa that he walked on the filthy wood and *tatami* floors only in his socks or slippers, the same footwear he would use in an office or in someone's home. Dilapidated though it may be, the set was "home" to his characters.[1]

Centuries-old texts and drawings prove that the practice of removing or changing footwear when entering a building has been around for a long time in Japan. It did not end during the modernizing, Westernizing years of the 1870s–1920s, or during the upheavals of the '40s and '50s. Instead the practice flourished as new varieties of footwear, like Western-style slippers, dress shoes, and sneakers became more available and affordable. When indoor plumbing became a standard fixture of Japanese buildings, another dimension of the footwear custom emerged as people placed designated "toilet slippers" in their restrooms. Homes with gardens often keep clean shoes near the garden entrance for residents and guests, since typical Japanese gardens are tidy, cultivated spaces distinct from the rest of the outdoors. At the entrance of most schools are shoe storage cabinets where students and teachers keep their outdoor shoes during school hours and store their indoor shoes when they leave for the day. Office buildings, hospitals, museums, nice restaurants, traditional-style hotels, and other indoor spaces also provide shoe cabinets and slippers for guests, and not to use them is a cultural *faux pas*.[2]

All of this shoe-switching helped make the Japanese shoe industry a robust survivor during an era when heavy industry and technology eclipsed most textile and handicraft production. According to MITI bureaucrats, clothing companies produced too much during the early part of the economic miracle when the government helped pay for their raw materials. Officials in the United States complained when a wave of "dollar blouses" from Japan flooded American department stores. In the mid–1960s the Japanese government, bowing to U.S. pressure to buy more American products and equalize the trade imbalance, began to remove trade protections for its manufactured goods, starting with old industries like clothing and later moving on to cars, machinery, and electronics. Business leaders worried that without protective tariffs and government assistance their products would not be able to compete on the domestic or international market.[3]

Yet shoes proved resilient. Domestic demand remained strong thanks in part to the practice of using different pairs of shoes for different purposes throughout the day. Even more importantly, exports of Japanese shoes kept increasing. That was true of most Japanese products in the 1960s as the government continued to promote overseas trade, especially to developing Asian countries. Shoes, however, benefited from especially lucky historical circumstances. The 1964 Summer Olympics in Tokyo raised the international profile of Japanese athletic goods, and shoe companies seized the moment by advertising Japanese track shoes and trainers around the world. In the same year, a young American entrepreneur named Philip Knight traveled to Japan on his father's money to pitch his idea for a line of affordable athletic shoes. He met with Onitsuka Kihachiro, the president of a shoe company called Tiger, and along with American track coach Bill Bowerman they formed a partnership to sell made-in-Japan running shoes in the United States. The resulting distribution company, Blue Ribbon Sports, eventually changed its name to Nike. During the economic miracle, even companies in less-favored, non-technological industries could thrive in the global marketplace.[4]

Heaven and Hell (*Tengoku to jigoku*, usually retitled *High and Low* in English), opens in the hilltop home of Gondo Kingo (Mifune Toshirō), an executive in a Japanese shoe company. He has an idea for a new, high-quality woman's shoe, but the other bigwigs don't like it. Manufacturing it is too expensive, they say, and "if shoes don't wear out, we don't sell any." They want Gondo to back a cheaper design over the objections of the company president, an old-fashioned man whose "ideal shoe is an army boot." If Gondo supports them, they will vote to make Gondo executive director. Gondo cites his own army experience and his many years in the business while rejecting both the shoddy shoe and the power grab, but he is motivated by more than just pride: he has a plan to take over the company on his own.

Gondo's young son and his chauffeur's son run into the living room playing "cowboy and outlaw" in generic Old West outfits familiar to 1960s audiences on both sides of the Pacific. Gondo's wife (Kagawa Kyōko) observes that their son is like his father: both of them enjoy being on the attack. Mifune's famous samurai movies, including the recent smash hit *Yōjimbō* which was remade as a western in 1964, lend his businessman Gondo a martial aura. When the boys switch costumes and Gondo's son takes on the role of the outlaw, Gondo instructs his child to fight rather than run because "a man must kill or be killed." Perhaps this attitude, like his belief in a sturdy pair of shoes, is a legacy of Gondo's military service, but it also applies to the business world in which Gondo is forever on the offensive against international and domestic competitors.

Then disaster strikes. The boys go play outside, and soon a kidnapper (Yamazaki Tsutomu) calls Gondo to say that he has his son. He orders the shoe magnate to pay a large cash ransom. Seconds later Gondo's son appears in the living room, perfectly safe, and the truth dawns on Gondo: the kidnapper abducted the chauffeur's child by mistake. Gondo is reluctant to pay a ransom for a boy who isn't his own, especially since he needs the money for his secret business deal. His entire fortune is bound up in his corporate takeover plan, and its failure would ruin him and his family. However, his legitimacy as a business leader, not to mention his reputation as a man, depends on his ability to look after his employees and their families.

Miracle-era bureaucrat Amaya Naohiro used the phrase *uchiwa*, "family circle," to describe Japan's approach to business management. Businesses were supposed to provide employment for the entirety of their employees' careers, offer pensions upon retirement, set salaries based on seniority, and promote from within except in the case of bureaucrats who "descended from heaven" (*amakudari*) into top corporate jobs after leaving government. Employees and their unions, in turn, were supposed to show loyalty and respect certain unwritten rules, such as that the rate of profit growth always exceeded the rate of wage increases. A union included only the employees of a particular company, not every employee across an entire industry, and this helped ensure that labor disputes stayed "in the family." The concept of *uchiwa* is especially applicable to Gondo and his chauffeur. Gondo's home is the chauffeur's workplace, and their children grow up as close friends. After an agonizing delay in which Gondo's wife reminds her husband of his ethical duty and the chauffeur meekly agrees to respect whatever decision his boss makes, Gondo decides to pay the ransom.[5]

Half a dozen detectives arrive at Gondo's home to monitor the kidnapper's phone calls and help Gondo prepare the ransom delivery. The cops' dialogue, especially Inspector Tokura's (Nakadai Tatsuya), highlights modern tools of the police trade like wiretapping, tracing serial numbers on yen notes, and the use of chemical compounds to track the briefcases holding the money. In the 1960s movies about detectives shared box office space with *yakuza* movies, and the two genres balanced titillation and reassurance at a time when Japan's overall crime rate dropped to historic lows. *Yakuza* movies like *Tokyo Drifter* (*Tōkyō nagaremono*, 1966), *A Colt is My Passport* (*Koruto wa Ore no Pasupōto*, 1967), and dozens of other low-budget but highly-sensory gangster pictures offered stylish depictions of organized crime. At the same time, Japan posted lower rates of homicide, rape, and theft than the United States and most of Western Europe, and the crime gap between Japan and the rest of the first world continued to grow wider. This trend had more to do with Japan's widely-distributed economic prosperity than with the effectiveness of its police, but the rarity of crime contributed to citizens' positive image of local and prefectural police forces even as it fed their appetite for fictional crime stories.[6]

Another area in which Japan outpaced the rest of the world in the 1960s was rail service, so it is appropriate that the next act of *Heaven and Hell* takes place on a train. Even as the United States phased out its passenger rail infrastructure in favor of cars, interstate highways, and domestic airlines, Japan opted to build new train lines at the same time that it increased automobile production. Local and express routes served the needs of commuters and often ran at full capacity, but from 1964 onward the jewels of the nation's rail system were its Shinkansen bullet trains. The super-high-speed lines were expensive to build and operate, and the loan that financed the first Shinkansen was not paid off until 1982, but they more than halved travel times between Japan's major cities and served 100 million passengers within their first three years of operation. Subsequent high-speed rail lines in Europe and Asia took inspiration from the Shinkansen's success and benefited from its technical innovations. *Heaven and Hell* debuted while the first Shinkansen was under construction, a little over a year before its maiden journey at the 1964 Tokyo Olympics, but the movie uses the speed of train travel to good effect in its tensest sequence. Following the kidnapper's instructions, Gondo takes an express train ride and tosses out the briefcases of money between stations. When the kidnapper releases the boy after receiving the money, the police begin their manhunt in earnest.[7]

Their first clue is an automobile. Evidence near the train tracks prove that the criminal drives a 1959 Toyopet from the car manufacturer Toyota. Toyopets were perennial best-sellers in Japan for several decades beginning in the mid–1950s, and car manufacturers contributed to the economic miracle in several ways. They were major employers, they satisfied a growing popular demand for high-end consumer goods, and they required machines, tools, and precision components that boosted many other technological industries. Slowly but surely Japanese cars also became crucial exports. In the late 1950s Toyota tried to sell Toyopets in the United States, but the cars were too low-horsepower to compete on the American market. It was a decade until a more powerful model, the Toyota Corona, finally became a common sight on American roads. In 1967 two Toyota cars, including a Toyopet, appeared in the Japan-themed James Bond movie *You Only Live Twice*—as good a sign as any that the brand had made it.[8]

In *Heaven and Hell*, the police's search for one Toyopet out of thousands is a reminder of how high Japan's average standard of living rose during the economic miracle. Trains provided cheaper, often faster commutes, and no country in the world produced more motorcycles than Japan, but as incomes rose and car production intensified, *maikā* ("my car," personal vehicles) became a must-have. Between 1960 and 1973 the number of cars in the country rose from 1.3 million to almost 25 million, and in 1970 over half of cars were personal-use rather than business-use vehicles. In the last four decades of the 20th century Japan was the world's second leading producer of vehicles after the United States.[9]

The police's next big break comes when they find the kidnapper's hideout and two people dead from heroin overdoses inside. The availability and use of illegal drugs is far lower in Japan than in the West, but some enters Japan despite strict policing at airports and seaports. In the mid–19th century, after seeing how opium and the so-called Opium Wars contributed to Western imperialism in China, the Japanese government announced that anyone caught with the drug in Japan would face the death penalty. However, during Japan's occupation of northern China

Japan's first Shinkansen bullet train debuted in 1964 (photograph by Roger Wollstadt).

during the 1930s and '40s, the Japanese military and its affiliated merchants sold opium to the Chinese in order to further subjugate them and make a tidy profit. Opium sales and an opium tax in Japan-occupied Manchuria accounted for much of the revenue generated there, and the paper money the Japanese created for the territory featured an image of a poppy, the plant from which opium derives. Drug use inside Japan peaked after the war when black markets sold illegal goods, *kasutori* culture celebrated debauchery (see Chapter 10), and people craved escape from widespread human misery. When the occupation ended, the Japanese government reimposed strict penalties for drug use and possession. The rate of drug use dropped in the 1960s and '70s, but the Japanese police remained vigilant for new drug-related behaviors like sniffing glue and abusing over-the-counter medicines. In accordance with a 1953 law, each prefectural and local police department maintains a narcotics division in order to keep illegal drugs from establishing a foothold. At the end of the 20th century the number of annual heroin-related arrests in Japan almost never exceeded double digits, whereas in the U.S., which had only twice Japan's population, they reached the upper hundreds of thousands. The numbers for other drugs showed similar discrepancies.[10]

The police's next clue—and, startlingly, the first use of color in a Kurosawa film—comes from a far more mundane activity than drug use: garbage disposal. The Gondo family and the detectives glance out Gondo's window and notice a plume of pink smoke rising from the black-and-white city below. A chemical the police put in the briefcases releases pink smoke when burned, so they know exactly when and where the kidnapper disposed of the evidence. At the time of the movie's release in

Toyota's Toyopet cars proliferated during the economic miracle. Several appear in this mid–1960s photograph, including the one second from left in the front row (Wikimedia Commons).

1963, Japan's rapid economic growth made trash management a pressing concern. More people and more goods meant more things to throw away, from packing material to old appliances to food waste. Japan enforced mandatory recycling laws near the end of the century, but even before that most trash did not go to landfills. Toward the end of the economic miracle Japan recycled 50 percent of its paper waste and almost all of its glass waste as opposed to American figures of 25 percent and 7 percent, respectively. What people could not recycle they burned. Processing centers that burned garbage often converted the heat into usable energy, and they disposed of the leftover ash more safely than American waste incinerators. Foreign visitors to Japan in the second half of the 20th century often remarked on the country's clean roadways and sidewalks, noticing that while Tokyo had a much larger population than New York City it did not have anything like New York's infamous rat-harboring trash piles.[11]

Following a lead from the trash facility, the police identify the kidnapper, but they do not arrest him right away. A conviction on kidnapping would lead to a long prison sentence, but the penalty Gondo and the police want is death. They must link the kidnapper to the heroin overdoses of his accomplices so that he will face drug dealing and manslaughter charges in addition to the kidnapping rap. Japan's commitment to the death penalty is markedly out of step with the rest of the first world; the United Kingdom abolished the death penalty in 1965, and the United

States placed a temporary moratorium on capital punishment in 1972. Dozens of inmates each year die in America's state execution chambers, but the federal government executed only three people between 1963 and 2020. By contrast, all executions in Japan take place at the national level, and all take place by hanging rather than the supposedly more humane lethal injection method that became standard in the United States in the 1970s. In a typical year Japan executes around half a dozen people. The process is highly secretive, so much so that the inmates themselves do not know in advance on what day they will die. Witnesses report that prerecorded Buddhist chants play during executions. Domestic and international human rights groups have repeatedly condemned Japan's approach to capital punishment to no avail. Kurosawa and his *Heaven and Hell* cowriters Kikushima Ryūzō (*Stray Dog*, *Scandal*), Oguni Hideo (*Ikiru*, *Record of Living Things*), and Hisaita Eijirō (*No Regrets for Our Youth*) usually used their movies to convey humanistic messages, but in *Heaven and Hell*, which they based in part on an American detective novel, they did not question the desirability of the death penalty as punishment.[12]

The police link the kidnapper to the deaths of his accomplices by tracing him to a nightclub where he purchases drugs. Like the nightclub in Kurosawa's occupation-era film *Drunken Angel* fifteen years earlier, this one pulses with loud Western music, and the Japanese men inside wear the Hawaiian shirts and dark sunglasses that suggest *yakuza* membership. The nightclub in *Drunken Angel* bore an English name but contained no foreign faces, since American censors did not allow Japanese movies to depict the occupiers. In *Heaven and Hell*, though, Kurosawa diversifies the club's clientele. Among the mass of people dancing and drinking are several foreigners, some of whom appear to be American soldiers. Black and white men in uniform flirt with Japanese women in tight skirts and beehive hair, raising the specter of miscegenation and mixed-race children, taboo topics in 1960s Japan.

During the American occupation over 5000 children were born to mixed-race unions, and in 1963 the oldest of these children were about to begin university. Most of them had a white American parent and a Japanese parent, but around 20 percent had a non-white American parent. In almost all cases the foreign parent was the father and the Japanese parent was the mother. Almost all of the children remained in Japan where the government granted them full citizenship rights and integrated them into public schools; in the United States many of the children would have been subject to segregation. Even after the occupation ended, the continued presence of American military bases in Japan and the increased ease of international travel meant that the number of mixed-race children steadily grew. A 1968 Japanese report put the number of half–Japanese, half–American children in the country between 20,000 and 25,000. As mixed-race children became adolescents and young adults, some found success in Japan's movie and music industries thanks to their exotic looks. There was a brief "mixed-blood children boom" (*konketsuji būmu*) in 1960s entertainment. Yet mixed-race children also faced discrimination in Japan, including unwelcome comments and generally "cold" treatment. Many Japanese people, including government officials, worried that these children and their future offspring posed a threat to Japan's supposedly homogeneous, harmonious culture. In the run-up to the 1964 Tokyo Olympics, some people worried that the looming influx of foreigners would lead to a new wave of miscegenation. *Heaven and Hell*'s use of diverse background actors in a sexually-charged setting that doubles as a haven for criminals is an unfortunate reflection of the suspicion with which some Japanese people viewed foreign fraternization.[13]

When the case against the kidnapper is as strong as possible, the police arrest him, and the court ultimately sentences him to death. Gondo visits him in prison where the kidnapper gloats at the news that Gondo has lost his position at the shoe company. The kidnapper's real purpose, he tells Gondo, was to make a wealthy man suffer. Gondo asks him if his own life was really that hard, and the expression on the kidnapper's face suggests that it was not after all. His small house in the shadow of Gondo's estate was hot in the summer and cool in the winter, he offers weakly, but that was true of most Japanese dwellings before, during, and after the economic miracle; due to the legacy of traditional Japanese architecture and widespread energy-consciousness, air conditioning has never been a high priority for Japanese homeowners. The kidnapper's attempt to explain his crimes in terms of economic inequality rings hollow in the context of overall prosperity, and he knows it.

Before the police drag him back to his cell, though, the kidnapper delivers a line that leaves Gondo frozen in contemplative silence. Going to hell is one thing, the condemned man says, but "if I had to go to heaven, then I'd really shake." The line is a reminder that the real conflict of the movie was not between the criminal and his victims, but between Gondo's ambition and his humanity. His great wealth only whet his appetite for more wealth, and he very nearly sacrificed a child to acquire it. The evils that *Heaven and Hell* decries are those associated with plenty, not with poverty: the soulless, corrupting world of business, the lure of recreational drugs, and the tendency to compare one's house and car with one's neighbors.' *Heaven and Hell* was a crime story for the boom years.

It was also Kurosawa's second-to-last black-and-white film and his second-to-last collaboration with the great Mifune. Their next and final movie, a *jidaigeki*, would mark the end of an era.

CHAPTER 23

Redbeard

In 1964 a state-of-the-art, 13,000-seat sports facility with a striking suspension roof opened in Yoyogi Park, Tokyo. Before and during the war, Yoyogi Park was a training ground for the Japanese army. Afterward it was the site of American military housing, an enclave of occupation forces in the midst of the busy Shibuya neighborhood. Now, less than two decades after Japan's surrender, the park was the site of a new stadium that symbolized progress, prosperity, and international cooperation. Designed by Japanese architect Tange Kenzō, the same man who created the Hiroshima Peace Memorial Park in memory of atomic bomb victims, the Yoyogi National Gymnasium hosted events during the Tokyo Olympics of 1964 and later served as a sports and concert venue. As the world looked to Japan for aesthetic inspiration and cutting-edge urban planning ideas, the stadium's futuristic design became a model for recreational facilities around the world. The Tokyo Olympics showcased a new Japan at the end of a decade of intense economic development.[1]

The 1964 Olympics marked the first time the games took place in Asia, and the event was a cultural touchstone for people who experienced it. Tokyo was supposed to host the 1940 Olympics, but due to World War II the International Olympic Committee moved and ultimately canceled those games. The committee did not allow Japan or Germany to compete in the first postwar games, the 1948 London Olympics. Tokyo's successful bid to host the 1964 games was therefore a redemptive moment, a symbol of atonement, closure, and new beginnings. The city that finished runner-up in the bidding was Detroit, hub of the American automobile industry, and Tokyo's triumph put a silver lining on Toyota's recent failure to crack the American car market (see Chapter 22). In the five years leading up to the games, construction of new venues, roadways, and rail lines went on nonstop. One Japanese observer said, "I felt the Japanese were fighting a war." The memory of World War II played a central role in the opening ceremony when 19-year-old university student Sakai Yoshinori, born in Hiroshima on the day of the bomb, carried the Olympic torch to the ceremonial cauldron. During the two weeks of games, Japanese athletes won more gold medals than any of the 94 participating nations except the United States and the Soviet Union, and the public displayed a "collective fervor" around the event as Japan proved itself capable of competing with the most powerful nations of the world. One of the country's leading filmmakers, Ichikawa Kon, captured the build-up and the games themselves in his documentary *Tokyo Olympiad* (*Tōkyō Orinpikku*, 1965), which frames the games as the culmination of Japan's post-occupation rebirth. The Olympics inspired more Japanese people to participate in sports, and over the next several decades the country hosted international events like the 1998 Winter Olympics in Nagano, the 2002 FIFA World Cup which Japan cohosted with South Korea, and the 2021 Tokyo Olympics that took place despite a global pandemic and its attendant safety concerns.[2]

In addition to showing off Japanese prosperity, the 1964 Olympics helped Japan brand itself as an international travel destination. The increase in Tokyo's tourist population made the city feel more cosmopolitan than ever. The long-running pictorial magazine *Asahi Graph* showed how during the Olympics "Tokyoites saw men and women from all the continents in the world at shopping centres, entertainment places and parks." Numerous Japanese periodicals and new English conversation schools for adults dispensed advice about how to interact with foreign visitors, including how to pursue romantic relationships. Tourists, meanwhile, "experienced firsthand the heart and energy of the Japanese people." TV coverage in the United States and Europe highlighted the games and the host country's unique cultural attractions. The tourism boom lasted beyond the games, and in 1966 the government began work on a new airport at Narita to handle the traffic. Landowners and anti-government groups fought it fiercely, but the airport opened in 1978.[3]

Progress and forging new relationships were themes of the 1964 Tokyo Olympics and of Kurosawa's 1965 film *Redbeard* (*Akahige*, usually written *Red Beard* in English). The movie takes place at a medical clinic in Edo before that city took the name Tokyo during the Meiji *jidai*. The clinic's doctor (Mifune Toshirō), known colloquially as Redbeard because of the ruddy and vaguely foreign color of his bushy facial hair, is a taciturn man who agrees to host an ambitious young doctor-in-training. Redbeard's clinic is also home to a number of long-term patients who suffer from a variety of physical and mental health problems. The evolution of Japanese politics and society provides context for the stories that play out in the clinic.

Doctor-in-training Yasumoto Noboru (Kayama Yūzō) arrives at Redbeard's clinic from the city of Nagasaki. For centuries before the Meiji *jidai*, Nagasaki was the only port in Japan where foreign trade and foreign books could enter the country. As a result the city became a haven of "Dutch learning," a catch-all phrase for European knowledge, most of which came to Nagasaki on Dutch ships. Technological and medical knowledge were useful, but the *shōgun*'s government did not welcome all Western concepts; Nagasaki became home to Japan's largest concentration of Christian converts, and they practiced their faith in secret because of strict and sometimes violent government oppression. Christianity became legal in 1873 and Nagasaki's Christian population went above ground, but the city's long association with the Western faith and Westernization in general did not prevent the United States from dropping an atomic bomb there on August 9, 1945. The blast destroyed the Urakami Cathedral, the largest Christian house of worship in all of

Atomic bomb survivor Sakai Yoshinori lights the cauldron to open the 1964 Summer Olympics in Tokyo (Wikimedia Commons).

Asia. *Redbeard* takes place a century before that event, but movie audiences associated Nagasaki with foreign influence both beneficial and disruptive. In the movie, the young doctor from Nagasaki hopes to use his exclusive knowledge to become the *shōgun*'s private doctor.

Yasumoto is struck by the lack of creature comforts in Redbeard's clinic. "Even poor people have *tatami*," a sick man complains, but Redbeard believes that the straw floor mats contribute to the spread of disease, so the clinic's floors are bare. The patients and doctors alike wear simple, neutral, unisex robes, and some of them long for clothes that are more dignified and colorful, but Redbeard is a strict man who values austerity. In Kurosawa's early postwar movies like *One Wonderful*

Sunday and *Drunken Angel*, poverty was the cause of characters' immiseration. In the middle of the comfortable 1960s, *Redbeard* presents different explanations for its characters' struggles. The doctors and even some patients are well-connected, and the clinic receives government funds, but in order to maintain a sterile environment Redbeard requires his patients and staff to live abstemiously. The cocky Yasumoto flaunts this rule by wearing his own clothes during his first several weeks at the clinic.

Yasumoto does not know, of course, that the government he wants to work for will soon fall, and that the new Meiji government will open the doors of Western learning to all. *Redbeard* came out nearly 100 years after the start of the Meiji *jidai*, and the anniversary celebrations were the biggest public event since the Olympics. The celebration of the Meiji centennial began in January 1968 and lasted all year. The media and the government of Prime Minister Satō Eisaku used the event to celebrate Japanese nationhood, and public expressions of patriotism during the Olympics and the centennial were the most open displays of Japanese nationalism since World War II. The Meiji emperor's birthday, November 3, was a public holiday that capped the celebrations, though it has gone by the name of "Culture Day" (*bunka no hi*) since 1948 when the American occupiers forbade emperor worship.[4]

As Yasumoto adapts to his new environment, the clinic's patients allow Kurosawa to take on new problems as well. In 1949's *Stray Dog*, the detective characters wondered about the connection between poverty and crime (see Chapter 9); in *Redbeard*, which came out amid historically low rates of crime and poverty, the doctors instead ponder the relationship between nature and nurture. A sequestered patient nicknamed "The Mantis" (Kagawa Kyōko) is famous among the clinic staff for "seducing" men and then stabbing them to death. She tells Yasumoto her story: as a child, she was raped by a man who said he would kill her if she told anyone. She then kisses and stabs Yasumoto, who barely escapes with his life. She implies that her experience drives her to murder, but Redbeard says she was born that way. Many people become ill due to misfortune, he says, but other girls experience what The Mantis did without becoming killers. Yasumoto remains silent. His "Dutch learning" gives him an edge in treating the body, but treating the mind is a trickier problem.

Unlike the 1940s when bacterial and viral diseases ran rampant in war-ravaged Japan (see Chapter 7), the most insidious health problems during the economic boom were psychological. From the 1960s on a host of mental illnesses received new attention, and new words to describe them entered common parlance. The term "masked depression" emerged as Japanese doctors sought to explain a rise in psychosomatic illnesses. Anxiety among children rose, too; in the 1970s people began to speak of "school refusal" to describe a phenomenon in which children experienced such severe stress that they could not attend school. By the end of the century there were perhaps a million people, mostly in their teens and twenties, who were total social recluses known as *hikikomori*. Pundits and scholars suggested that Japanese

The Meiji Centennial Observation Tower on Tokyo Bay was one of many ambitious, modernist construction projects of the miracle years (photograph by Yamamoto Yukiko, Wikimedia Commons).

culture, with its pressure on individuals to conform to the group, was partly to blame, but that did not explain why psychological problems seemed to worsen during and after the economic miracle. Neither nature nor nurture alone seemed to explain mental illness, but rather some combination of the two.[5]

A common thread in *Redbeard*'s patients' stories is fractured relationships. One old man passes away shortly before his grown daughter comes to see him for the first time in years; his wife had alienated the two by forcing the daughter to marry her father's enemy. In another storyline, a landslide in a neighborhood near the clinic unearths a human skeleton, and a patient on his deathbed confesses that it was his wife. She killed herself out of shame, he explains, when he discovered that she was secretly married to another man. Most dramatically there is The Mantis, whose short-lived relationships are defined by violence. Even Yasumoto has a troubled romantic history—he had a fiancée while he was a student in Nagasaki, but she left him for someone else. The scandal caused her own father to disown her.

Redbeard's preoccupation with troubled couples and families spoke to real anxieties about the state of marriage in Japan. The institution of marriage reached a tipping point just as the movie came out. Between 1965 and 1970, for the first time in Japan's recorded history the number of "love marriages" surpassed the number of arranged marriages, and by the end of the century the former would almost entirely replace the latter. Young people were choosing their own spouses with or without parental approval and without the assistance of marriage brokers. Of course, choosing one's own partner did not guarantee a successful marriage. Japan's divorce rate remained comparatively low until the 1990s, but several categories of marriage problems received national attention during the economic boom. "Retired-husband syndrome" or "husband-at-home stress" described psychosomatic illnesses that wives developed as a result of being in close proximity to their husbands, from whom they had grown distant during the years when the husbands worked outside the home. Husbands who felt uncomfortable in the company of their families developed "refuse-to-go-home syndrome" and spent even longer stretches of their days and nights in the office or at the bar with friends. "In-house divorce," whereby husbands and wives remained legally married but lived separate lives and rarely saw or spoke to each other, became increasingly common. Even relatively happy Japanese couples had sex infrequently compared to their counterparts in other countries, and Japan's fertility rate continued its infamous long-term decline. The use of the word "syndrome" (shōkōgun) to describe these psychological and sexual phenomena implied that doctors could or should be able to fix them, but like Redbeard and Yasumoto, the doctors of the late 20th century did not have all the answers.[6]

The *Redbeard* character with the most challenging symptoms is Otoyo (Niki Terumi), a 12-year-old girl who works in a brothel. Redbeard and Yasumoto visit the brothel to treat a syphilis case and notice the girl obsessively scrubbing the floor. The madam, the closest thing Otoyo has to a mother, routinely beats the girl. Otoyo is virtually mute, and she focuses intently on her repetitive chore to avoid human interaction. She does not yet "entertain" clients, but the atmosphere of the brothel is clearly not healthy for her. Redbeard forcibly removes Otoyo from the establishment and tasks Yasumoto with curing the girl's near-catatonic mental state. When Yasumoto falls ill after caring for her around the clock, Otoyo comes out of her shell to care for him. They become a kind of constructed family, finding in each other a connection that they lack.

At the same time that he takes on the role of father to Otoyo, Yasumoto apologizes to Redbeard for the haughty attitude he adopted when he first arrived at the clinic. The two doctors also create a relationship similar to that between a parent and a child. After stubbornly wearing his personal clothes for weeks, Yasumoto finally dons the plain robes of a clinic doctor, signifying to everyone that he has joined Redbeard's *de facto* family. He acknowledges Redbeard as a patriarch who inspires loyalty in the resident staff and patients. The film shows that even when "normal" family structures fall apart, new configurations can fill the void.

Yasumoto decides to marry his ex-fiancée's sister, who often visits him at the clinic, and several father figures play a role in their wedding. There is Redbeard, who instructs Yasumoto in wedding etiquette and chides the young doctor for making his bride wait while he dons his ceremonial robes. There is the bride's father, a prestigious physician who finally secures Yasumoto his long-coveted position as the *shōgun*'s personal doctor. Then there is Yasumoto's biological father, of whom Yasumoto grumbles, "He's always making plans for me without asking, but I have my own ideas." Yasumoto has a surfeit of paternal influences, but like many young people in postwar movie audiences he asserts his independence when it comes to love and career. Yasumoto announces during his wedding that he intends to stay at the clinic rather than work for the *shōgun*. The clinic offers little prestige and only a modest salary, but it is his calling, and in front of their relatives and patrons he asks his bride if she will accept him under these conditions. Both bride and groom assent to the match and the path that lies before them.

Yasumoto's optimism and independence make him an avatar of the Japanese spirit during the era of high-speed growth. The economic miracle that began in the 1950s and peaked in the 1960s helped transform Japanese society beyond what the American occupation achieved between 1945 and 1952. During the boom, class distinctions flattened as incomes rose, and people challenged traditional norms in areas such as marriage. Japanese industries moved toward global competitiveness, and Japan redefined itself as a peaceful, independent player in international affairs. It also became an attractive destination for international travelers and events like the Olympics. Yet the nation also experienced new problems like mental health crises, and its people continued to wrestle with old ones like the controversial relationship between Japan and the United States. The ten movies Kurosawa directed between the end of the occupation and the start of the 1970s reflected both the good and the bad of the miracle years. *Redbeard*, with its balance of pain and sweetness and its focus on endings and new beginnings, was a fitting final entry in this period.

Kurosawa waited five years to release his next film, by far the longest break in his career to date. When *Dodesukaden* finally came out in 1970, both the director and Japan were on the cusp of a new era.

PART FOUR

The Global Years

CHAPTER 24

Dodesukaden

Of all Japan's exports and contributions to international society, the most valuable have been the intangibles: art and idealized images of Japanese culture. A global fascination with Japan and its aesthetics grew apace with the Japanese economy, but it continued to grow even when the economic miracle ended. Kurosawa's last seven films, released between 1970 and 1993, exist in part because of the global fascination with all things Japan to which they also contributed.

In 1968 the Nobel Prize for Literature went to its first-ever East Asian recipient, Japan's Kawabata Yasunari. The Nobel committee said that Kawabata's novels like *Snow Country* (published in stages between 1935 and 1948), *Thousand Cranes* (1952), and *The Old Capital* (1962) expressed "the essence of the Japanese mind." Kawabata embraced that praise in an address he delivered upon accepting the prize, and his remarks attracted a lot of attention in Japan. Kawabata's address, titled "Japan, the Beautiful and Myself," described the Japanese spirit in romantic terms. Japanese people, he argued, were sensitive to nature, deeply moved by simple beauty, and found transcendence in the sensation of loneliness. His examples were the refined displays of Japanese culture that flourished in the middle ages: the tea ceremony, flower arranging, *bonsai* tree cultivation, gardening, Zen meditation, short-form poetry, and calligraphy. Westerners found these Japanese arts fascinating, and many fell in love with the version of Japan that Kawabata described as "mysterious," "suggestive," and "evocative." Kawabata's flattering portrait of Japan was well-received in his home country, where the media and readers and non-readers alike celebrated his Nobel in a spirit of "national jubilation."[1]

In stark contrast, Kurosawa's 1970 movie *Dodesukaden* (usually rendered *Dodes'ka-den* in English) could hardly have presented an uglier picture of Japan. During the 5 years since *Redbeard*, Kurosawa had an international film project fall through when the Japan-Hollywood war production *Tora! Tora! Tora!* replaced him as co-director shortly into the shoot. The Japanese press attributed it to disharmony between Kurosawa and the American producers. In the long interval between films, Kurosawa also fell out with his longtime star Mifune. Kurosawa's productions were growing longer, often lasting more than a year, and Mifune reportedly became frustrated at having to decline other lucrative jobs in film and television. After *Redbeard*, their 16th movie in 17 years, the two never worked together again. Kurosawa struggled to raise money for his next project, so he and his fellow directors Kinoshita Keisuke, Kobayashi Masaki, and Ichikawa Kon formed a new company, Yonki no Kai ("The Club of Four Knights" or "The Four Horsemen Club"), through which they secured funding for Kurosawa's first all-color motion picture. Rather than use color to highlight Japan's beauty, modernity, and charm, though, as Ichikawa did in 1965's *Tokyo Olympiad* and Kinoshita did in 1967's *Eyes, the Sea and a Ball* (*Natsu-kashiki fue ya taiko*, "My Dear Flute and Drum"), *Dodesukaden* uses sickly hues to depict the lives of people who live in a toxic slum. The source material for the movie was a 1962 Yamamoto Shūgorō novel, *The Town Without Seasons* (*Kisetsu no nai machi*). Yamamoto's title explicitly rejected one of the most important foundations of Japanese art—the colorful representations of spring, summer, fall, and winter that Nobel laureate Kawabata cited in the first line of his famous speech.[2]

In terms of challenging convention, *Dodesukaden* has much in common with the Japanese New Wave, a trend in filmmaking that peaked in the 1960s and early '70s as niche production companies emerged to give young storytellers opportunities outside of the conservative studio system. New Wave movies rebelled against norms in content and form, like Ōshima Nagisa's *Sing a Song of Sex* (*Nihon shunk-akō*, "A Treatise on Japanese Bawdy Songs," 1967), which revels in taboo sexual and political topics, and Shinoda Masahiro's *Double Suicide* (*Shinjū: Ten no Amijima*, "The Love Suicides of Amijima," 1969), which applies puppet theater techniques to live actors. Kurosawa belonged to an older generation than the prominent New Wave directors, but with *Dodesukaden* he expanded his visual style by filming in full color, and he focused intently on the emotional lives of people on the margins of society, a common concern of Japanese New Wave movies.

Dodesukaden opens with a young man (Zushi Yoshitaka) looking wistfully at a train from the window of his shack while his mother maintains a ceaseless chant in front of their family altar. The windows of the shack are papered over with childish drawings of trains that shine brightly as morning light pours in. The young man, boyish but not a child, joins his mother in her fervid prayers and then heads off to his "job" driving an imaginary train through the shanty town. As he stomps along non-existent tracks, fiddling with controls that only he can see, he recites an invented onomatopoeia for the sound of wheels on rails: *dodesukaden, dodesukaden*. His behavior suggests autism, but in 1970 autism diagnosis, treatment, and awareness were at early stages of development. Contemporary moviegoers might have understood the young man as a particularly extreme kind of *densha otaku*, or "train geek." Japan has many thousands of *densha otaku* who obsessively memorize engine statistics, rail routes, and train color schemes, collect train figurines, and travel to see rare trains like an all-yellow Shinkansen nicknamed "Dr. Yellow." Like geeks anywhere, *densha otaku* and other kinds of *otaku* with their own areas of obsession are subject to teasing, and the young man in *Dodesukaden* receives cruel taunts of "*densha baka*" (train fool) from a group of young children.[3]

The theoretical train runs near a cluster of shacks housing a motley assortment of impoverished neighbors, including a group of women who do their dishes at a communal water tap. Despite the ubiquity of indoor plumbing and potable urban water systems, Japan still boasts many community wells, some active since before the Meiji *jidai*. At the famous Genchi Well in Nagano prefecture people still gather nightly to draw water for household consumption, mostly by choice rather than need. It is also not unusual that the women of *Dodesukaden* do not have automatic dishwashers. Even after washing machines, refrigerators, TVs, and cars became commonplace in Japanese homes during the 1950s and '60s, dishwashers remained rare, and at the turn of the 21st century barely a quarter of households had them. Countertop dishwashers, dryers, and sanitizers are available in stores for less than a hundred dollars, but many Japanese kitchens simply lack space for such appliances, and given the country's high cost of electricity most people prefer energy-efficient alternatives. The need to minimize expenses is a major motivator for the house-wives of *Dodesukaden*, who experience a level of poverty that is very unusual for the period in which they live.[4]

One of the local women, Mrs. Shima (Tange Kiyoko), takes her parsimony to anti-social extremes. She rudely barters with the neighborhood vegetable vendor, whose prices are already low. Farmers markets and food stalls are popular alternatives to grocery stores in Japan, both for their competitive prices and because of strong consumer support for locally-grown goods. In fact, even when locally-produced food is costlier than imported food, Japanese shoppers have a marked preference for buying local when they can. In rural areas vendors often leave road-side food stands and money boxes unmanned due to shoppers' general trustworthiness. This approach might not work for the poor grocer in *Dodesukaden*, though, whose stall Mrs. Shima practically robs in broad daylight.[5]

Turning Kawabata's picture of "Japan, the Beautiful" on its head, *Dodesukaden* repeatedly satirizes Japanese institutions and cultural points of pride. The movie's non-existent train seems to mock the advent of high-speed rail, and it raises the question of whether Japan's technological achievements are meaningful signs of social and economic progress or merely give the illusion of progress. The vegetable stand where rural producers and urban consumers are supposed to forge a mutually-supportive relationship is instead the site of strife and resentment. As the movie progresses, it becomes clear that every home and family contains at least one disturbing abnormality. Inside one of the shantytown's houses, a mute young woman named Katsuko (Yamazaki Tomoko) robotically prepares artificial flowers for sale while her uncle (Matsumura Tatsuo) berates her for being unattractive and unproductive. The scene pointedly contains none of the "feminine elegance" or "delicate sensibilities" that Kawabata spoke of when describing the Japanese art of flower arrangement.

Exacting attention to detail is an element of Japanese art that often draws praise and wonder, but in *Dodesukaden* it is a darkly humorous liability. A hairbrush maker (Minami Shinsuke) pedantically counts the number of bristles in each of his brushes, explaining to his wife (Kusunoki Yuko) that he does it for the sake of the

Baby stroller and street market, c. 1970s (Wikimedia Commons).

craft rather than for customers who may not notice or care. While he counts hairs, his pregnant wife sleeps with most of the men in town. The young children he raises even begin to suspect that he is not their biological father.

The most poignant satirical content in *Dodesukaden* involves architecture. In a broken-down jalopy on the outskirts of town, a daydreaming father (Tonomura Toshiyuki) and his young son (Minami Shinsuke) plan a house they will never build. The father tells his somewhat skeptical child that Japanese people are weak because they live in fragile wooden houses in gentle, sheltered valleys. People abroad, he says, live in concrete structures on rocky ground, and this makes them more resilient. Therefore, the father reasons, he must build a concrete house on a hill in order to give his son a better life. The man's glassy-eyed, far-seeing stare and unkempt appearance make it plain that he is mad. *Dodesukaden*'s audience all remembered the 1966 debut of Japan's latest architectural marvel, the concrete-and-steel Olympic stadium built on former American military land at Yoyogi Park, and many of them lived in concrete apartments that rose in long, gray lines from the ruins of postwar cities. The change in architecture had not changed the national character that Kawabata and many others still called "beautiful."

If there is beauty in *Dodesukaden*'s Japan, only the insane, the desperate, and the intoxicated can see it. Instead of run-down houses and junk heaps, the young *densha otaku* sees a glorious sunset in crayon colors, a rainbow in the mist, and bright stars above. At night the town's lovers search for romance, but their only options are with people as dilapidated as the town. The housewives whisper about a gaunt, hollow-eyed man (Akutagawa Hiroshi) who was once handsome. His name, Hei, is a homonym for soldier, so perhaps he served in the war. Now Hei's hollow voice, pale color, and shuffling gait remind them of death, but with little better to do one woman tries to seduce him anyway. Meanwhile, two husbands swap wives after drinking so much alcohol that they can hardly tell which is which. Kawabata's "warm, deep, delicate compassion ... [and] deep quiet of the Japanese spirit" exists only for drunks, dreamers, and fools in *Dodesukaden*. The movie views the country through the lens of mental illness, lecherousness, alcoholism, and the lingering echoes of wartime collapse.

There were, in fact, dark undercurrents in Japan in 1970. Even though incomes had more than doubled in the last ten years, tensions lurked below the surface and sometimes broke through in frightening ways. The economy entered a recession in the middle of the year that would last until the end of 1971, the longest downturn since the 1940s. Near the end of the year, author Mishima Yukio, who was in the running for the Nobel Prize that Kawabata ultimately won, attempted to take over a Self Defense Forces base in Tokyo as the first part of a planned coup. He committed ritual suicide in the base commander's office after delivering a nationalistic, emperor-worshipping speech to the soldiers that failed to win him any followers. Less than a month later, a riot outside an American military base in Okinawa turned violent. Unlike the security treaty protests ten years earlier (see Chapter 19), none of the estimated 5000 Japanese citizens or hundreds of American soldiers involved in the riot died, but there were many injuries and arrests and a great deal of property damage. As the nation's unprecedented run of prosperity slowed, old anxieties and debates came to the fore.

The Japanese phrase *mottainai* loosely translates to "it would be a waste," and in the last quarter of the 20th century the expression referred to everything from food waste to the improper disposal of trash and recycling. Japanese restaurants and grocery stores threw out relatively little food in the 1960s, but beginning in the mid–70s the amount of food available in Japan rose faster than consumption. Much uneaten food went into garbage incinerators rather than becoming compost or livestock feed. At the turn of the 21st century, the Japanese government passed the Food Waste Recycling Law in an effort put more leftover food to good use, and neighborhood organizations, restaurants, and food banks created no-waste campaigns and "salvage parties" to encourage appropriate serving sizes and creative food reuse. In *Dodesukaden* Kurosawa stresses the immorality of letting food go to waste in a time of plenty by following the young boy with the mad father as he scrounges for food. The boy takes what he can carry from a restaurant that throws out deep bowls of ramen noodles and huge plates of *tonkatsu* pork while the uncharitable restaurant owner hurls threats at him.[6]

Dodesukaden's use of very young characters alongside older ones helps Kurosawa shift his focus to a new generation. One simple scene distills the despair that the director explored in the first three quarters of his career, then lays them to rest.

Two old men sit in an unadorned living room while one of them (12-time Kurosawa actor Fujiwara Kamatari) rattles off a list of woes. His wife, sons, and house all perished in the war, mistresses came and went, and jobs felt futile. After living with this pain for so long, suicide seems like the best way out for the old man. In response, the other man produces a deadly poison from his storage room, which the depressed man quickly consumes. Moments later, the suicidal man realizes that if he dies the memory of his family will die with him, and he begs for an antidote to the poison. His friend admits that the "poison" was only a digestive aid. The depressed man is relieved to remain among the living, but during this short scene something did indeed die; his suffering, and by extension the suffering of the wartime generation, now belongs to the past. Meanwhile the movie's younger generation, exemplified by the boy with the lunatic father and the girl who ties flowers day and night for her taskmaster uncle, must endure or escape their elders in order to live full lives in the present.

One problem that is specific to young people is child sexual abuse. In *Dodesukaden*, Katsuko, the flower-making girl, is raped by her uncle. There were few systematic studies of child sexual abuse in Japan before the year 2000 when the government enacted the Child Abuse Prevention Act, but it was always a substantial problem. Since the early 20th century the Japanese rail system has offered optional, separate train cars for women and children commuting to work and school in order to reduce the likelihood of sexual assault by *chikan*, "perverts" who invade the privacy of young girls and women on public transit. A great deal of sexual abuse, though, takes place in the home, and research suggests that Japan's efforts to combat it

In 1970, novelist Mishima Yukio's ultranationalist coup attempt ended in his suicide (Wikimedia Commons).

are still inadequate. Japanese media frequently sexualizes young women and girls, and the age of consent in Japan is only 13, comparable to several Asian nations but lower than the West's average. With little legal recourse against her uncle, *Dodesukaden*'s Katsuko must take her safety into her own hands.[7]

The young boy, by contrast, lacks the ability to protect himself from his well-meaning but foolish father. Against an ironically-beautiful impressionistic backdrop of a sunset, the movie's darkest plotline sees the child waste away from preventable disease and malnutrition, something that happened to too many children a quarter of a century earlier during war and occupation, while his father continues to fantasize about foreign architecture and modern luxuries that he cannot acquire. *Dodesukaden* ends with tragedy for the boy, marginal improvement for Katsuko, and an unchanged status quo for most. The film's message is that the much-celebrated beauty and modernity of contemporary Japan are at best surface-deep, and at worst they are distractions from persistent social problems.

This was not a message that people wanted to hear. Some foreign critics appreciated *Dodesukaden*, but its bleak perspective did not resonate with Japanese audiences or critics who preferred more escapist stories like the *jidaigeki* Mifune continued to make without Kurosawa. In addition, worldly Japanese audiences of the Olympics generation increasingly bought tickets to Hollywood or European films rather than those made in Japan. Imported films earned more money in 1970 than in any previous year on record, and by the end of the decade Japanese movies would account for barely 50 percent of Japanese box office revenue—a trend that had dire implications for domestic film budgets. Troubled by the failure of his first movie in five years, and suffering from failing eyesight, chronic pain, and other demons, Kurosawa attempted suicide in 1971. He recovered, but the production company that he and his colleagues formed to make *Dodesukaden* soon broke apart. The future of Kurosawa's career was in doubt. Then, at a key moment in the Cold War, the director traveled to the Soviet Union to tell a story he had fallen in love with as a young man.[8]

CHAPTER 25

Dersu Uzala

During the first months of the American occupation of Japan the number of U.S. troops in the country reached around 430,000. If there had been no more wars in Asia, most of them might have gone home when the occupation ended in 1952. Yet by 1953, the last year of fighting in Korea, there were still over a quarter of a million American soldiers in Japan. The renewal of the controversial U.S.-Japan security treaty in 1960 ensured that the substantial American presence would continue indefinitely (see Chapter 19). By the late 1960s the United States was deep into another war in Asia, this time in Vietnam, and once again Japan served as a base of operations. The number of American military personnel in the country climbed higher, and at their bases they stockpiled nuclear weapons—possibly over a thousand nukes in Okinawa alone—plus biochemical weapons like "Agent Orange" that endangered people who came in contact with them, including tens of thousands of Japanese base workers. The year of 1975 marked the 30th anniversary of Japan's last war, but war remained a daily reality for the country.

The Korean War had kick-started Japan's economy, but the effects of the Vietnam War were less propitious. U.S. president Lyndon Johnson pressured his Japanese counterpart, Prime Minister Satō Eisaku, to increase financial aid to Southeast Asia, fund the construction of hospitals in the region, send televisions and other consumer goods to South Vietnam, and buy half a billion dollars' worth of U.S. government bonds to support the war effort. In response, many Asian countries criticized Japan as a facilitator of American imperialism. On top of that, the Vietnam War years saw the beginning of the end of Japan's economic miracle. Inflation set in as government spending increased, and people began to complain about "crazy prices" that had not been seen since the early 1950s.[1]

The Japanese public took a dim view of American actions in Vietnam. In a 1965 poll nearly half of Japanese citizens named the United States their favorite foreign country—an impressive number considering the fierce opposition to the renewal of the Japan-U.S. security treaty just five years earlier. When pollsters asked the question again in 1973 after years of diligent coverage of the Vietnam War in the Japanese press, only 18 percent of respondents preferred the United States to all other foreign countries. Neutral Switzerland was the most popular response. Japanese people were, on the whole, decidedly anti-war, and many protested their country's involvement in Vietnam. For "the first time in the history of our country," wrote historian Inoue Kiyoshi at the time, "the overwhelming majority of people have opposed a war the government supports."[2]

Japan had little power to influence American foreign policy, a fact that came home in dramatic fashion courtesy of "the Nixon shocks." In 1971 American president Richard Nixon opened diplomatic relations with communist China, ending over twenty years of official silence between the Cold War rivals. Nobody in Nixon's administration bothered to inform Japan of this sudden reversal of U.S. policy. China's leaders claimed that they would not normalize relations with "imperialist" Japan, and at the same time Nixon announced new tariffs on Japanese imports into the United States. Nixon's decision to take the U.S. dollar off the gold standard threw the future of the yen into doubt, since Japan's currency had been pinned to

America's since the end of World War II. Japan's leaders lost face due to their lack of preparedness for these situations, and Japanese journalists warned that the special relationship between Japan and the U.S. was in danger of collapse.[3]

On the bright side, by 1975 it seemed that the Cold War might soon reach a peaceful end. The United States withdrew from Vietnam without defeating the communists there, and the American and Soviet governments forged new agreements on trade, weapons development, and space exploration. American troops still guarded the border between North and South Korea, but the number of soldiers there fell as tension between the superpowers relaxed. People in Japan breathed a bit easier,

Prime Minister Satō Eisaku and President Richard Nixon in 1972. Satō's tenure saw frequent scandals and worsening relations with the United States (photograph by Bob Moore).

the anti-war protests faded away, and the United States slowly regained its popularity in Japan as the threat of regional and global war felt less imminent. Yet Russia, a nemesis of Japan since the war of 1904–5, continued to present challenges. Its troops still occupied islands at the northern end of the Japanese archipelago that it seized in 1945. Soviet ships in the Sea of Japan grew so numerous that the head of Japan's Self Defense Forces archly suggested renaming it the Sea of Russia. The rival nations fought an unproductive war of words over fishing and territorial rights that lasted throughout the Cold War thaw, but at least they were talking.[4]

In the midst of this cautious détente, Kurosawa went to Siberia. Neither Japanese nor American studios were eager to work with the director after his abortive stint on *Tora! Tora! Tora!*, the commercial failure of *Dodesukaden*, and his recent suicide attempt (see Chapter 24), but the heads of the Soviet movie studio Mosfilm knew that Kurosawa could still reach a global audience. They offered him the chance to direct a project of his choosing. The studio wanted Mifune to star in the movie, but Kurosawa and Mifune's long association had ended a decade earlier and would not be renewed.

A lifelong admirer of Russian writers, Kurosawa first read Vladimir Arsenyev's 1923 memoir *Dersu Uzala* in the late 1930s or early '40s. The book tells the story of Arsenyev's surveying missions to the Russian Far East between 1902 and 1907 and how a woodsman named Dersu Uzala, a member of the Nanai ethnic group, taught Arsenyev and his men how to survive in the vast taiga. Arsenyev served in the Russian military under Czar Nicholas II and did not support the Russian communists when they came to power, but his true-life adventure books made him a popular figure in the Soviet Union long after his death in 1930. His image appeared on a Soviet stamp even after the U.S.S.R. executed his widow and sent his daughter to a gulag for allegedly carrying on Arsenyev's anti-communist work. The book *Dersu Uzala* had already received a major Russian film adaptation, but in the mid–70s the easing of Cold War tensions and the availability of Asia's most acclaimed director allowed for a grander and more international version of the classic travelogue.

The Soviet Union allowed Kurosawa to film in parts of the country that were usually off-limits to foreigners, specifically the regions of Primorsky and Khabarovsk at the easternmost edge of the Siberian biome, very near where the real Dersu had lived. Kurosawa arrived in the port of Vladivostok where "it was a rare sight to see a foreigner … let alone someone of his stature," according to a Soviet scholar who saw him there during filming. Despite the respect that Kurosawa commanded, the Soviet police closely watched the Japanese film crew during their year-long stay in the U.S.S.R., and Mosfilm tried without much success to keep Kurosawa within a tight budget.[5]

Actor Maxim Munzuk, born near the border of Mongolia and Russia, played Dersu, and Yury Solomin, born even further east along the same border, played Arsenyev. Their disparate appearances were crucial to the story Kurosawa wanted to tell; Munzuk's Asian features convey Dersu's deep roots in the Far East, while

Solomin's European look marks Arsenyev as an outsider to the region. The story's 1902–1907 timeframe spans the Russo-Japanese War, an event in which the Asian nation proved its technical superiority over the European one in a decisive clash of modern navies. In similar fashion the Far Easterner Dersu proves that he is more adept than the St. Petersburg man Arsenyev at navigating the taiga.

The men's ancestral differences remind movie audiences of the racial dimensions of exploration and imperialism. The Russian Far East was trackless and unmapped from the perspective of Moscow and St. Petersburg, but natives of the region knew it well. Japan's 20th-century experience helped Kurosawa and Japanese viewers identify with both the Russian and the Nanai perspectives. As an empire Japan used the tools and language of modernity to subjugate its neighbors, and its leaders claimed superiority over other Asian cultures. Yet in 1975 Japan was also a formerly-occupied nation, and as largely-powerless observers of the Cold War its people increasingly identified with the non-aligned and formerly-colonized nations of Asia.

Dersu Uzala begins with the observation that 20th-century progress often meant the loss of hallowed landscapes and landmarks of the past. In the opening scene, which takes place after the other events of the movie, an older Arsenyev visits the area where he buried his friend Dersu. To his dismay he cannot find the gravesite. The trees that once marked it are gone, cleared to make way for new roads and buildings. In Japan, which has far less land to develop than Russia, graves also sometimes make way for urbanization. Buddhist temples and municipal cemeteries free space through the practice of *hakajimai*, or "closing graves." This involves removing old headstones and the urns beneath them, sometimes putting them in new locations and sometimes disposing of them in legal or illegal ways. Until the late 1990s it was illegal to scatter ashes in the sea or other public places in Japan, but a growing need for space and a rise in "abandoned" graves that family members failed to maintain led to a loosening of restrictions. Some dismantled graves and cremated remains are converted into building materials, thus furthering the urbanization that prompted their removal.[6]

In 1975, for the first time, over three-quarters of Japan's population lived in urban rather than rural areas, and within the next 40 years the proportion of Japanese people living in cities would top 90 percent. This was a significant increase from the early postwar years when the urban share of the population was well under 50 percent. The large-scale exodus of people from their ancestral villages meant more abandoned graves. Despite the annual observance of Obon, a late summer holiday in which Japanese people visit family graves, people in the late Shōwa *jidai* found it increasingly inconvenient to visit and maintain old tombs.[7]

People's severance from the places of their past could increase their longing for the rhythms of pastoral life. Japanese consumers supported locally-grown foods, took weekend trips to scenic mountains and lakes, and participated in tree-planting and other wilderness stewardship activities with a growing number of forestry associations. The number of people applying for and receiving hunting licenses in Japan peaked in the 1970s, and the practice of "forest bathing" (*shinrin yoku*), a meditative approach to walking in the woods, gained adherents in the 1980s and beyond. The desire to reconnect with nature was an important motivator for Kurosawa during the year he spent in Siberia filming *Dersu Uzala*. The director summarized the film's message by saying, "If nature is destroyed, human beings will be destroyed too. So we can learn a lot from Dersu." The movie's depictions of low-tech hunting and tracking are heavily romanticized, but they are also evocative and inspirational.[8]

It is significant that when the film flashes back to Dersu and Arsenyev's first meeting, the frontiersman's first lesson to the greenhorn is how to make the wilderness more welcoming for others. At Dersu's urging the Russian survey team leaves some of their own food, wood, and fuel in an abandoned shelter; one never knows who might need it, and they themselves might benefit from the same kind of help one day. Dersu does not jealously guard his forest from outsiders, but freely shares his backwoods wisdom. In a much broader sense, the film's depiction of free exchange of goods and knowledge in a place where different ethnicities comingle speaks to the relaxed international environment that made the film possible.

Few Japanese moviegoers in 1975 had experience with wilderness survival, but they eagerly consumed stories about their countrymen and women who blazed trails in the rugged Asian hinterland. Just five years earlier the first Japanese team reached the summit of Mount Everest, but at a steep cost: eight people died, including seven hired Sherpas and one Japanese climber. A member of the expedition, Miura Yūichirō, became the first person to descend the mountain on skis, and the footage his teammates shot became the first sports documentary to win an Academy Award. Another milestone occurred in 1975 when Japanese climber Tabei Junko became the first woman in the world to reach the top of Everest. Along the way a Sherpa saved her life by digging her out of the snow after an avalanche. Audiences who saw *Dersu Uzala* that same year might have felt more admiration for these achievements—and remembered the critical contributions of unsung native guides—after watching Dersu keep Arsenyev alive through a night of snow and freezing wind.

Dersu has a spiritual worldview that overlaps with Japanese tradition and emphasizes environmental consciousness. For Dersu, the sun, the moon, water, fire, and wind are all "people"—"very great people" capable of feelings like anger. This animistic notion is deeply rooted in Japan as well as in mainland Asia, and the idea of treating the natural world with reverence retained an elemental appeal even in the comparatively-secular 20th century. In the 1970s a growing number of people became aware of how their motorized, mechanized lifestyles posed risks to the environment and to their own wellbeing. Japanese citizen groups advocated for "sunshine rights"—the right to see the sun as opposed to smog and high-rises—and successfully pushed for anti-pollution laws to protect Japan's air, water, and soil. People brought lawsuits against major polluters like the Yokkaichi petrochemical complex and the company responsible for "Minamata Disease," a kind of mercury poisoning. Environmentalist messaging in the 1970s had moral and religious components. In a series of provocative public demonstrations, a group of activist Buddhist monks went so far as to invoke death curses against the owners of dirty factories. On the less confrontational end of the spectrum, villages across the country continued to hold time-honored celebrations of local gods said to inhabit mountains and streams. When Dersu spoke of the natural world in spiritual terms, personifying the earth and the heavens, his words resonated with viewers contemplating their own relationships with nature.[9]

In the second half of *Dersu Uzala* nature be-

Vladimir Arsenyev (left) and Dersu Uzala (right), frontiersmen of the 1910s, inspired weekend woodsmen of the 1970s (from the collected works of Vladimir Klavdievich Arseniev).

comes all-encompassing as the Siberian forest visually swallows Dersu and Arsenyev. Like *Rashōmon*'s otherworldly grove (see Chapter 11), the ensnaring wood in *Spiderweb Castle* (see Chapter 16), and the glorious countryside of *The Hidden Fortress* (see Chapter 19), *Dersu Uzala*'s taiga is a character in its own right. Kurosawa captured Siberia's seasonal changes in real time, filming in the region for a full year amid summer greens, winter ice, and spring and autumn glow. In wide shots the movie's human characters look like insects under the thick forest canopy, and tangled branches and heavy mist often obscure them. There is danger within this elemental beauty, and Dersu experiences a profound crisis of confidence when he shoots at a tiger, an act that he believes will bring him bad luck. Yet it is in this wild environment that the characters find happiness and purpose. The close bond that develops between the Nanai trapper and the Russian captain as they explore the wilderness together is possible because the power of the environment makes their national and ethnic differences trivial. The men's relationship is not the same outside of that environment, nor can Dersu survive apart from it, as the movie's sad coda shows.

In the mid–1970s the combination of a Cold War thaw and an emerging environmental movement suggested that internationalism and conscientious approaches to modernity might increase global wellbeing. *Dersu Uzala* captured that hope, and the film met with success on both sides of the Cold War; it won the Oscar for Best Foreign Language Film and the gold medal at the Moscow Film Festival. Yet the bookends of the movie, which depict the deforestation of the taiga and the death of the indigenous hero on the outskirts of a town, reminded audiences of how much had already been lost. This tension between hope and cynicism would also figure in Kurosawa's epics in the 1980s.

CHAPTER 26

Kagemusha

Three men sit in the frame, and two of them are identical. One of them is the lord of a grand, besieged medieval domain (Nakadai Tatsuya), and he sits on his dais in samurai armor. His apparent twin (also Nakadai), a captive thief in rags, sulks below him. A trusted military advisor sits to one side as the lord contemplates his doppelganger. In this long, trick opening shot of *Kagemusha*, Kurosawa's characters hatch a plan to fool their enemies—and their friends, family members, and future historians as well. To expunge his crime and save his life, the thief will serve as the lord's body double, his *kagemusha*. The movie, whose title means "shadow warrior," raises questions about identity, memory, and the caprice of high politics.

Kagemusha is set in the late 16th century when the mighty warlords Oda Nobunaga, Toyotomi Hideyoshi, and Tokugawa Ieyasu tried to bring all Japan under their rule. To do so they had to conquer powerful rivals like Takeda Shingen, the real-life *daimyō* (feudal lord) at the center of Kagemusha's historical fiction. They also had to contend with the growing influence of foreigners on Japanese soil, particularly Portuguese traders and missionaries who brought guns that could change the tide of war and Bibles that could upend Japan's social foundations. Lastly, they had to keep an eye on each other; alliances between neighboring domains in Japan's feudal period were apt to change suddenly. Tokugawa and Takeda were allies until Tokugawa switched sides, and after the defeat of Takeda the alliance between Oda and Tokugawa also came near collapse.

When *Kagemusha* came to theaters in 1980, Japan enjoyed remarkable political stability. The country's last civil war had happened over a hundred years earlier. The aged Emperor Hirohito, longest-serving monarch in Japanese history and by the 1980s the longest-serving monarch anywhere in the world, was in the middle of his sixth decade on the throne. One political party, the center-right Liberal Democratic Party (*Jiyū Minshutō*) or LDP, had held power continuously since 1955, with each of the 10 prime ministers in that timeframe coming from its ranks. In the United States during the same 25-year stretch the White House seesawed between the major parties three times. The United States ratified five new constitutional amendments between the end of World War II and 1980, while Japan did not alter its postwar constitution in any way. After a tumultuous start to the 20th century, Japan had become more predictable than its chief ally.

Yet the world outside Japan was changing fast when *Kagemusha* delivered its story of conspiracy and state-building. The 1979 Soviet invasion of Afghanistan and the Iranian Revolution that same year put Asia at the center of a new phase in geopolitics. Relations between the United States and the Soviet Union worsened after their polite diplomacy of the 1970s. China and the United States, bitterly opposed during the 1950s and '60s, now cooperated to resist Russian aggression in Asia, and China and Japan came to terms with a Treaty of Peace and Friendship that was years in the making. Soviet and Chinese relations reached a new low after years of animosity, and the partnership between Japan and the United States showed new signs of strain as well. Japan joined the U.S. in boycotting the 1980 Moscow Olympics, but its leaders resisted pressure from American presidents Jimmy Carter and Ronald Reagan to buy new anti-missile technologies and increase Self Defense Force patrols in the northwest Pacific. Japan also disappointed American leaders by continuing to purchase oil from Iran in defiance of an American trade embargo on the new regime there.[1]

Trade was the thorniest issue dividing Japanese and American leaders. For Japan there was a silver lining to oil crises and instability in the Middle East: American drivers became more willing to buy fuel-efficient Japanese cars. American car manufacturers and politicians feared disruption. Honda opened its first American factory in 1979 and Toyota followed suit in 1986, but it was not enough to offset hundreds of thousands of layoffs at American-owned car makers. The Japanese trade ministry agreed to a temporary cap on automobile exports to the United States, and they agreed to phase out tariffs on U.S. agricultural goods to reduce the overall trade imbalance between the two countries, but the trade situation remained decidedly in Japan's favor. American pundits criticized the "unfair" policies that helped enrich Japan, like subsidies to key corporations and an undervalued yen. The Japanese media in turn reported on growing "trade friction" (*bōeki masatsu*) between the longtime allies, which grew along with "defense friction" (*bōei masatsu*).[2]

At this tense moment, *Kagemusha* illustrated the nexus of international trade and national defense with a familiar historical example. Kurosawa's first samurai movie in 15 years features two of the most famous samurai of all time, the national unifiers Oda and Tokugawa, in pivotal roles. Over drinks of *sake* and European wine, Oda (Ryū Daisuke) explains to Tokugawa (Yui Masayuki) his plan to defeat the Takeda clan. The presence of wine reminds the audience that Oda united Japan with the help of powerful foreign allies. Tokugawa's preference for *sake* over the alien drink foreshadows the anti-foreign policies his government later pursued. After uniting Japan under his rule, Tokugawa's government severely limited the import of foreign goods and sought to stop the spread of foreign ideas like Christianity. For the moment, though, the foreigners are useful. Looking over his shoulder at his Jesuit priest allies, Oda smiles and says, "Amen."

Japan's ancient and modern leaders understood the role of ideology in great power politics. As a Christian convert, Oda used personal connections with

European missionaries and traders to procure guns which he used to overwhelm his rivals. The prime minister of Japan at the start of the 1980s, Ōhira Masayoshi, was also a Christian, like five of his predecessors in the office stretching back to the Taishō *jidai* (1912–1926). Christians make up only 1 percent of Japan's population, but religious identity is rarely an issue at the ballot box, and men who identified as Christian held the office of prime minister for 14 out of 35 years between 1945 and 1980. Their travel experiences, Western education, or marriages to women who adopted Christianity during their own Westernized upbringings partially explain this phenomenon, but there was also a pragmatic dimension to political leaders' faith. Recalling Oda and the more recent example of Jiang Jieshi (Chiang Kai-shek) in China, whose Christianity American politicians praised while supporting his war against communism in the 1930s and '40s, Japan's Christian leaders might have hoped that their faith would enhance their relationship with American presidents. In truth, though, Japanese and American leaders' shared religion did little to smooth over problems that emerged around trade, defense, and relations with the wider world.

In *Kagemusha*, the actual identity of rulers is surprisingly unimportant to the way history unfolds. When an anonymous gunman in Oda's army kills the real Takeda Shingen at the end of an indecisive battle, the doppelganger thief immediately takes over as head of the Takeda clan and its army. We never learn the thief's original name. The only name that matters is the name that comes with the job: Takeda. His task is not to distinguish himself, but to look and act and think exactly like his predecessor. The late lord's adult son, Katsuyori, craves the power and prestige that should rightfully be his, but the Takeda generals overrule him in order to maintain the illusion that the great Shingen is still alive.

A ruse like this is the stuff of historical legend, but the ideal of perfect continuity was also important in contemporary Japanese politics. In June 1980, just two months after *Kagemusha* came to theaters, Prime Minister Ōhira died of a heart attack while fighting one of the toughest political campaigns in recent memory. During Ōhira's tenure, a power struggle within the LDP created an opportunity for the minority Socialist Party to win more seats in the Diet. Since the LDP had been in power since its creation in 1955, a loss to the Socialists could have heralded a major departure from the norm in Japanese politics. Ōhira's death may have saved the LDP's majority. His deputy, whose name was also Masayoshi, took over as interim prime minister, and a wave of "sympathy votes" resulted in the biggest LDP victory in years. The next man the LDP selected as prime minister, Suzuki Zenkō, was a former Socialist Party member, but during his tenure he closely followed the policies of previous prime ministers. He negotiated with newly-elected American president Ronald Reagan to keep Japan's defense budget low and its trade profits high. Neither the death of a prime minister nor factionalism in the legislature altered Japan's essential political posture.[3]

In *Kagemusha* the transition in leadership is so smooth that it goes almost unnoticed. Shingen's son complains and his concubines joke among themselves, but Shingen's adoring grandson has only a passing suspicion, and the Takeda soldiers go about their business as usual. Knowing that Shingen was shot, Oda and Tokugawa's spies investigate the matter, and from the shore of a lake they observe Takeda men dispose of a large urn that they correctly guess contains the late lord's body. Yet the spies later see the Takeda leader apparently alive and well, and they duly report that information to their superiors. The appearance of continuity proves indistinguishable from continuity itself as the new Takeda lord successfully preserves the status quo.

The movie's handling of identity and espionage also parallels one of the most mysterious incidents of the Cold War: the kidnapping of Japanese citizens by the government of North Korea in the late 1970s and early 1980s. The victims were men and women of all ages, from older bachelors to young couples to children. One thirteen-year-old girl disappeared just 800 feet from her home. Most of the abductees lived along the Sea of Japan, which Korean maps call the East Sea, and their abductors transported them a thousand kilometers to Korea by boat or submarine. Many of the victims, including the young girl, apparently died in North Korea under unknown circumstances, but others worked for decades as translators and spies for the dictatorial regime. Few ever returned to Japan, but those who did spoke of years of psychological manipulation and loneliness. Like a darker version of the thief's crash course on Takeda clan history and philosophy in *Kagemusha*, the kidnapping victims internalized North Korean propaganda and learned to take on new roles in service of the state.[4]

The idea that North Korea was behind the disappearance of dozens of Japanese citizens—as well as thousands of South Korean citizens and a few more far-flung kidnappings—spread like a conspiracy theory in the 1980s and '90s, but many found it difficult to believe. Some in the Japanese government knew the truth thanks to their own spy operations, but to avoid international scandal they did not publicly address the North Korean kidnappings until journalistic investigations and confessions from former spies produced overwhelming evidence. Songs, books, documentaries, and even animated movies about the kidnappings proliferated in Japan when the truth came to light. In the early 2000s North Korea finally returned some of the surviving abductees to Japan, along with spouses and children that some of them gained in captivity, but relations between Japan and North Korea remained chilly partly because of the anger and unresolved questions surrounding the kidnappings.

The kidnappings were still largely unknown when *Kagemusha*'s audiences watched the Takeda clan capture an unfortunate thief, indoctrinate and train him in the ways of medieval warfare, and use him as a pawn in their political game. If viewers in 1980 made any connection at all between the film and Korea, it was likely because the actor Daisuke Ryū, who played the famous warlord Oda, was of Korean descent, or because they remembered that Oda's ally Toyotomi Hideyoshi had led two failed invasions of the Korean peninsula in the 1590s. In hindsight, though, the

Families worked for decades to learn the fates of relatives abducted by North Korea. A photograph of Yokota Megumi, kidnapped in 1977 at the age of 13, is displayed by her brother Takuya and mother Sakie at a 2019 event in Tokyo (photograph by Shealah Craighead).

protagonist's journey gains a new and tragic dimension through its eerily-timed similarities to one of the Cold War's strangest, saddest episodes.

Hindsight is crucial to *Kagemusha*'s approach to nationalism. As Oda and his allies plot to bring Japan's warring kingdoms under a single banner, the Takeda clan's survival depends not only on using the thief to disguise their weakness, but on envisioning their domain as an independent nation. Despite complex alliances and hierarchies between Japan's medieval domains, each territory was its own kingdom. The medieval nationalism of Takeda prefigured the 20th-century version with its focus on military strength and powerful leadership, but it existed within a decentralized medieval system, so it also stood in the way of nationalism's development. After Takeda's defeat and the eventual unification of Japan under the Tokugawa clan, the idea of "nation" acquired a larger meaning than what domain rulers like Takeda could claim. Words for "nation" like *kuni* and *kokka* were used interchangeably for domains and for Japan as a whole during the 17th, 18th, and 19th centuries, but each domain acknowledged that the *shōgun* had the exclusive authority to impose his policies anywhere in Japan and to control interactions between Japan and the outside world. This modern idea of a "nation" was natural to people who grew up in the Meiji, Taishō, and Shōwa *jidai* when powerful central governments remade Japan as a modern state, waged war on the world, then remade it again. Looking back on Japanese history after a century of extreme change, *Kagemusha* highlights a key moment in the shift from many nations to one nation.[5]

With full knowledge of the later significance of nationhood, *Kagemusha* stresses the Takeda clan's efforts to assert its political identity. What distinguishes them from their enemies, on a practical level, are their flags—the vertical banners that Takeda samurai carry into battle. In *Kagemusha* the flags are of numerous designs, including red, blue, and green ones bearing the words for fire, wind, and forest, respectively. These banners refer to the particular ideology of the Takeda clan, which they borrowed from Chinese military strategist Sun Tzu: "Swift as the wind, silent as the forest, sweeping as fire, immovable as a mountain." The Takeda leader is the mountain, and his armies are as awesome as nature itself. Through emblems and slogans that conflate the Takeda regime with the order and harmony of the natural world, the Takeda nation makes the case that it is a rightful, unassailable, unassimilable fixture of Japan's landscape. Governments of future centuries also claimed to be inevitable, like the governments of the Meiji, Taishō, and Shōwa periods that used a rising sun flag to represent Japan and its military and taught that the emperor was descended from the sun goddess Amaterasu. Yet everyone in 1980 knew that these governments had been as ephemeral and subject to defeat as the Takeda clan 400 years before.

The Japanese government of the 1980s, fighting battles over international trade and internal politics, redefined the Japanese nation once again. The longest-serving prime minister of the decade, Yasuhiro Nakasone, described Japan as an "international state" (*kokusai kokka*): not an empire, as it was decades earlier, nor a rehabilitating client state, as it was in the 1950s and '60s, but an expansive and cooperative leader in a globalized world. Some Japanese politicians were reluctant to use the word "alliance" to describe the relationship between Japan and the United States, and increasingly they turned their attention to issues like the "special relationship" between Japan and South Korea. Nakasone's trip to South Korea in 1983 was the first time a postwar Japanese prime minister visited that country, and he showed his "flair for personal diplomacy" by speaking and even singing in Korean. At the G7 summit of the world's largest economies Nakasone conducted "multilateral diplomacy" with all participants, not just with American president Ronald Reagan. In 1989 a government minister and the chairman of Japan's corporate giant Sony collaborated on a book called *The Japan That Can Say No: Why Japan Will Be First Among Equals*, which argued that Japan was no longer the United States' "yes man" and would soon become the benevolent moral, technological, and economic leader of an integrated international community. Japanese leaders defined their nation not as a neutered ex-empire or a lesser power punching above its weight, but as a new kind of global state.[6]

Like *Dersu Uzala* in the mid–1970s, *Kagemusha* owed its existence to international cooperation and the status that Kurosawa enjoyed as one of the world's leading filmmakers. *Kagemusha*'s projected budget went beyond what Kurosawa could raise in Japan, so the director agreed to let two young Americans, George Lucas and Francis Ford Coppola, make up the gap and arrange the movie's international

In the 1980s Japan's leaders sought to redefine Japan as an "international state." Prime Minister Nakasone Yasuhiro is pictured here with other world leaders at the 1985 G7 summit. From left to right: Jacques Delors of the European Commission, Bettino Craxi of Italy, François Mitterrand of France, Margaret Thatcher of the United Kingdom, Helmut Kohl of West Germany, Ronald Reagan of the United States of America, Nakasone of Japan, and Brian Mulroney of Canada (National Archives).

distribution. Lucas and Coppola became passionate about Kurosawa after seeing his black-and-white samurai movies in film school and in arthouse theaters, and these "exotic" films inspired them when they began to make their own movies. Thanks to the enormous success they enjoyed in the 1970s with films like *Star Wars* and *The Godfather,* they now had the influence and the means to help one of their heroes. To make additional money during production, Coppola and Kurosawa appeared together in several Suntory Whiskey commercials. Lucas and Coppola received executive producer credits for helping fund and distribute *Kagemusha,* and their investment paid off when the film received two Oscar nominations and one of the most coveted prizes in film, the Cannes Palme d'Or. It was also the top-grossing film of the year in Japan, making it Kurosawa's most financially successful movie since the 1960s.

Things do not end as happily for the nameless thief. Shingen's son eventually forces the imposter out and leads the Takeda army to a disastrous military defeat. The thief does not return to his old life, but watches helplessly as the Oda and Tokugawa forces slaughter the people he briefly ruled. Ashen-faced and raving, he flies from the carnage of the battlefield and sees a fallen Takeda banner floating down a river. He gives chase, hoping to save the symbol of his adoptive house from the flow of the water and the flow of time, but he dies before he reaches it. His body and the flag float out of sight and into history. Such is the fate of all nations and people, from the highest to the lowest. The lordly thief was both.

Tragic endings on screen and international collaboration behind the scenes became hallmarks of Kurosawa's work in the 1970s and '80s, so it was little surprise that he selected one of the most famous Western tragedies of all, *King Lear*, for the subject of his next film.

CHAPTER 27

Ran

In 1879, in the midst of its modernization program, the Meiji government addressed the need for moral education in Japanese schools. "We set out to take in the best features of the West and bring in new things," read the Imperial Rescript on Education, but "the danger of indiscriminate emulation of Western ways is that in the end our people will forget the great principles governing the relations between ruler and subject, and father and son. Our aim, based on our ancestral teachings, is solely the clarification of benevolence, justice, loyalty, and filial piety." A century and a half later, moral education, *dōtoku*, remains a fixture of Japanese schools.[1]

There are mandatory *dōtoku* classes in the public school curriculum, and activities that take place between and after classes reinforce the lessons imparted there. Cleaning the school, for example, is the daily responsibility of students rather than hired janitors. Donning scrubs to clean their space together, explains scholar Sugimoto Yoshio, teaches Japanese children "to be both humble and hard-working through sweeping with a broom, wiping the floor with a damp cloth, and getting their hands dirty. This routine is supposed to train pupils to be compliant, cooperative, and responsible citizens." *Dōtoku* classes and extracurricular activities with moral dimensions do not primarily teach Shinto or Buddhist doctrine or the Confucian substructure of concepts like filial piety—what the Meiji government called "our ancestral teachings"—but they instill in students a sense of civic morality that stresses healthy habits and basic social responsibility. In a country where people seldom attend religious services, *dōtoku* lessons help create a common moral frame of reference.[2]

Ran ("chaos") is a *jidaigeki* set in medieval Japan featuring Buddhist imagery, but there is a universality to its morality tale that transcends national and religious identity. The movie, financed in part by French producer Serge Silberman, closely follows Shakespeare's *King Lear*, a tragedy in which the fictional title character disinherits his youngest and most faithful daughter while his two older daughters and their husbands destroy each other and bring the kingdom to ruin. Kurosawa locates the story in feudal Japan and changes the name of the ruler to Ichimonji Hidetora (Nakadai Tatsuya), a warlord with three quarrelsome sons, but the moral content of the story survives the transition intact. Greed, fratricide, and parental neglect were wrong in Elizabethan England when Shakespeare wrote the story, in medieval Japan where Kurosawa set his version, and in the mid–1980s when the movie debuted domestically and internationally. Justice, loyalty, and honoring one's parents were righteous ideals in all of these contexts, cultural differences and centuries of change notwithstanding.

Yet many Japanese people perceived contrasts between their sense of morality and the outside world's. Japan in the 1980s was, in the words of its leaders, an "international state" that practiced peaceful diplomacy, hosted international celebrations, and contributed to global material wealth and artistic culture, but a powerful sense of exceptionalism still allowed Japanese people to feel that they were in the world but not of it. In the 1970s and '80s a genre of writing called *nihonjinron*, "discourses on Japanese people," became a major industry as writers tried to explain the country's postwar transformation and link it to Japan's past and future by focusing on supposedly unique cultural traits. A recurring idea in *nihonjinron* was that consensus-oriented Japanese people were not as selfish as individualistic foreigners; this idea also appeared in Japanese students' *dōtoku* classes. *Nihonjinron* and

dōtoku texts characterized Japanese culture as homogeneous in comparison to other, more eclectic countries. A strong collective identity supposedly encouraged Japanese people to abide by informal social rules as well as official laws. In other words, mainstream morality was valid precisely because it was mainstream. There were moral authorities beyond the wisdom of the crowd— the enlightened Buddhas of the past, the Shinto *kami* (gods), and the souls of departed ancestors— but students of *nihonjinron* and *dōtoku* argued that Japan's moral universe was specific to Japanese culture and not universal.[3]

Elementary school students in Karakuwa, Japan scrub the floor after classes in this 2006 snapshot (photograph by the author).

The casting of *Ran* raises a "moral" issue on which Japan and the West had differences as well as similarities: homosexuality. The character who functions as an audience surrogate is Hidetora's court jester, a young man named Kyōami. He is played by an actor who goes by the single English name "Peter" because of his resemblance to the character Peter Pan—both are slim, spritely, and androgynous. The actor Peter frequently plays queer roles on film and television. Apart from *Ran*, his most notable role is in the 1969 arthouse film *Funeral Parade of Roses* (*Bara no sōretsu*) by Matsumoto Toshio, a hyperkinetic modern retelling of the Greek play *Oedipus Rex*. Written and pictorial depictions of homosexuality go back to ancient times in Japan, and during the 20th-century Japan had no laws against same-sex relationships, whereas in the United States such laws remained in effect until the early 2000s. Japan is also different from the West in that there is no powerful religious opposition to homosexuality. Yet there is cultural pressure in Japan to conform to "traditional" gender roles, and this makes it difficult for homosexual and non-cisgender men and women to express their identities publicly. Much of Japan's gay culture remained underground throughout the 20th century, but in 1971 the country's first professionally-published and ad-supported gay magazine, *Barazoku*, appeared, and others followed. The popularity of openly-gay entertainers on screen grew in the last decades of the Shōwa *jidai*. The cross-dressing tradition in all-male Noh and kabuki theater and the all-female Takarazuka Revue continued to attract admirers; Takarazuka, an invention of the progressive Taishō *jidai*, particularly emphasizes the gender-bending dimension of its cabaret-style musical productions. In direct and indirect ways, Japanese queer men and women asserted their existence in defiance of culture norms that sought to minimize them.[4]

Kyōami, Peter's character in *Ran*, stands out from the crowd. Other characters in the tragedy are sober and still, and the men and women alike have proud bearings, but Kyōami is lively, loudly-attired, and intensely emotive. In this and in the implicit queerness that Peter brings to the character, Kyōami channels the heightened world of contemporary Japanese theater. In the 1980s, even as traditional theater remained popular with mainstream audiences and tourists, young theatergoers and niche-seekers gravitated towards avant-garde playhouses and their "sumptuous display[s] of diverse and provocative visions." Japanese theater directors and some of their most acclaimed counterparts from overseas staged innovative and challenging works at venues such as the Toga International Arts Festival, first held in 1982, and at "little theaters" (*shogekijō*) both permanent and impromptu. Contemporary critics observed that 1980s Japanese theater was a "young people's theater" and compared it to the early years of kabuki when itinerant actors performed it in the alleys of Kyoto and Edo's entertainment districts. The directors, actors, and patrons of 1980s theater grew up during Japan's economic boom, and they were open to experimentation. Their plays dealt with subjectivity, sexuality, communal experiences of "shared sentiments," and post-apocalyptic themes that stemmed from Cold War tensions and environmental consciousness. In the 1984 play *Tabula Rasa and the Monster with Multiple Heads* (*Massara na basho to tatō no kaibutsu*) by Kawamura Takesha, the world after Armageddon becomes a blank slate in which the distance between history, myth, and present reality collapse. In a 1985 staging of Kōkami Shōji's *With a Rising Sun Which Looks Like a Setting Sun* (*Asahi no yō na yūhi o tsurete*), a similar premise comes to life through singing, dancing youths who strive for new expressions of identity in a confusing world. In Kurosawa's *Ran*, Peter's outlandish and often jarring performance as Kyōami reflects the youthful, vivid, searching nature of modern Japanese performance art, as well as the increased visibility of queer performers in Japan.[5]

When *Ran*'s patriarch Hidetora falters, Kyōami proves more useful to him than his own flesh and blood. Hidetora's two oldest sons, Tarō (Terao Akira) and Jirō (Nezu Jinpachi), plot to destroy each other, and the youngest son Saburō (Ryū Daisuke) enters exile after criticizing their father's decision to retire. Only Kyōami stays by the lord's side when Hidetora finds himself powerless to heal the rift between his children. Kyōami keeps his master alive during the destruction of the Ichimonji clan, and he prevents the lord from taking rash, violent actions. He also communicates unpleasant truths through jokes, songs, and irreverent metaphors, though this puts him in danger when the targets of his mockery take offense. Kyōami plays the role of fool and conscience in the Ichimonji clan, similar to the way avant-garde theater in the 1980s used fanciful premises and expressive choreography to discuss social problems and deliver warnings about the future.

Tarō has a more malevolent voice at his shoulder in the form of his wife Kaede (Harada Mieko). Years before, Hidetora conquered Kaede's family and she had to marry Tarō. Now Kaede avenges her family by manipulating Tarō and Jirō into destroying their father, each other, and the entire Ichimonji kingdom. In personality Kaede is reminiscent of the Lady Macbeth character in *Spiderweb Castle* who goads her husband to rebel against his lord, but in the 30 years since Kurosawa made that movie changes in Japanese gender ideology helped make Kaede a more sympathetic villain. When *Spiderweb Castle* came out in 1957, arranged marriages were still the norm, but by the time of *Ran*'s debut in 1985 young people regarded them as old-fashioned. Kaede's monologue about her forced marriage to Tarō creates context for her decision to instigate a civil war—context that the Lady Macbeth character in *Spiderweb Castle* did not have.

In the 1970s and '80s a women's liberation movement in Japan sought to build on women's postwar gains like voting rights and marriage choice. Activists paid close attention to the American women's liberation movement that was happening at the same time, and they borrowed its terminology for the phrase *ūman ribu* ("woman lib" in Japanese syllables). *Ūman ribu* leaders like Tanaka Mitsu advocated for greater understanding of women's sexual pleasure and bodily autonomy, access to birth control, and support during pregnancy and motherhood. Yet the movement struck a conservative attitude toward lesbians, ignoring them and sometimes actively excluding them from *ūman ribu* organizations in order to appear more respectable to mainstream society. Still, by writing and speaking against patriarchal practices in homes and workplaces, *ūman ribu* activists inspired an increasing number of women to seek greater financial autonomy and to became their own bosses. The rooms that Kaede occupies in *Ran* are suggestive of old-fashioned, upscale hotels called *ryōkan*, which at the turn of the 21st century gave women opportunities to live "without the need of a man" ("*otoko wa hitsuyo ga nai*," in the words of one *ryōkan* employee). Female *ryōkan* employees wore traditional clothing like Kaede's medieval finery, and they lived and worked in rooms with *tatami* and artfully-decorated sliding doors like the ones where Kaede plans her revenge. Despite this strict and antiquated aesthetic, female *ryōkan* owners and their predominantly-female workers reported feeling more control over their workspaces than women in ordinary offices, where men often referred to female colleagues by the term "office flowers." The fact that *ryōkan* offered majority-female working environments as well as room and board contributed to a sense of independence that was all too rare among women in corporate and household settings.[6]

In *Ran*, Kaede also uses her feudal space as an instrument of power. She shows her husband precisely where her mother committed suicide, and she sits on a dais that elevates her above her father-in-law, thereby making the castle seem more hers than the Ichimonji men's. She also conspicuously raises the status of her female attendants by ordering them not to bow to Hidetora's concubines, whom he blusteringly refers to as "my women."

The 1970s and '80s also saw the rise of a new industry in which women played central roles—the pop idol industry. Idols (*aidoru*) like Yamaguchi Momoe and Matsuda Seiko won legions of fans with their bubbly, upbeat songs and appearance of innocence and vulnerability. Their girlish and conspicuously "pure" public images were manufactured and tightly controlled by entertainment managers who were usually men, and these managers pocketed most of the money that idols earned through music sales, concerts, and public appearances. Having a boyfriend or getting married could end an idol's career, since part of their appeal was that men could imagine themselves in relationships with the virginal idols. This fetishization of innocence known as *moe* also influences depictions of women and girls in *manga* and *anime*.

In *Ran*, part of what marks Kaede as a villain is the extent to which she is not vulnerable and does not cater to the men around her. Her background elicits sympathy, but her actions defy social expectations and enrage the movie's male characters. Hidetora angrily criticizes her for her insubordinate attitude and blames her for his sons' rebellion. Near the end of the movie an Ichimonji samurai executes her when she confesses to orchestrating the war between Hidetora's sons. Kaede's death is the bloodiest in the movie, as if to emphasize her guilt for all the blood shed by the Ichimonji armies.

There is a woman in *Ran* who is designed to elicit *moe*. Jirō's wife Sue (Miyazaki Yoshiko) is the opposite of Kaede: she is demure and submissive, and she is both a caregiver and someone who is in need of care. Like Kaede, she became an orphan

Ōhashiya, an active, 300-year-old *ryōkan* in Toyokawa (Wikimedia Commons).

when Hidetora conquered her parents' castle. Yet she loves and respects Hidetora, calling him "father" and welcoming him warmly when he visits her at Jirō's castle. She is deeply religious, and when Hidetora asks why she does not hate him like Kaede does, she explains that the events of her life and the roles that people play in it are part of a karmic cycle of birth and rebirth under the gaze of a benevolent Buddha. In addition to bearing her own fate in good spirits, Sue takes care of her blind, exiled brother. She is a model daughter-in-law and sister, but as a wife she has little political utility for Jirō. When war breaks out and Tarō dies in battle, Jirō takes Kaede as a lover, effectively displacing Sue from her home. The innocent, helpless Sue finds herself bereft of protection in a world in which violent demons (*asura*), not Buddha, have the upper hand. Her meekness, her simple faith, and her beauty provoke *moe*, causing viewers' hearts to go out to her.

Hidetora proves as vulnerable as Sue, but *moe* applies to young female characters, not to old men. Instead of targeting viewers' romantic or paternalistic impulses, Hidetora's arc speaks to their shame about their treatment of elderly family members. In the mid–1980s when *Ran* came to theaters, Japan's working-age population hit its postwar peak. After that the number of working adults and the number of children in the country steadily declined while the elderly population continued to grow. There was a longstanding cultural expectation that elderly adults should live with one or more of their adult children. Japanese culture values "protection and predictability, rather than autonomy and independence," in the words of one Japanese scholar, so in-home elderly care is a broadly-accepted ideal. Modern lifestyles, however, make the arrangement difficult. Many working adults live in small urban apartments rather than in their hometowns where their aging parents reside, and relocation and cohabitation can cause discomfort for everyone involved. Whether they live alone or with their children, elderly people worry about burdening their families, and they commit suicide at about twice the rate of people in their twenties and thirties. There is an uncomfortable familiarity in the way the mentally- and physically-declining Hidetora moves from one son's castle to the next and finds them unwilling or unable to accommodate him.[7]

Hidetora finally finds shelter with someone even worse off than he is: Sue's brother Tsurumaru (Nomura Mansai), whom Hidetora blinded years earlier after conquering his family. Tsurumaru lives in a simple shack with few possessions except for a *shakuhachi* flute. By the late 20th century, improvements in healthcare had made blindness among young people quite rare in Japan, and after 1959 virtually all blind adults were eligible for disability pensions. Starting in the late 1960s Japan led the world in the development of tactile paving for the vision-impaired, and by the mid–1980s designer Miyake Seiichi's "Tenji bricks"—textured blocks on sidewalks and train platforms—were commonplace in Japan and beginning to appear in other countries as well. At the same time, the blind occupied a place of prominence in Japanese fiction. Blind virtuosos like the ancient musicians Semimaru and Hōichi and the 1960s action movie hero Zatoichi had household name recognition, and audiences liked imagining that the sense of sight could be traded for other abilities.

Other kinds of disabilities did not receive the same level of attention or support. People with cognitive disabilities were not included in the disability pension system until 1964, and until 1986 people with disabilities other than blindness or loss of limbs received smaller pension payments. There were no special education services for Japanese schoolchildren with multiple disabilities or mental handicaps until 2007. On the other hand, the tendency of Japanese schools to integrate abled and disabled students as much as possible showed advantages in terms of enriching all students' experiences.[8]

Ran places marginalized people—the implicitly queer Kyōami, the woman Kaede, the elderly Hidetora, and the disabled Tsurumaru—in central roles. The privileged male samurai who vie for control of the Ichimonji domain are supporting players who fight and die in spectacular but indecisive battles. The real protagonists, all ostensibly powerless, cut through the noise of politics and warfare by establishing alternative hierarchies and embodying eternal truths that outlast the chaos of the moment. Kyōami the fool says to Hidetora the fallen lord, "Speak your nonsense and I will speak my truth" as he guides him through a war-torn landscape. The absence of Hidetora's sons and the loss of his faculties highlights his total reliance on Kyōami. Kaede's power over Tarō and then Jirō is strong, and the men's advisors warn against her in vain. She uses the ambitions of men to achieve her own purpose, though it costs her her life. Hidetora finds himself superfluous as he experiences his kingdom from the perspective of its meekest subjects, and he learns to value people like Kyōami and Sue not as pawns in a political game but as companions on a journey that ends the same way for both conquerors and conquered. After a short and painful life, the blind Tsurumaru stands alone on a ruined castle in the film's final shot. He carries his sister's scroll painting of the Buddha, a reminder that while suffering is inevitable, the roles people fill in one life may not be the roles they take on in the next life.

Tsurumaru drops the painting into a chasm as the sun sets, and its gold-leaf glints up like a ray of hope in a darkening world. As the last decade of the 20th century approached, a persistent hope for queer people, women, the elderly, and the infirm was that the benefits of modern Japanese society would apply equally to all citizens regardless of sexuality, sex, age, or ability.

Kurosawa's movies routinely deal with people who feel powerless, from the poor to victims of crime to social outcasts, but in his next film he would take on a new subject: himself. The 1990 movie *Dreams* offers a surrealistic take on the 80 years of Japanese history that Kurosawa experienced as a man of position and influence.

CHAPTER 28

Dreams

Emperor Hirohito died in January 1989 at the age of 87. His record-breaking 64 years on the throne included the incomparable pain of defeat in World War II as well as some of Japan's greatest years during the economic miracle of the 1950s, '60s, and '70s. The name for Hirohito's era, the Shōwa *jidai*, meant "peace and enlightenment," and at times the name was darkly ironic. When his son Akihito took the throne, the Japanese calendar started over. The name of the new *jidai*, Heisei, also signified peace, and it represented the hope that Japan's darkest days were truly in the past.

Almost on cue, the Japanese economy crashed. Its growth had slowed during the 1970s when a pair of oil crises sent shockwaves through the economy, and there had been brief recessions even amid overall growth, but the bubble that burst at the beginning of the Heisei *jidai* was like nothing in recent memory. Japan's stock market lost half its value by the summer of 1990. Consumers cut spending and deflation set in. Several businesses and banks failed, and others survived only after government bailouts. Many residential and commercial properties became vacant. The slump was not short-lived; it wore on to the end of the century and beyond. The 1990s, the first full decade of the Heisei *jidai*, received the nickname *ushinawareta jūnen*: "the lost decade."

Even in a country with a large elderly population, most people could not remember the last calendar change in the mid–1920s. Kurosawa could. He turned 80 years old in 1990, and he was in a mood for reflection. His new film, *Dreams* (*Yume*), gave him a chance to consider nearly a century's worth of Japanese history from a very personal perspective. Kurosawa borrowed the title and the structure of the movie—several short segments that each begin with the phrase "I had a dream" (*konna yume o mita*)—from a 1908 novella by writer Sōseki Natsume. Sōseki died in 1916, but from 1984 to 2004 his face appeared on Japanese 1000-yen bills, and he remained very well known. The dreams in Kurosawa's movie, though, are very different from the dreams in Sōseki's book; they are specific to Kurosawa's interests and to Japan's 20th-century experiences.

Kurosawa cast Terao Akira, a gangly actor he had worked with in *Ran*, as his doppelganger "I." I wears the same kind of floppy fisherman's hat that the director wore in the heyday of his career. Terao plays I in six of the movie's eight dreams. In the other two, younger versions of I are played by child actors Isaki Mitsunori and Nakano Toshihiko, each of whom Kurosawa cast again in his final two films. Much later Isaki would contribute his voice to one of the most financially successful Japanese films of all time, the 2004 *anime Howl's Moving Castle* (*Hauru no ugoku shiro*). In the late 1990s and early 2000s Japanese animation became a nearly $5 billion per year industry in the United States, making it one of the country's most successful exports ever even as the overall economy stagnated. Kurosawa admired *anime*, but he also lamented that "many talents nowadays whom I would have loved to have kept for movies have gone to the animation industry…. We, the movie industry, must not be lazy. We must make pictures that stimulate young talents' interest in movies." As if to show how this might be done, Kurosawa's *Dreams* contains the kind of magical, brightly-saturated imagery that is much more common in *anime* than in live-action movies. From impossibly-perfect rainbows over postcard fields of flowers to a symphony of nuclear explosions around Mt. Fuji, the aesthetic of *Dreams* draws on the heightened unreality of imagination, wonder, and nightmare.[1]

Like most of Kurosawa's projects over the last 20 years of his career, *Dreams* was only possible because of international assistance. Bringing Kurosawa's surreal visions to life was costly, especially at a time when money was tight. A growing number of Japanese storytellers were choosing animation rather than traditional film as their medium, like award-winning director Ōtomo Katsuhiro who dabbled in live-action but found more success with *anime* features like 1988's *Akira*. The most expensive anime made to date, *Akira* was still millions of dollars cheaper to produce than Kurosawa's *Dreams* or *Ran*, and it was more successful at the box office too. Kurosawa and his American admirers, though, still believed there was value in making fantasy the old-fashioned way. American director Steven Spielberg, responsible for live-action fantasies like *E.T.* and the *Indiana Jones* series, acted as executive producer for *Dreams*. *Star Wars* creator and *Kagemusha* producer George Lucas's visual effects company, Industrial Light & Magic, helped to create the special effects that Kurosawa required.

In the opening dream, set in the early 20th century, the young I goes out exploring on a day when the sun shines and the rain falls. This is the kind of weather in which fox spirits hold their weddings. Kurosawa previously wrote about fox spirits in his script for *Ran*, but in *Dreams* he actually shows them in their otherworldly, perilous, irresistible glory. When the boy enters a forest he sees human-sized foxes conducting a ritualistic wedding procession. When he returns to his family's large, old-fashioned home, which looks like Kurosawa's childhood home and bears the name Kurosawa on its plaque, I's *kimono*-clad mother refuses to let him back in. She tells the boy that he offended the fox spirits by observing their secret ceremony, and now he must beg their forgiveness or else commit *seppuku*. The young child sets out to find the foxes in a dazzling, virginal landscape overflowing with color, and with adventure or death waiting for him the dream ends.

"Fox shrines" (*inari jinja*) both great and very, very small dot Japan, and the

Fox figures at Fushimi Inari shrine (photograph by Immanuel Giel, Wikimedia Commons).

folkloric role of foxes as shapeshifters and trickster gods is still widely recognized. The worship of fox spirits takes place at Shinto shrines like the sprawling Fushimi Inari Shrine in Kyoto and at private, dollhouse-sized shrines tucked away in copses of trees throughout the countryside. In 1990 one of the Fushimi Inari shrine's yearly festivals attracted as many as 80,000 people who each paid the equivalent of anywhere from $120 to $4000 for a keepsake box representing their own personal fox spirit.[2]

Fascination with Japanese mythology survived and thrived as a century of modernization and cosmopolitanism came to a close. The opening episode of *Dreams* revels in it, and most of the subsequent dreams also borrow heavily from Japanese folklore. So do several of the most popular *anime* of the 1990s, as well as titles from the fast-growing Japanese video game industry, whose international success was a bright spot amid the economic downturn. 1988's best-selling game *Super Mario Brothers 3* and 1994's hit *anime Pom Poko* (*Heisei tanuki gassen ponpoko*) from Studio Ghibli, for example, both reference *tanuki*, another mischievous creature in folklore. For young people, these innovative forms of entertainment are key sources of information about Japanese legends and fables.

The second dream also deals with a cherished bit of Japanese culture. Every March 3 it is customary for families with pre-teen girls to display a large set of dolls representing the emperor, the empress, and their attendants. The dolls' costumes, hairstyles, and accessories emulate the fashion of the Heian *jidai* (794–1185), when imperial court culture was at its peak. The dolls sit in a particular order on a raised, multi-tiered dais. Often very expensive or antique heirlooms, the doll sets are not toys, but young girls and their friends often sit near them while playing games, eating traditional snacks like rice crackers and rice cakes, and dressing up in *kimono*. This holiday is called *Hinamatsuri*, "Girl's Day" or "Doll's Day."

As a boy, the young dreamer is not a full participant in Girl's Day; the holiday that was once Boy's Day, now Children's Day, takes place on May 5 and involves carp streamers rather than dolls. His duty during *Hinamatsuri* is to serve tea and snacks to his sister and her female friends. The young I soon notices that one of the girls is visible only to him. She is a spirit, and he follows her outside to the place where his family's peach orchard once stood. There, arranged on the terraced hillside like dolls in a *Hinamatsuri* set, are the spirits of an emperor, empress, and members of their court. They remind the boy that the timing of Girl's Day originally coincided with the blossoming of peach trees. The spirits are angry that the boy's family razed their orchard, but they take pity on him and allow him to see the trees in bloom one last time. As a rain of peach blossoms washes over the hill, the spirits transform into living trees and then into dead stumps. Only one tree, the one into which the young girl transforms, still has life in it at the end of the dream.

The boy weeps for the loss of his family's orchard, a loss experienced again and again in 20th-century Japan as farms gave way to urbanization and young members of rural households left agriculture for commercial and industrial jobs. By the 1990s farming was primarily the work of the elderly, and often it supplemented other sources of income. The Japanese government subsidized and protected farming as much as it could, but it faced constant pressure from American politicians and agribusinesses to import cheaper American food. The World Trade Organization negotiations of 1986 to 1993 resulted in Japan allowing more food imports that further reduced the viability of Japanese farms. Between 1990 and 2005 the percentage of abandoned Japanese farmland rose from about 3 percent to nearly 10 percent. Kurosawa's placement of a young boy and a young girl at the center of his dream about a razed orchard emphasizes the magnitude of this change in the Japanese landscape. The boy's deep sadness about the loss of the orchard, and the enduring popularity of of Girl's Day with its subtle reminder of seasonal rhythms, implies that the survival of Japanese agriculture and other traditions depends on the nation's youth. Today farming is part of the curriculum in many Japanese elementary and middle schools, and even urban schools often maintain small plots of rice or vegetables for students to cultivate.[3]

The third dream features a folklore character whose fame increased in the 20th century thanks to a bit of international give and take. Three mountain climbers, including an adult I, get caught in a high-altitude blizzard and encounter a beautiful but malicious spirit called *yukionna*, a woman of the snow. Tales about *yukionna* date back centuries, and each region of Japan has its own local version of the ghoul, but the most well-known is the one from Lafcadio Hearn's 1903 book *Kwaidan: Stories and Studies of Strange Things*. Hearn was a lifelong immigrant who was born in Greece, raised in Ireland, and moved around the United States before traveling to the West Indies and finally to Japan. In 1890 he became one of the first Europeans to marry a Japanese woman. His *yukionna* story deals with a marriage between the snow woman and a mortal man. They live happily together for several years before he discovers her true identity. *Kwaidan* was popular in Japan, and Hearn's *yukionna* appears in Kobayashi Masaki's memorable 1962 movie adaptation of the book. Kurosawa's *yukionna* straddles different planes of reality—"I" is the dreamer's dream self, and he dreams the encounter with the *yukionna* while dying. It also straddles time, bringing the folklore of eons past into a contemporary setting as the spirit haunts modern mountaineers.

Of course, some things are better left in the past. That's the message of the fourth dream, in which the dreamer is a World War II Imperial Army officer. Though Kurosawa himself did not serve in the military, rather contributing to the war as a propagandist (see Chapters 1, 2, and 3), everyone from the wartime generation carried memories of bombing raids and lost loved ones. Kurosawa's uniformed dreamer emerged from the war unscathed, the only one of his company to do so, but he suffers from survivor's guilt. At the beginning of the dream he walks along an empty road and enters a long, dark tunnel guarded by a snarling dog. When he reaches the other end of the tunnel he hears footsteps behind him, and the ghost of one of the soldiers he commanded emerges from the tunnel in full uniform. Soon the rest of the dead company marches out as well, all with pale skin and hollow expressions. They seem to need something from the dreamer, and I gives them an emotional speech in which he apologizes for their deaths and expresses his sorrow at being alive. Between sobs he begs them to accept their deaths and not to wander the earth, and finally he orders them to march back into the darkness of the tunnel, which they do without a word. Consigning the dead to the past does not rid I of memory or regret, though; at the end of the dream, the snarling dog appears once again to growl and snap at him.

Forty-five years after surrender, the shadow of war still hounded Japan in personal and collective ways. Atomic bomb survivors talked about their experiences from victims' point of view, but ex-soldiers had belonged to an aggressor army and could not easily claim the moral high ground. A few veterans published memoirs, including some written in collaboration with American veterans, but for the most part they spoke of the war only to family and friends, if at all. Nor could Japanese politicians speak of veterans' sacrifices the way Americans valorized "the greatest generation," especially not in the 1990s when there was intense international pressure on Japan to atone for the war. At that time the Yasukuni Shrine in Tokyo, which is dedicated to Japan's war dead, became a flashpoint of criticism due to the addition of convicted war criminals to its official registry. China, South Korea, and other countries that Japan invaded during the war expressed outrage, and the emperor stopped his regular official visits to the shrine. Prime Minister Miyazawa Kiichi's personal visit there in 1991 remained a closely guarded secret for several years. It was also in the early 1990s that Korean women's organizations and the South Korean government began to demand that Japan apologize and make restitution for forcing thousands of Korean "comfort women" into sexual slavery during the war. It is appropriate that the soldier segment of *Dreams* focuses on unresolved guilt.[4]

Two later dreams deal with the controversial subject of nuclear power. In 1985 Kurosawa told a foreign journalist, perhaps mischievously, that his samurai epic *Ran* was about nuclear weapons. When he made *Dreams* five years later, the Cold War was all but over; the Soviet Union would dissolve in 1991. Tens of thousands of nuclear weapons still existed in the United States, Russia, and a handful of other nations, but for the moment nuclear war seemed a remote possibility. The 1986 nuclear meltdown crisis at Chernobyl, however, reminded the world that nuclear disasters could happen even without a war, and in *Dreams* Kurosawa channels his pessimism toward Japan's own nuclear power plants.

Several nuclear reactors came online in Japan during the 1960s, '70s, and '80s, and the Japanese government hoped to replace most of the nation's imported oil with nuclear power by the end of the 21st century. This goal suffered a setback in 2011 when a deadly earthquake and tsunami triggered reactor meltdowns at a plant in Fukushima prefecture. The area around the plant became depopulated as entire towns fled the leaking radiation. Public opinion, never very supportive of nuclear power, turned even more strongly against it, and all of Japan's reactors temporarily shut down. The government insisted the plants were safe and slowly brought them back online, but the danger the plants posed to Japan was now much more widely appreciated.

Twenty-one years earlier, *Dreams* eerily foreshadowed these events in a segment set on Mt. Fuji. From a distance, as from Tokyo on a clear day, Fuji looks blue. Up close, though, the dirt that covers its slopes has a red hue. Artistic depictions of Fuji in red, called *akafuji*, usually symbolize good luck, but Kurosawa turns this imagery on its head. His Fuji is bathed in red from the simultaneous explosion of half a dozen nuclear reactors. As mushroom clouds and vividly-colored radiation envelop the mountain, a throng of people race to escape, but there is no easy escape from an island nation. Everyone but the dreamer and a mother with two children leaps into the sea, choosing a quick death over slow radiation poisoning. The dream is unapologetically polemical, and with its dream logic and use of special effects it exaggerates the spectacle of nuclear meltdowns. In hindsight, though, it has an undeniable emotional resonance with the nuclear crisis of 2011 and the years of impassioned debate about nuclear power that followed.

The next dream also takes place on Mt. Fuji, this time long after the nuclear disaster. Gigantic, mutant plants now cover the mountain. Humans also survived in a fashion, but their daily existence is indistinguishable from sinners in a Buddhist hell. They groan and writhe in agony on the shores of a sickly lake like the damned souls in Akutagawa Ryūnosuke's famous short story "The Spider's Thread" (*Kumo*

Japan's 16th nuclear power plant, in Tomari, Hokkaido, came online in 1989, one year before *Dreams* (photograph by Mugu-shisai, Wikimedia Commons).

no ito, 1918). Kurosawa's nuclear mutants even grow horns out of the tops of their heads like folkloric *oni* (demons). The worst sinners, including those responsible for the nuclear meltdown, grow the most horns and experience the most pain. Fleeing this horrifying post-apocalypse, the dreamer goes tumbling down Mt. Fuji.

Bookending the Fuji dreams are two segments containing Kurosawa's thoughts on his life's work and its impending end. As an 80-year-old man he knew that he had few years left. Yet, tireless creator that he was, he felt the urgent need to say what he had to say while time remained. His dreamer stand-in studies Vincent van Gogh paintings in a museum and then enters life-sized versions of the paintings, wandering through swirls of flowers along impressionistic country lanes until he meets the one-eared master himself. Van Gogh, played by American movie director Martin Scorsese, paints frantically and explains to the dreamer that he must do as much work as he can while the sun still shines. When the dreamer asks about van Gogh's head bandage, the painter explains that he could not get the ear right in his self-portrait, so he cut it off. Kurosawa, too, was a prolific oil painter in the impressionistic mode, especially late in life when he spent months making elaborate storyboards for *Kagemusha, Ran,* and *Dreams.* Van Gogh's fanaticism, self-sacrificing perfectionism, and determination to create without rest all mirror Kurosawa's approach to moviemaking. During his last years Kurosawa worked at a faster rate than he had since the mid–1960s, and his painted storyboards ensured that nearly every frame of them burst with color.

In the final dream, I enters an idyllic village and chats about life, death, and memory with someone even older than Kurosawa: a centenarian played by 85-year-old actor Ryū Chishū. Their dialogue is heavily didactic. When the dreamer asks why the local villagers place flowers on a large stone near the river, the man replies that long ago a traveler came to the village and died on that spot. Now it is a tradition to leave flowers there even though young people don't remember why. Kurosawa based this idea on a similar tradition in his father's home village, and it echoes the second dream in which the dreamer learns about the ancient association between Girl's Day and the seasonal blossoming of peach trees. Rather than condemning forgetfulness like the peach tree spirits, the centenarian accepts all loss with grace. He speaks of a long-lost love with a smile, and he even meets death with good cheer. In his village, funerals are occasions of joyous song and dance, and one happens to be taking place that very day. Its celebrants wear colorful clothes like those that Kurosawa saw on farmers in a remote village in his youth. What makes this idyllic life possible, the old man says, is living close to nature. The dream ends, and the credits of *Dreams* play over a long, still shot of weeds under a flowing river. The plants float and dance with the current yet remain rooted to the riverbed, gentle, flexible, and eternal.[5]

For Kurosawa, the changes he witnessed during Japan's past century were antithetical to both nature and memory. Industrialization, war, and nuclear horrors altered the landscape and created deep cleavages with the past. Yet there were comforting continuities as well. The Japanese system of reckoning years still existed alongside the Western calendar and brought a fresh *jidai* in 1989, concepts from Japanese folklore continued to survive with the help of new media, and people still acknowledged the spirits and the natural world with esoteric fox shrines and local festivals.

Kurosawa had eight years left to live, and he spent them wisely. Working with remarkable speed, he completed his penultimate film just one year after *Dreams*.

CHAPTER 29

Rhapsody in August

During his last years Kurosawa often told friends and colleagues that a person only becomes free after the age of 80. He spoke of a favorite Noh actor who'd kept performing into his 80s, and he cited the example of a Meiji *jidai* painter who upon reaching 80 "suddenly started painting pictures which were much superior to the previous ones, as if he were in magnificent bloom." Kurosawa wrote a letter to Swedish director Ingmar Bergman, seven years Kurosawa's junior, saying "[I] am convinced that my real work is just beginning." In copious video from the period, as documentary filmmakers captured the elderly master at work and in moments of reflection, a picture emerges of a smiling, laughing, confident Kurosawa. With lifetime achievement awards and production money flowing to him from admirers abroad, his ability to make movies had never been so secure. He was without question the leading communicator of the Japanese condition to the world, and he had no peers in experience and acclaim.[1]

With scarcely a break after the demanding production of *Dreams*, Kurosawa made *Rhapsody in August* (*Hachigatsu no kyōshikyoku*). His subject matter was the atomic bomb, which he saw as one of the most critical topics not only in Japanese history but in human history. Yet his approach this time was fresh. For the first time since the 1940s when he made *The Most Beautiful* and *No Regrets for Our Youth*, he cast a woman as his central character. Perhaps this decision honored his late wife Yaguchi Yōko, star of *The Most Beautiful* (see Chapter 2), who died in 1985 after 40 years of marriage. Kurosawa's oversized photograph of Yōko in old age sits behind him in a 1990 documentary, and his face tightens to prevent tears when he mentions her and the movie they made nearly 50 years earlier.[2]

The aged matriarch of *Rhapsody in August* is Kane Haruno (Murase Sachiko), a survivor of the atomic bombing of Nagasaki on August 9, 1945, in which her husband, the father of her two young children, perished at the elementary school where he taught. The movie takes place in the summer of 1990 when Kane's four grandchildren come from Tokyo to stay with her while their parents visit a distant relative in Hawai'i. Kane still lives in an old-fashioned, thatched-roof house in the hills overlooking Nagasaki, and her rural lifestyle poses challenges for her urban, American-fashion-wearing grandkids. They fill their days tooling around with arcane house fixtures and complaining about Kane's plain cooking, and they are

213

easily frightened in the mountain's dark nights and dim woods. Small-town Japan is almost alien to them, as it was for many kids who grew up in sprawling Japanese cities in the 1980s and '90s.

When the kids trek to nearby Nagasaki in search of better food than grandma's, what strikes them is not the modern city on the surface, but the remnants of the destroyed city that came before it. They visit Nagasaki's enormous, rebuilt Catholic cathedral and see the marks the bomb left on its statues. They see the huge fountain at Nagasaki Peace Park with its inscription about those who died in agony in the minutes and hours after the blast. They count the memorial statues sent by nations like Portugal (which has strong historical ties to Nagasaki), Italy, Poland, China, and the Soviet Union, but they notice that there is no statue from the United States; a statue from Nagasaki's American sister city, St. Paul, Minnesota, finally arrived in 1992 a year after *Rhapsody in August* came out. Finally the children visit the site of the school where their grandfather died and see its humble memorial: a warped and melted jungle gym left *in situ* with a plaque that gives the exact time of the nuclear explosion.

Nagasaki's Urakami Cathedral, photographed here with bomb damage in 1945, was rebuilt in 1959 (photograph by U.S. Army Corps of Engineers photographer).

Seeing Nagasaki firsthand gives the kids a new respect for their grandmother the *hibakusha*. The precise legal definition of *hibakusha* ("people affected by bombs") was still evolving 45 years after the war. Through a series of laws passed in the 1950s, '70s, and '90s, hundreds of thousands of people eventually qualified for official *hibakusha* status, including people present in Hiroshima or Nagasaki at the time of the bombings, people who entered those cities in the weeks thereafter, people born to *hibakusha* soon after the bombings, and people within the radiation zone that extended for kilometers around the atomic epicenters. Kurosawa's *hibakusha* character, Kane, lived close enough to Nagasaki to see the blast from her door, and she entered Nagasaki soon thereafter to search for her husband's remains. As a result of her exposure to radiation, much of her hair fell out and never grew back. Many *hibakusha* developed physical symptoms from their exposure to the nuclear blasts, but even those who remained asymptomatic qualified for governmental assistance.

In the early 1990s there was substantial popular interest in Japan, the United States, and around the world to hear *hibakusha* tell their stories, and many of them wrote or gave talks about their experiences. Though Kane is a fictional *hibakusha*, her story captures the essence of many real first-hand accounts. She remembers the nuclear blast as a horrific "eye" in the sky, an eye that one of her brothers drew obsessively for the rest of his life. Art was a cathartic outlet for many *hibakusha*, and thousands of their untrained but haunting illustrations of the bomb's aftermath have appeared on Japanese television and in museums and books. In 1984 a gallery in Los Angeles became the first venue in the United States to host an exhibition of *hibakusha* artwork. Kane's vivid stories inspire her youngest grandchild to draw the "eye" in the sky as well. Her descendants internalize her stories and even act them out, making her a compelling example of the power of survivor testimony in preserving the memory of the bombs.[3]

Growing international dialogue about the bombs caused one previously-overlooked group of *hibakusha* to receive new attention in the early 1990s. Around 70,000 Koreans lived in Hiroshima and Nagasaki at the time of the bombs, mostly laborers whom the Japanese military conscripted in Korea and brought to Japan by force to work for low or no wages. Only about 30,000 of them survived the blasts. Some Korean *hibakusha* stayed in Japan after the war despite economic and social discrimination, but many returned to North or South Korea and received no hibakusha benefits from the Japanese government. As late as the 1970s the Japanese government encouraged Koreans

Artwork by *hibakusha* Takakura Akiko depicts a woman drinking the "black rain" that fell on Hiroshima and Nagasaki after the blasts (illustration by Takakura Akiko, Wikimedia Commons).

still living in Japan to repatriate to North Korea, where many became victims of the oppressive regime there. Korean *hibakusha* who returned to Japan illegally to seek medical treatment for their injuries and illnesses faced the possibilities of arrest and deportation. The South Korean government and Korean *hibakusha* organizations pleaded with the Japanese government for years for recognition and assistance, and in 1990 the issue was a major point of discussion during Korean President Roh Tae-woo's visit to Tokyo. Japanese Prime Minister Kaifu Toshiki pledged millions of dollars' worth of aid to surviving Korean *hibakusha*, and later in the decade Japan placed a memorial to Korean bomb victims in Hiroshima Peace Memorial Park.[4]

Rhapsody in August does not broach the subject of Korean *hibakusha*, but its story does have a strong international dimension. Kane was one of at least a dozen children, and though most of her siblings died young or lost touch over the years, one elderly brother in Hawai'i wants to reconnect with her. Kane has little or no memory of her brother Suzujirō, and she is not eager to reestablish a relationship with him. She considers him a foreigner since he moved to Hawai'i in 1920, married a white American woman, and raised an American son named Clark (Richard Gere). Kane's grandchildren initially encourage her to go to Hawai'i because they want a vacation, but after touring Nagasaki and hearing Kane's stories about the bomb, they begin to resent their American relatives for living in the country whose weapon caused so much pain. Kane's adult children, on the other hand, are very solicitous of their Hawaiian family members because Suzujirō owns a lucrative business. The Hawaiian relations have no idea that so many of their long-lost Japanese kin are *hibakusha*, and Kane's grown children wish to keep it that way to avoid causing them feelings of guilt, shame, or resentment. Nearly half a century after the end of the war the bombs remained a sensitive subject, particularly when it intersected with international relations.

Kane eventually agrees to visit her ailing brother in Hawai'i, saying that she will make the trip after her annual observance of her husband's death. The cities of Nagasaki and Hiroshima each hold ceremonies on the dates of the atomic attacks, usually with survivors, political leaders, and dignitaries from Japan and other nations in attendance. Smaller, more local observances also take place, and *Rhapsody in August* depicts one of these at the school where Kane's husband died. Kane's own annual tradition is even more private, taking place where few outsiders tread. Every August 9 she and her neighbors gather to chant Buddhist sutras at a small wooden temple— little more than an open-air shelter housing a few Buddhist statues. This kind of "private religious practice," along with prayers and offerings to family shrines in the home, is far more common in Japan than the large gatherings with formal officiants that characterize much of Western religious observance. Older women like Kane belong to the demographic most likely to engage in religious worship. When an outsider—an American, no less—comes to Kane's mountain on August 9 to attend the humble prayer ceremony, he draws curious stares from the men and the younger attendees. Meanwhile, Kane and the other elderly women maintain strict focus, chanting in unison in memory of their lost loved ones.[5]

The foreigner who comes to visit is Clark, the American nephew Kane never knew she had. When Clark received Kane's message about visiting Hawai'i after the bomb anniversary, he suddenly realized that his Japanese relatives were *hibakusha*—something his father Suzujirō never told him. He travels to Japan to spare his aunt the trip and commemorate the bomb with her. Clark is a *nisei* ("second generation"), a person born abroad to a Japanese emigrant, and he is also a *hāfu* ("half"), half Japanese and half non–Japanese. He is unmistakably an outsider in Japan with his white phenotypes and limited Japanese vocabulary, but Hawaiian-born *nisei* and *hāfu* who visit Japan sometimes receive warmer welcomes than their counterparts from elsewhere in the world. Romantic ideas about Hawai'i, its popularity as a vacation destination, and its comparatively large *nisei* population can make it easier for Japanese people to acknowledge Japanese-Hawaiians as their distant kin than *nisei* and *hāfu* from the continental United States, Brazil, and elsewhere.[6]

By coincidence, *Rhapsody in August* came to theaters at a time when more foreigners than ever were visiting rural Japan and staying for years at a time. This was due to an ambitious government initiative, the Japan Exchange and Teaching (JET) Programme, which began in 1987 and quickly became the largest teacher exchange organization in the world. Every year the program hires thousands of foreigners, most of them Americans just out of college, and places them in Japanese primary schools as assistant English teachers. The JET Programme encourages its young recruits to integrate into their host communities, particularly in rural areas whose residents have few opportunities to interact face-to-face with people from outside Japan. Cultural exchange is at least as important a goal of the JET Programme as raising Japanese students' English proficiency. Neither teaching qualifications nor Japanese language skills are required, and the program does not accept applicants who have already spent a great deal of time in Japan; the idea is to foster authentic cross-cultural communication. After spending from one to five years in the program, JET participants often return to their home countries as informal, grassroots ambassadors for Japan, furthering Japan's "soft power" overseas by touting its appeal as a travel destination, its unique food and entertainment, and the personal enrichment opportunities it presents. The character Clark has a more intimate connection to Japan than the average JET teacher, but his interactions with Kane's grandchildren and neighbors ring true for foreign viewers who have lived and worked in rural Japan.

Rhapsody in August makes Clark a bridge between cultures. Overcoming a language barrier and preconceived notions, Clark and his Japanese relatives forge close ties. The Hawaiian *nisei* sits with Kane under the stars and tells her how sorry he is for not realizing what the bomb did to his extended family so many years ago. She responds graciously, saying that she blames the war, not Americans, for what happened in Nagasaki. Clark promises to share his father's wealth with his Japanese relatives, and Kane's adult children feel ashamed that they tried to wheedle what the American freely gives. Clark is fun and casual with Kane's grandchildren, playing up his Americanness and laughing with them at his missteps in Japanese. Together these characters reunite a family, achieve some degree of closure for the lingering pains of the past, and point the way toward a more global and harmonious future. The graying of the World War II generation and the end of the Cold War did not mean the end of the complex relationship between Japan and America, but they did create an opportunity for new beginnings.

Nevertheless, the dominant theme of the film is not hope or anticipation, but loss. No sooner has Clark settled into his surroundings then he receives a telegram saying that his father has passed away. He returns to Hawai'i abruptly, leaving Kane to mourn her last sibling, whom she barely knew. After this Kane begins to lose her faculties. First she mistakes her son for one of her brothers. Then she mistakes a lightning storm for a bomb blast and frantically attempts to cover her astonished grandchildren with white sheets to protect them. The stories she tells her grandchildren earlier in the movie are full of references to local myths: a *kappa* water imp that rescued a child from drowning, a grove with charred trees that represent doomed lovers, and the urban legend that people wearing white were more likely to survive the atomic blast. In the movie's final scene Kane takes on almost mythical proportions herself by trying to run to Nagasaki in a raging typhoon. She believes it is the day of the bomb and that she must save her husband. As "Heidenröslein" by Franz Schubert plays, Kane's grandchildren chase after her, stumbling in the wind and rain while Kane charges forward unbowed. Whatever kind of world the children will inherit, whatever global relationships they will forge, whatever great or terrible events they will experience are still in the future, but their grandmother the *hibakusha* now belongs entirely to the past.

Soon, so would Kurosawa. In his final film, released just two years after *Rhapsody*, he was even more determined to depict 20th-century Japanese history through a witness's eyes.

CHAPTER 30

Mādadayo

Kurosawa made seven movies based on Western source material, from Shake-speare to pulp novels, but he adapted even more Japanese works. Eleven of his 30 movies derive from books, short stories, or plays by Japanese writers. His first foray into color film, 1970's *Dodesukaden*, was one of them, and his last movie, 1993's *Mād-adayo* ("not yet"), was another. By coincidence, these films coincided with two major events in the history of Japanese literature. *Dodesukaden* came out less than two years after the Nobel Prize committee first recognized a Japanese author for contri-butions to world literature. The honored author, Kawabata Yasunari, titled his Nobel acceptance speech "Japan, the Beautiful and Myself" (see Chapter 24). In 1994, the year after *Mādadayo*, the literature Nobel went to its second-ever Japanese recipient, Ōe Kenzaburō. Though Ōe was a generation younger than Kurosawa the two artists had a great deal in common, from living in the same neighborhood outside Tokyo to their passionate and frequent statements against nuclear weapons.[1]

Ōe's Nobel acceptance speech, "Japan, the Ambiguous, and Myself," compli-cated and updated Kawabata's message. Where Kawabata linked his work to time-honored Japanese aesthetic traditions like the seasonal poetry of medieval Zen poets, Ōe said that his books reflected the scars of 20th-century "insanity." After the ups and downs of the last 100 years, Ōe said, Japan had developed a bipolar per-sonality. It was part of Asia, but during the 20th century it largely interacted with Asia only in war or as a proxy for the United States. Japan had spent 120 years since the beginning of the Meiji *jidai* borrowing the culture and technology of the West, but its leaders also insisted on preserving "traditional culture." After the devasta-tion of World War II Japan reconnected with the world through "electrical engineer-ing and its manufacture of automobiles," but the technological horrors that visited Hiroshima and Nagasaki cast long shadows. The miracle economy of the 1950s and '60s was an answer to postwar prayers, but the century closed amid gnawing anxiet-ies about environmental decay and Japan's aging society. Ōe and his peers, human-ist and realist writers of the wartime and postwar generation, tried to heal these rifts in themselves and their nation through writing, and the literary world responded appreciatively.[2]

Kurosawa, one of cinema's great humanists, worked toward the same goal for fifty years and met with the same appreciation. He received the highest honors available to him, from international awards to the praise of his peers. At the end of his career he made one final effort to capture the awesome and terrifying Japanese Century on camera, and he turned to one of his nation's most widely-read authors to help him do it—Uchida Hyakken, who lived from 1889 to 1971. Uchida's short stories and diaries enjoyed a renaissance toward the end of the century as a new generation of readers discovered and analyzed them for what they revealed about change and constancy in modern Japan. Much of Uchida's work dated to the prewar, wartime, and early postwar periods, and its renewed popularity in the 1980s and '90s was part of a "World War II boom" in popular culture as Japan approached the 50th anniversary of the war's end.[3]

Mādadayo is based not only on Uchida's fiction and nonfiction writings, but on episodes from the author's actual life, a life that in some ways mirrored Kurosawa's own. Yet in Kurosawa's hands *Mādadayo* becomes neither a biopic nor a semi-externalized autobiographical film like 1990's *Dreams*, but a record of a generation. Its lead character lives through the war, experiences defeat and occupation, and witnesses the birth of a new kind of Japan that he sometimes struggles to understand. The film is a tribute to a specific and well-known literary figure, but also to everyone who experienced and contributed to Japan's 20th century, each of them doing their parts in good times and bad, for better and worse, without knowing what the outcome of their efforts would be.

The movie begins with an ending as Uchida (Matsumura Tatsuo) leaves his post as a German language teacher during World War II. Before postwar Americanization, and even before the wartime alliance between militarist Japan and Nazi Germany, many in Japan looked to Germany as an exemplar of high culture and modern know-how. Bureaucrats admired German military organization and the German educational system, while intellectuals like Uchida were drawn to the aesthetics of German Romanticism and the German idealization of *Kultur* (culture) that flourished between the wars. In the Taishō and early Shōwa *jidai* Japanese writers like Uchida, his mentor Sōseki Natsume, and humanist authors from the so-called White Birch movement were almost fanatical in their pursuit of "culture," "art," and "spirit," which they valued more highly than politics and other "practical" concerns. Later commentators, looking back from the other side of the war, sometimes accused men like Uchida of retreating into private worlds of soul-searching fiction rather than using their talent and influence to resist Japan's descent into ultranationalism. During the war writers who engaged with politics usually did so only in support of the military regime, for example by joining the government-sponsored Japanese Literature Patriotic Association. Most authors could not get their works published unless they belonged to this body of "writers of the empire." Uchida was one of the few who could; he did not join the militarists, but neither did he openly condemn them. His wartime writings like *Tokyo Diary* (1938) convey nostalgia for the prewar years, especially the progressive, internationalist culture of the Taishō *jidai* (see Chapter 2), and in his praise for the past it is possible to infer criticism of the present.[4]

Uchida's retirement from teaching was not the end of his contribution to Japanese intellectual life, nor was it the end of his relationship with his students. Uchida's role as teacher continued in a fashion thanks to the tradition of esteemed writers hosting informal schools in their homes. Traditionally, a revered master's *monkasei*, his disciples, take on the burden of housing their *sensei* in exchange for perpetual, personalized instruction and discussion. The 17th-century wandering poet Matsuo Bashō typified this practice. Bashō's followers, young authors who learned the art of *haiku* from him, built or purchased houses for their *sensei* in the various places where he resided, and at these houses the circle of poets gathered to hone their craft. This tradition survived into the 20th century. In the 1900s and 1910s, Uchida and other aspiring writers met weekly at Sōseki's house in Tokyo to discuss Sōseki's philosophies and techniques and test their own ideas. When Uchida became a full-time writer decades later, the cycle continued. In the first act of *Mādadayo* Uchida's students help him move into a new home, and he posts a sign on the door announcing his scheduled "visiting days." Twice a month Uchida's *monkasei*, including some of his closest former classroom students, gather to learn, chat, or simply think. *Monkasei* can be translated as "pupils below the gate," and in Uchida's first retirement house this meaning is literal. He jokingly tells his amused disciples that he wants his writing desk near the entrance so that he can guard the property "against you riffraff."[5]

At first, Uchida, his *monkasei*, and his wife (Kagawa Kyōko) live in a world of genteel isolation, conspicuously unaffected by the war that is destroying Japan. On the occasion of Uchida's 60th birthday his students come to drink and dine with him. The horse meat that Uchida purchases for the event is not ersatz food or a last resort during straitened times; horse is an accepted part of the Japanese diet, and restaurants serve it both raw and cooked. While eating, Uchida tells his *monkasei* an amusing story, which Kurosawa presents in flashback, about a horse that a soldier led past the butcher shop where he bought the meat. In the movie's spoken dialogue, though, Uchida describes only the horse and omits the soldier's existence. When Uchida remarks over dinner that he hates air raids, it isn't because of the destruction American bombs cause, but because he dislikes having to turn out the lights in his house. To the best of his ability he pretends that the war itself doesn't exist. The life of the mind that Uchida and his followers cultivate is a pleasant and serene one, full of books and *bon mots* and pleasant evenings over food and drink, seemingly a world away from the barbarism of politics and war.

The cozy retirement house inevitably falls victim to one of the air raids, and Uchida and his wife relocate to a one-room shack. The old man rescues just one of his books, *An Account of My Hut* by a 13th-century Buddhist monk, and it brings him comfort in his deprivation. So do visits from his *monkasei*, who promise to build him a new home as soon as they can. The real Uchida spent three years in the hut, which was just three *tatami* mats wide, and he eventually published a diary titled *A New Account of My Hut* in reference to the well-known classic.

Even when dealing with periods as unhappy as the war and occupation, the dominant mood of *Mādadayo* is nostalgia. The scenes that take place at Uchida's shack have an elemental beauty that stands in juxtaposition to the rudeness of the dwelling. Kurosawa creates a picturesque seasonal montage at the location, surrounding it with autumn leaves, new-fallen snow, and plum and cherry blossoms. When the hut's sliding doors are open the moon shines in brightly, and Uchida and his wife and *monkasei* enjoy *tsukimi*, moon viewing. Moon-viewing is the subject of many Japanese poems and songs, and even great lords used to do it in small tea houses and rustic huts not so different from Uchida's shack.

Uchida and his disciples frequently commune over alcohol, a cherished social lubricant in Japan. As the scion of a *sake*-brewing family in a heavy-drinking culture, Uchida was no stranger to beer and spirits. In *Mādadayo* his former students remember drinking with him while he was still their teacher, and after the war they create an annual *nomikai* in his honor. *Nomikai*, or "drinking parties," are among Japan's most cherished cultural institutions, and they serve several important social functions. They are more-or-less required parties through which colleagues bond over abundant amounts of food and drink in rented event spaces or private sections of beer halls and restaurants. The dress code is often rather formal, particularly for office workers, and *Mādadayo*'s *nomikai* attendees wear coats and ties. Subordinates and superiors who normally interact on unequal terms can communicate on a more relaxed basis at *nomikai* where alcohol breaks down inhibitions. The parties provide space for people to be franker and more demonstrative than ordinary social rules allow. Shouting, singing, showing off personal talents like mimicry, and of course getting drunk are not merely tolerated at *nomikai*, they are the events' overt goals. Ordinary relationships between participants grow stronger because of the release that *nomikai* provide.

The name of the *nomikai* in *Mādadayo* is a pun that reflects the event's dual nature as formality and fun. It is the "Māda Fest," and each of the letters in the name refer to a Buddhist deity, but it also sounds like the refrain in a children's hide-and-seek game meaning "not yet." The wordplay combines the sacred and the simplistic, the cerebral and the childish. This combination suits the atmosphere of the *nomikai*, which is an organized and calculated way to achieve a spirit of joyous camaraderie, and it also suits Uchida's personality, which is both dignified and at times quite childlike. The *nomikai* slogan is also an irreverent reference to Uchida's mortality; every year it celebrates that he is "not yet" dead, and Uchida takes great pleasure in proving the fact by out-performing his students in feats of drinking and revelry.

The inaugural Māda Fest, which takes place early in the American occupation, is not only an opportunity for Uchida and his *monkasei* to enjoy each other's company, but a chance for Kurosawa to speak more frankly about Japan's midcentury experience than ever before. The doctor in *Drunken Angel* and the detectives in *Stray Dog* spoke about hard times in a general sense, but they could not explicitly refer to the American management of Japan or the relationship between political leadership and the state of the nation's health and economy. As a result, early postwar cinema is an incomplete record of the beginning of the special relationship between Japan and the United States. The movies that Kurosawa and his peers made then were products of an environment that they could not fully describe. In *Mādadayo*, Kurosawa's last opportunity to make up for his medium's deficiencies on the topic, he devotes several minutes to a full-throated condemnation of the American occupation. As the *monkasei* march around their rented beer hall venue, Uchida leads them in an improvised song accusing the Americans of prattling about democracy while allowing cor-

People viewing the moon from a field of pampas grass, a nostalgic and quintessentially Japanese scene by Ishikawa Toyomasa, c. 1767.

ruption, crime, inequality, and disease to fester. Uchida's students laugh loudly and knowingly at their *sensei*'s seditious song, and even a normally stone-faced Buddhist priest joins in with the song lampooning American *warui yatsu* ("bad guys"). At one point American MPs burst into the room to check on the noise, causing some beer hall patrons to shrink in fear, but the soldiers conclude that the party is harmless and move on without investigating more deeply. Uchida, who a few years earlier got away with criticizing Japan's military regime in subtle literary works, now gets away with flagrant criticism of the American occupation under the guise of an old man's drinking party. Through him Kurosawa belatedly has his say as well. The occupation's progressive achievements like land reform (see Chapter 5) and the constitutional ban on war (see Chapter 11) remained broadly popular at the end of the 20th century, but the memory of early postwar hunger, disease, and suffering remained strong as well.

At a later Māda Fest in the 1960s, Uchida's students change the satirical song to target the scandal-ridden Japanese governments of the economic miracle years. Laughing as giddily as before, the celebrants threaten to march into the streets singing about bribery and corruption at the top of their lungs; Kurosawa had made the same critiques in the middle of his career (see Chapter 19). Meanwhile, the grandchildren of some of the aging *monkasei* sing "Happy Birthday" to Uchida in English, much to the *sensei*'s delight. He has, it seems, made peace with the Japan-U.S. relationship that survived the low points of war and occupation.

Uchida's most popular contribution to Japanese literature is not his comparatively political work like *Tokyo Burning* or *Hyakkien's Postwar Diary* ("Hyakkien" was one of Uchida's pen names), but his amusing and heartfelt pieces about something both simpler and more enigmatic: the common housecat. Stories about cats captivated Japanese audiences well before the internet and its cat memes became global trend-setters. Uchida's mentor Sōseki wrote the classic novel *I Am a Cat* toward the end of the Meiji *jidai*, and children still commonly read the feline-narrated satire in school. In the 1930s, *The Cat, Shōzō, and Two Women* was a popular comedic novel by acclaimed writer Tanizaki Junnichirō. The 1950s and '60s saw the release of at least a dozen cat-themed Japanese horror movies, the most

Kurosawa Akira (from *Eiga no Tomo*, December 1953).

famous of which, 1968's *Kuroneko*, won multiple domestic film awards. The 1980s had its own cat-themed literary phenomenon, *Tama ya* by Kanai Mieko, whose title was a reference to Uchida's 1957 cat book *Nora ya* ("Oh Nora"). *Nora ya* is about Uchida's search for his missing cat Nora, whose name means "Stray." The book includes reproductions of the reward signs that Uchida posted around town during his ultimately unsuccessful search.[6]

Kurosawa's depiction of Uchida's love for Nora and his nearly obsessive quest to find the cat captures the sentimental flavor of the story, but it also has a larger meaning. In a philosophical sense, the loss of the cat speaks to the inevitability of change and sorrow in the world, a core tenet of Japanese Buddhism and an inspiration for much Japanese art. The saga of Nora places this concept in the specific context of the postwar period. Nora goes missing around the time that Uchida's *monkasei* attempt to prevent development on a lot near their *sensei*'s new home. A greedy builder wants to erect a three-story structure that will block the sunlight from Uchida's garden, recalling the notion of "sunshine rights" that emerged amid 1960s urbanization (see Chapter 25). The students buy the lot to try to keep it as it is: an island of stasis in a fast-changing metropolis. Holding back change, though, is like trying to keep a stray cat at home. Uchida loves Nora like he loved old Tokyo and old Japan, but all his love cannot bring back what is gone. His wife and students search the city's busy shops, crisscross its crowded streets, visit its schools and talk with children, and pound the pavement as midcentury music wafts from windows. Though they never find the cat, Uchida compares the friends and strangers who help him search for it to Daikokuten, a god of wealth. As Japan rebuilds itself—a painful process as well as an enriching one—its people help each other heal as well.

What's past is past, but life goes on, and a new cat soon enters Uchida's garden. It is different, but it is here, and he and his wife give it a loving home. People who lived through the Meiji, Taishō, Shōwa, and Heisei *jidai* understood change as well as anyone in Japanese history or world history, and it is that intimate familiarity with loss and renewal that gives Uchida's cat story and Kurosawa's film their power.

The movie's final scene takes place near the end of Uchida's life. A gorgeous sunset fills the frame as the old man remembers an idyllic scene from his childhood. "*Mādadayo*"—not yet—says a boy as he gazes into the flaming sky that changes from pink and yellow to blue and green, and finally to gold.

Just off camera, Kurosawa sat motionless while the final scene of his career played out in front of him. After a period of silence he announced "cut," then stood and walked away.

Epilogue

Kurosawa Akira died in 1998 at the age of 88. Shimura Takashi (21 movies) and Mifune Toshirō (16 movies), the stars who accompanied him for most of his cinematic journey, died in 1982 and 1997, respectively. If these artists and hundreds of other collaborators are immortalized in the movies they made together, so too is the Japan that they knew.

TIME, the American magazine that declared the 20th century "The American Century" before it was half over, ran a "Person of the Century" issue in 1999. Among the finalists were seven Asians and one Japanese man: Morita Akio, founder of tech giant Sony. The news channel CNN, *TIME*'s younger cousin in the TIME-Warner media empire, refined the formula to name several "Asians of the Century": people from the world's largest and most populous continent who "saw the way forward a little more clearly than others" and "who found better paths … to help us on our way." In the category of Arts, Literature, and Culture, CNN named Kurosawa the top Asian of the last hundred years. "He remains Asia's greatest exponent of what has been the major art form of the century," the global outlet proclaimed. This list making was at once a grandiose and trivial exercise, but it showed that even the sometimes-parochial American media could not let the century mark pass without considering the ways Asia and Japan had reshaped the world's economy and culture.[1]

Pondering Japan's outsized influence on cinema, British critic John Gillett once asked Kurosawa how it was that Japan produced so many great films and filmmakers during the 20th century. Kurosawa marveled at it as well; near the end of his life the director undertook his own "best of" list, a list of the 100 greatest films of all time, and nearly a fifth of them were Japanese (none of them his own). "It was really good times when Mr. Ozu, Mr. Naruse, and Mr. Mizoguchi were all making movies," Kurosawa reflected. The explanation Kurosawa gave Gillett emphasized conditions in Japanese movie studios that allowed great directors to flourish, but there was a deeper reason why auteurs like Kurosawa emerged when and where they did and found so many powerful stories to tell. Simply put, Japan's intense experiences with modernization, destruction, rebirth, and reinvention provided storytellers with both the tools and the inspiration to create monumental works of art one after another.[2]

Japan's centrality to 20th-century global culture could scarcely have been guessed in the Meiji *jidai*, when the country's leaders set a goal of catching up to the Western world in terms of civil society, economic power, and technology. *Sanshirō Sugata* (1943) and *Sanshirō Sugata Part II* (1945), Kurosawa's purest *Bildungsromane*, are about the making of a man, but they are set during the making of a nation. Their Meiji trappings recall the era when Japan first began to conceive of itself as an international state, and their wartime themes are reminders of the nation's intemperate ambition.

The comparatively brief Taishō *jidai* felt like a Meiji coda until the horrors of depression, war, and occupation made people nostalgic for its stylish "New Women," its department store indulgences, and its liberal democracy that proved all too fragile. The hardworking women of *The Most Beautiful* (1944) are too young to remember how their Taishō forebears entered the workforce in large numbers and pushed for greater social equality, but the protagonists of *No Regrets for Our Youth* (1946) know exactly what they lost when fascism targeted the freedoms of Japanese universities and tragically redirected the course of young lives in the post–Taishō backlash.

What Japan gained during the first fifty years of the century seemed to be lost, perhaps forever, with the end of the war and the beginning of the American occupation. The pretensions of global power that led Japan to war in the early Shōwa *jidai* now took a backseat to mere survival. American authorities tried to bury Japan's distant and recent past alike, a policy illustrated in a small way by their decision to ban Kurosawa's film *The Men Who Tread on the Tiger's Tail* (1945). Although censorship restricted their content, movies like *One Wonderful Sunday* (1947), *Drunken Angel* (1948), *The Quiet Duel* (1949), *Stray Dog* (1949), and *Scandal* (1950) created a potent record of the grim postwar years.

Japan emerged from the seven-year occupation uncertain about what the future would bring. Its new, close relationship with the United States offered opportunities, like the Korean War which stimulated Japan's economy, and risks, like the presence of dangerous American weapons on Japanese soil. It remained to be seen whether Japan's post-occupation leaders would distribute the benefits of recovery broadly through society, or whether political and corporate corruption would make it a recovery only for the few. After American media censorship lifted, *Rashōmon* (1950) insisted on the inevitability of doubt, an ex-soldier tried and failed to adjust to postwar life in *The Idiot* (1951), and a bureaucrat found redemption by working for the good of the people in *Ikiru* (1952).

Japan's post-occupation recovery was, in the end, more than a recovery; it was a miracle. To be sure, there were intractable problems. Anxiety about nuclear weapons and Japan's position in the Cold War only intensified, as reflected directly in *Record of Living Things* (1955) and indirectly in *Yōjimbō* (1961). Corruption proved a recurring feature of Japanese politics, as dramatized in *The Bad Sleep Well* (1960). And nobody knew just how long the miracle would last, as Kurosawa subtly reminded audiences with *The Lower Depths* (1957). Yet the period of rapid economic growth—an astonishingly high rate of growth from the mid–1950s to the early 1970s, and more modest growth for years after that—proved utterly transformative for Japan. People's quality of life soared, crime plummeted, technological advances came rapidly and spread widely, Japan exported high-quality products that changed lifestyles globally, and the nation wowed the world with the 1964 Tokyo Olympics, a symbol of everything Japan had accomplished in less than a generation since war and defeat. Films like *Seven Samurai* (1954), *Spiderweb Castle* (1957), *The Hidden Fortress* (1958), *Tsubaki Sanjūrō* (1962), *Heaven and Hell* (1963), and *Redbeard* (1965) engaged with many aspects of the period, good, bad, and neutral, but beyond their content they are entertaining showcases of a culture flush with confidence. Their high production values, rich narratives, and powerful characterizations made them instant classics of world cinema.

Change did not stop when the miracle ran its course, but the end of high-speed growth prompted soul-searching. Japan had won the world's attention, respect, and even envy, but it faced new challenges from without and within. The aging of Japan's population, growing awareness about environmental degradation, lingering controversies about the war, an apparent rise in mental illness, and other societal challenges raised concerns. The Cold War waned, old alliances frayed, and Japan's leaders prepared for a more multilateral and globalized era to come. Japan's artists, like its two Nobel literature laureates, rethought what it meant to be Japanese. Kurosawa's films in this period became increasingly introspective, but they also grew grander and more experimental. To make *Dodesukaden* (1970), *Dersu Uzala* (1975), *Kagemusha* (1980), and *Ran* (1985) he had to find new sources of support, often from foreign admirers.

The long Shōwa *jidai* ended 1989 and the Heisei *jidai* began with a painful economic recession, but Japan's global cultural influence continued unabated. Creators connected with international audiences in new ways through *anime* and video games, and the Japanese government pursued a policy of "pop-culture diplomacy" (*poppu karucharu gaikō*) to maintain and strengthen its positive image abroad—an image that came into focus in large part because of Kurosawa. Using films, TV, and games, as well as "traditional culture, language education, intellectual exchange and people-to-people exchange programs," Japan positioned itself as a cultural powerhouse and leading international travel destination. Active until the end, Kurosawa looked back in wonder at a century of foibles, failures, resiliency, and adaptability with *Dreams* (1990), *Rhapsody in August* (1991), and *Mādadayo* (1993).[3]

Kurosawa's legacy lives on in the 21st century. Contemporary filmmakers Alejandro González Iñárritu, Bong Joon Ho, Julie Taymor, and many others have expressed debts to him. In 2018, Steven Spielberg used a digital avatar of Mifune, clad in armor like his *Hidden Fortress* character, as a major character in his tech-heavy adventure film *Ready Player One*. Retrospective screenings of Kurosawa's movies attract enthusiastic crowds, and online fan groups dedicated to the director boast hundreds of thousands of followers, many of whom were not yet born when

Kurosawa made his final film. The Tōhō movie studio, which frequently tussled with Kurosawa over budgets and schedules, commissioned a large *Seven Samurai* mural that now towers over its front entrance.[4]

By the dawn of the Reiwa *jidai* (2019–?), large Chinese companies regularly surpassed Japanese ones in global revenue. Korean exports, including high-profile movies and wildly popular music, made rapid inroads overseas in the early decades of the new millennium. Japan's neighbors will help define the 21st century. When we remember the highs and lows of the 20th century, though, we remember Japan's profound experiences and enduring contributions, of which Kurosawa was both a chronicler and a creator.

Chapter Notes

Introduction

1. Henry R. Luce, "The American Century," *Time*, February 17, 1941, 61–65.
2. Bert Cardullo, ed., *Akira Kurosawa Interviews*. (Jackson: University Press of Mississippi, 2008), 175.

Chapter 1

1. *Akira Kurosawa: My Life in Cinema*, directed by Sato Shizuo, DVD (1993; New York: The Criterion Collection, 2006).
2. Stephen Prince, "A Career Blooms," *Sanshiro Sugata* DVD liner notes (New York: The Criterion Collection, 2010).
3. John Dower, *Embracing Defeat: Japan in the Wake of World War II* (New York: W.W. Norton & Co./New Press, 2000), 150.
4. Patrick Galvan, "Sanshiro Sugata: The Deleted Scenes," Toho Kingdom, https://www.toho kingdom.com/blog/sanshiro-sugata-the-deleted-scenes/, accessed May 10, 2021.
5. Scott Allen Nollen, *Takashi Shimura: Chameleon of Japanese Cinema* (Jefferson, N.C.: McFarland & Company, 2019), 18.

Chapter 2

1. Joyce Capman Lebra, "Women in an All-Male Industry: The Case of *Sake* Brewer Tatsu'uma Kiyo," in *Recreating Japanese Women, 1600–1945*, ed. Gail Lee Bernstein (Berkeley: University of California Press, 1991), 131–48; Sharon H. Nolte and Sally Ann Hastings, "The Meiji State's Policy Toward Women, 1890–1910," in *Recreating Japanese Women, 1600–1945*, ed. Gail Lee Bernstein (Berkeley: University of California Press, 1991), 151–74.
2. Mark Metzler, "Woman's Place in Japan's Great Depression: Reflections on the Moral Economy of Deflation," *Journal of Japanese Studies* 30, no. 2 (2004): 322; Laura Rasplica Rodd, "Yosano Akiko and the Taishō Debate over the 'New Woman,'" in *Recreating Japanese Women, 1600–1945*, ed. Gail Lee Bernstein (Berkeley: University of California Press, 1991), 175–198; Margit Nagy,

"Middle-Class Working Women During the Interwar Years," in *Recreating Japanese Women, 1600–1945*, ed. Gail Lee Bernstein (Berkeley: University of California Press, 1991), 199–216.
3. Yoshiko Miyake, "Doubling Expectations: Motherhood and Women's Factory Work Under State Management in Japan in the 1930s and 1940s," in *Recreating Japanese Women, 1600–1945*, ed. Gail Lee Bernstein (Berkeley: University of California Press, 1991), 267–295.
4. Cardullo, 91.
5. Gary R. Saxonhouse, "Country Girls and Communication Among Competitors in the Japanese Cotton-Spinning Industry," in *The Pacific in the Age of Early Industrialization*, ed. Kenneth Pomeranz (London: Routledge, 2009), 41–69.
6. Stuart Galbraith, *The Emperor and the Wolf: The Lives and Films of Akira Kurosawa and Toshiro Mifune* (New York: Faber and Faber, 2003), 35; Stephen Prince, "Doing His Part," *The Most Beautiful* DVD liner notes (New York: The Criterion Collection, 2010); Cardullo, 91.

Chapter 3

1. Mitsuhiro Yoshimoto, *Kurosawa: Film Studies and Japanese Cinema* (Durham: Duke University Press, 2000), 93.
2. Akira Kurosawa, *Something Like an Autobiography*, trans. Audie E. Bock (New York: Vintage Books, 1983), 136–37; Scott McGee, "Sanshiro Sugata Part 2," TCM, accessed October 26, 2020, https://www.tcm.com/tcmdb/title/491264/sanshiro-sugata-part-2#articles-reviews?articleId=290058.

Chapter 4

1. Sato, *My Life in Cinema*.
2. *Nippon Sengoshi—Madamu Onboro no seikatsu* にっぽん戦後史―マダムおんぼろの生活 [*History of Postwar Japan as Told by a Bar Hostess*], directed by Imamura Shōhei 今村 昌平, 1970; Dower, 104–5.
3. James Hornfischer, *The Fleet at Flood Tide: America at Total War in the Pacific, 1944–1945* (New York: Random House, 2016), 471–72; Imamura.

231

4. Galbraith, 61.

5. Kyoko Hirano, *Mr. Smith Goes to Tokyo: The Japanese Cinema Under the American Occupation* (Washington: Smithsonian Institution Press, 1992), 44.

6. Eiji Takemae, *Inside GHQ: The Allied Occupation of Japan and its Legacy*, trans. Robert Ricketts and Sebastian Swann (London: Continuum, 2002), 390–91; Kurosawa, *Something Like an Autobiography*, 143–44; Sato, *My Life in Cinema*.

7. Junko Miyawaki-Okada, "The Japanese Origins of the Chinggis Khan Legends," *Inner Asia* 8, no. 1 (2006), 123–134.

Chapter 5

1. Dower, 190–95.

2. Susan Townsend, *Yanaihara Tadao and Japanese Colonial Policy* (East Sussex: Psychology Press, 2000), 231.

3. Ōgai Tokuko, "The Stars of Democracy: The First Thirty-Nine Female Members of the Japanese Diet," English Supplement, U.S.-Japan Women's Journal 11 (1996), 81–117.

4. David Conrad, "'The Greatest Good for the Greatest Number': American Land Redistribution in East and Southeast Asia, 1945–1969," (PhD diss., The University of Texas at Austin, 2016), 8.

Chapter 6

1. Dower, 90–97.

2. Dower, 99–101.

3. Dower, 47–8, 61–3, 101.

4. Takemae, 126.

5. Joseph L. Anderson and Donald Richie, *The Japanese Film: Art and Industry* (Rutland: C.E. Tuttle Co., 1959), 224–25.

6. Dower, 112, 115.

7. "Japan's Citizen Kane," *Economist* (London), Dec. 22, 2012; Takemae, 397.

8. Dower, 153–54.

9. Hornfischer, 296.

10. Takemae, 398, Dower, 149–51.

11. Kurosawa, *Something Like an Autobiography*, 153; Dower, 61–3.

Chapter 7

1. Galbraith, 20–22, 67–69; Kurosawa, *Something Like an Autobiography*, 160.

2. Nollen, 11–12.

3. *Kurosawa and the Censors*, DVD (2007; New York: The Criterion Collection, 2007).

4. Dower, 103–4, 131.

5. *Kurosawa and the Censors*.

Chapter 8

1. Dower, 65.

2. Joint Chiefs of Staff, *Basic Initial Post-Surrender Directive*; Dower, 79, 532–33.

3. Hirano, 205–6; Dower, 269.

4. Hirano, 226.

5. Barbara Jelonek, "Rethinking Gender, Rethinking Migration: Statistical trends and law regulations of Japanese marriage," *Miscellanea Anthropologica et Sociologica* 17, no. 3 (2016): 103–9; Dower, 105–7.

6. Newsreel, *The Quiet Duel*, DVD (1949; Newbury Park, CA: BCI Eclipse Company, 2006).

7. Kurosawa, *Something Like an Autobiography*, 158–59.

Chapter 9

1. Mark Metzler, *Capital as Will and Imagination: Schumpeter's Guide to the Postwar Japanese Miracle* (Ithaca: Cornell University Press, 2013), 19, 10, 122–24, 128, 134.

2. Chalmers Johnson, *MITI and the Japanese Miracle: The Growth of Industrial Policy, 1925–1975* (Stanford: Stanford University Press, 1982), 192; Dower, 154.

3. Harry Emerson Wildes, "The Postwar Japanese Police," *Journal of Criminal Law, Criminology & Police Science* 43, no. 5 (1953): 655.

4. Dower, 143–44.

5. Wildes, 660.

6. Dennis Snelling, *Lefty O'Doul: Baseball's Forgotten Ambassador* (Lincoln: University of Nebraska Press, 2017), 87.

7. W. Macmahon Ball, *Japan: Enemy or Ally?* (New York: The John Day Company, 1949), 94–95; Dower, 51–54.

8. *Kurosawa and the Censors*.

9. Kurosawa, *Something Like an Autobiography*, 173–74.

Chapter 10

1. Michael Schaller, *The American Occupation of Japan: The Origins of the Cold War in Asia* (New York: Oxford University Press, 1985), 33–38; Takemae, 76–77, 164–65; Dower, 117–19.

2. Takemae 387, 392, Dower, 432–33.

3. Takemae, 242–43.

4. Eri Hotta, *Pan-Asianism and Japan's War, 1931–1945* (New York: Palgrave Macmillan, 2007), 131–32.

5. Dower, 148–58.

6. Dower, 149.

7. Junko Kimura and Russell Belk, "Christmas in Japan: Globalization Versus Localization," *Consumption Markets & Culture* 8, no. 3 (2005): 325–38.

8. Dower, 533–34.

9. Donald Richie, *The Films of Akira Kurosawa*, rev. ed. with additional material by Joan Mellen (Berkeley: University of California Press, 1984), 65.

10. Takemae, 485.

Chapter 11

1. Takemae, 126, 487.
2. Takemae, 286, 289–91.
3. Takemae, 489–93.
4. Takemae, 485–86.
5. Hirano 245–48; Takemae 391–92.
6. Hornfischer, 406–9; Dower, 124, 130–31, 211; Takemae, 67–71.
7. William Fairchild, "Shamanism in Japan," *Folklore Studies* 21 (1962): 1–122.
8. Ronald Dore, *Shinohata: A Portrait of a Japanese Village* (New York: Pantheon Books, 1978), 257, 260–65; Jolyon Baraka Thomas, *Faking Liberties: Religious Freedom in American-Occupied Japan* (Chicago: The University of Chicago Press, 2019), 17, 45-46.

Chapter 12

1. Dower, 61.
2. Sandra Wilson, "War, Soldier and Nation in 1950s Japan," *International Journal of Asian Studies* 5, no. 2 (2008): 196–200.
3. R.P. Dore, *Land Reform in Japan*, rev. ed. (New York, Schocken Books, 1985), 7.
4. Dower, 447–54, 508–21.
5. Ayumi Ishijima, "The Discourse of Mistress in Modern Japan," 이화여자대학교 아시아여성학센터 학술대회자료집 [Ewha Womans University Asian Women's Studies Center Academic Conference Materials] (2006): 79–83.

Chapter 13

1. Takemae, 301–3.
2. Takemae, xlii, 159, 332.
3. Dower, 549–51.
4. Pico Iyer, "*Ikiru* Many Autumns Later," *Ikiru* DVD insert (New York: The Criterion Collection, 2015).
5. Takemae, 423–25.
6. Emiko Takagi, Merril Silverstein, and Eileen Crimmins, "Intergenerational Coresidence of Older Adults in Japan: Conditions for Cultural Plasticity," *The Journals of Gerontology: Series B* 62, no. 5 (Sep. 2007): S330-S339.
7. Noriyuki Takayama, "The Japanese Pension System: How It Was and What It Will Be," Paper presented at *International Conference on Pensions in Asia: Incentives, Compliance and Their Role in Retirement, Tokyo, Hitotsubashi Collaboration Center, Hitotsubashi University, Feb. 2004* (Tokyo: Institute of Economic Research, Hitotsubashi University), https://hdl.handle.net/10086/14318.
8. Eric C. Sedensky, "Pachinko Passion," *Japan Quarterly* 39, no. 4 (Oct. 1992): 457; "1949 Dainippon Beer is split up," Sapporo Beer, accessed October 14, 2020, https://www.sapporobeer.jp/english/company/history/1949.html.

Chapter 14

1. Dore, *Shinohata*, 3.
2. Dore, *Shinohata*, xix–xxi.
3. Dore, *Shinohata*, 209–13; Dower, 94–95, 146.
4. Dore, *Shinohata*, 307–8.
5. Takemae, 461.
6. Kenji Hasegawa, *Student Radicalism and the Formation of Postwar Japan* (Singapore: Palgrave Macmillan, 2019), 2–10; "Bloody May Day (May 1, 1952)," Cross Currents, accessed May 26, 2021, http://www.crosscurrents.hawaii.edu/content.aspx?lang=eng&site=japan&theme=work&subtheme=UNION&unit=JWORK007.

Chapter 15

1. Nobumasa Akiyama, "Disarmament and the non-proliferation policy of Japan," in *Routledge Handbook of Japanese Foreign Policy*, ed. Mary M. McCarthy (London: Routledge, 2018), 176.
2. Sato, *My Life in Cinema*.
3. Akira Kurosaki, "Japanese Scientists' Critique of Nuclear Deterrence Theory and Its Influence on Pugwash, 1954–1964," *Journal of Cold War Studies* 20, no. 1 (2018): 101–2.
4. Jacques Hymans, "Veto Players, Nuclear Energy, and Nonproliferation: Domestic Institutional Barriers to a Japanese Bomb," *International Security* 36, no. 2 (2011): 162–63, 187–189.
5. Ernani Oda, "Family narratives and transforming identities: three generation of Japanese Brazilians living between Brazil, Japan and beyond," *Social Identities* 16, no. 6 (2010): 776.
6. Colin P.A. Jones, "Japan's discriminatory koseki registry system looks ever more outdated," *Japan Times* (Tokyo), Jul. 10, 2016.
7. Kuniko Fujita and Richard Child Hill, *Japanese Cities in the World Economy* (Philadelphia: Temple University Press, 1993), 191–92.
8. Sato, *My Life in Cinema*.

Chapter 16

1. Osamu Ito, "The International Environment and Domestic Structure of Postwar Japan's Rapid Growth," in *Japanese Economy and Society Under Pax-Americana*, eds. Hiroshi Shibuya, Makoto Maruyama, and Masamitsu Yasaka (Tokyo: University of Tokyo Press, 2002),76–77.
2. Ito, 80, 83, 93.
3. Masamitsu Yasaka, "American Impacts on Agriculture and Foods," in *Japanese Economy and Society Under Pax-Americana*, eds. Hiroshi Shibuya, Makoto Maruyama, and Masamitsu Yasaka (Tokyo: University of Tokyo Press, 2002), 340–41.
4. *Akira Kurosawa: It Is Wonderful to Create*, "Throne of Blood," directed by Nogami Teruyo, 2002, Blu-ray (New York: The Criterion Collection, 2014).
5. Stephen Prince, *The Warrior's Camera: The Cinema of Akira Kurosawa* (Princeton: Princeton

University Press, 1991), 147–48; Helen Westgeest, *Zen in the Fifties: Interaction in Art Between East and West* (Zwolle: Waanders Publishers, 1997), 43–72.

6. Cardullo, 65.

7. Michael Dylan Foster, *Pandemonium and Parade: Japanese Monsters and the Culture of Yōkai* (Berkeley: University of California Press, 2008), 162–64.

8. Johnson, 36, 45, 49–50.

9. Kunio Fukumoto 福本邦雄, *Kanryō* 官僚 [Bureacrats] (Tokyo: Kobundo, 1959), 157–59; Johnson, 51, 56–57, 68–69.

10. Kanji Haitani, *The Japanese Economic System: An Institutional Overview* (Washington, D.C.: Lexington Books, 1977), 181.

Chapter 17

1. Mark Metzler, "Capitalist Boom, Feudal Bust: Long Waves in Economics and Politics in Pre-Industrial Japan," *Review* 17, no. 1 (Winter 1994), 61–62.

2. Metzler, "Capitalist Boom," 76–78, 92; Johnson, 190–91.

3. Dore, *Shinohata*, 11, 282–83.

4. Dore, *Shinohata*, 311; Johnson, 239.

5. Dore, *Shinohata*, 259–61.

Chapter 18

1. Cherie Wendelken, "Aesthetics and Reconstruction: Japanese Architectural Culture in the 1950s," in *Rebuilding Urban Japan After 1945*, eds. Carola Hein, Jeffry M. Diefendorf, and Ishida Yorifusa (Hampshire: Palgrave Macmillan, 2003), 189–90, 201.

2. Asanobu Kitamoto, "Digital Typhoon: Typhoon Damage List," accessed October 15, 2020, http://agora.ex.nii.ac.jp/cgi-bin/dt/disaster.pl?lang=en&basin=wnp&sort=dead_or_missing&order=dec &stype=number.

3. Mark Metzler, *Lever of Empire: The International Gold Standard and the Crisis of Liberalism in Prewar Japan* (Berkeley: University of California Press, 2007), xiv–xv, 239.

4. "Natural Resources and Japan: Gold, Timber, Urban Mining and Metal Thieves," Facts and Details, accessed October 15, 2020, http://factsanddetails.com/japan/cat24/sub159/item932.html.

5. *Natural Park Act*, Act No. 161 of 1959, http://www.env.go.jp/en/laws/nature/law_np.pdf, accessed October 15, 2020; John Knight, "Competing Hospitalities in Japanese Rural Tourism," *Annals of Tourism Research* 23, no. 1 (1996): 168, 344; Millie Creighton, "Consuming Rural Japan: The Marketing of Tradition and Nostalgia in the Japanese Travel Industry," *Ethnology* 36, no. 3 (Summer 1997), 239, 244; Oliver R.W. Pergrams and Patricia A. Zaradic, "Evidence for a fundamental and pervasive shift away from nature-based

recreation," https://www.ncbi.nlm.nih.gov/pmc/articles/PMC2268130/pdf/ zpq2295.pdf, accessed October 15, 2020.

6. Creighton, 245–46.

7. Catherine Russell, "A Princess and Three Good Men," *The Hidden Fortress* DVD insert (New York: The Criterion Collection, 2014).

Chapter 19

1. Takemae, 556.

2. Johnson 202, Takemae 539.

3. Tsuneo Watanabe, *Japan's Backroom Politics: Factions in a Multiparty Age*, trans. Robert D. Eldridge (Washington, D.C.: Lexington Books, 2013), 251.

4. *Akira Kurosawa: It Is Wonderful to Create*, "The Bad Sleep Well," directed by Nogami Teruyo, 2002, DVD (New York: The Criterion Collection, 2006); Cardullo, 141.

5. Walter Edwards, "Something Borrowed: Wedding Cakes as Symbols in Modern Japan," *American Ethnologist* 9, no. 4 (Nov. 1982): 699–711.

6. Eiji Yoshioka, Yasuaki Saijo, and Ichiro Kawachi, "An analysis of secular trends in method-specific suicides in Japan, 1950–1975," *Popular Health Metrics* 15, no. 14 (2017).

7. Francesca Di Marco, *Suicide in Twentieth-Century Japan* (London: Taylor & Francis, 2016), 118, 121.

8. Hasegawa, 199; Michael Tai, *China and Her Neighbors* (London: Zed Books, 2019), 35.

Chapter 20

1. Kweku Ampiah, "Japan at the Bandung Conference: The Cat Goes to the Mice's Convention," *Japan Forum* 7, no. 1, 20–21; Sakamoto Kazuya, "Conditions of an Independent State: Japanese Diplomacy in the 1950s," in *The Diplomatic History of Postwar Japan*, ed. Makoto Iokibe, trans. Robert D. Eldridge (London: Routledge, 2011), 69.

2. Winston Davis, "Buddhism and the Modernization of Japan," *History of Religions* 28, no. 4 (1989): 329–30; Sakamoto, 69.

3. Tadokoro Masayuki, "The Model of an Economic Power: Japanese Diplomacy in the 1960s," in *The Diplomatic History of Postwar Japan*, ed. Makoto Iokibe, trans. Robert D. Eldridge (London: Routledge, 2011), 81.

4. Dore, *Shinohata*, 113, 116.

5. Charles Yuji Horioka, "Why is Japan's Household Saving Rate so High?: A Literature Survey," *Journal of the Japanese and International Economies* 4, no. 1 (Mar. 1990): 49–92; Kent E. Calder, "Linking Welfare and the Developmental State: Postal Savings in Japan," *The Journal of Japanese Studies* 16, no. 1 (Winter, 1990): 31; John A. James and Isao Suto, "Early Twentieth-Century Japanese Worker Saving: Precautionary Behaviour Before a Social Safety Net," *Cliometrica* 5, no. 1 (Jan. 2011):

1–25; "Personal Saving Rate in the United States from 1960 to 2019," Statista, accessed October 18, 2020, https://www.statista.com/statistics/246234/personal-savings-rate-in-the-united-states/; Metzler, *Capital as Will and Imagination*, 141–43, 208; Johnson, 14–15, 208; Dore, *Shinohata*, 63–64.

6. Ampiah, 45–47.

Chapter 21

1. Roger H. Brown, "Yasuoka Masahiro's 'New Discourse on *Bushidō* Philosophy': Cultivating Samurai Spirit and Men of Character for Imperial Japan," *Social Science Japan Journal* 16, no. 1 (2013): 107–129.

2. Bennett Alan Weinberg and Bonnie K. Bealer, *The World of Caffeine: The Science and Culture of the World's Most Popular Drug* (London: Routledge, 2001), 79–87; Boye De Mente, *Passport's Japan Almanac* (Lincolnwood, IL: Passport Books, 1987), 43.

3. Junichi Tanaka, "Japanese Tea Breeding History and the Future Perspective," in *Global Tea Breeding: Achievements, Challenges and Perspectives*, eds. Liang Chen, Zeno Apostolides, and Zong-Mao Chen (Berlin: Springer Berlin, 2012), 228; Bennett and Bealer, 84.

4. Michael Hoffman, "The long road to identity," *Japan Times* (Tokyo), Oct. 11, 2009.

5. Satoshi Imazoto, "Household Fee Ranking System and Clans' Social Order Change in a Japanese Village in Nagano Prefecture," *Journal of Rural Studies* 13, no. 1 (2006): 13–24; Sonia Ryang, *Japan and National Anthropology: A Critique* (New York: Routledge, 2004), 101–38; Dore, *Shinohata*, 282–341.

6. Miho Ogino, "From Natalism to Family Planning: Population Policy in Wartime and the Post-War Period," in *Gender, Nation and State in Modern Japan*, eds. Andrea Germer, Vera Mackie, and Ulrike Wohr (London: Routledge, 2014), 203; Ilse Lenz, "From Mothers of the Nation to Embodied Citizens," in *Gender, Nation and State in Modern Japan*, eds. Andrea Germer, Vera Mackie, and Ulrike Wohr (London: Routledge, 2014), 217; Hiroko Hirakawa, "Maiden Martyr for 'New Japan': The 1960 Ampo and the Rhetoric of the Other Michiko," *U.S.-Japan Women's Journal* 51 (2017): 17, 21.

Chapter 22

1. *Akira Kurosawa: It Is Wonderful to Create*, "The Lower Depths," directed by Nogami Teruyo, 2002, DVD (New York: The Criterion Collection, 2004).

2. Midori Kuriyama 栗山 緑, *Nihon no "ashi bunka" no takakuteki kōsatsu—nihonjin no "hakimono" no chakudatsu* 日本の「あし文化」の多角的考察 -日本人の「はきもの」の着脱 [A multifaceted consideration of Japanese "foot culture"—Japanese people's taking on and off of "footwear"], *Journal of Japanese Culture* 70 (Aug. 2016): 41–55.

3. Johnson, 249–52.

4. "The Unlikeliest Shoe Empire," *Los Angeles Times* (Los Angeles), Feb. 13, 1992; Johnson, 252.

5. The Mitsubishi Corporation, *Japanese Business Language: An Essential Dictionary*, rev. ed. (London: Routledge, 2011), 187; Johnson, 11.

6. Tetsuya Fujimoto and Won-Kyu Park, "Is Japan Exceptional? Reconsidering Japanese Crime Rates," *Social Justice* 21, no. 2 (1994): 110–135; Masahiro Tsushima and Koichi Hamai, "Public Cooperation With the Police in Japan: Testing the Legitimacy Model," *Journal of Contemporary Criminal Justice* 31, no. 2 (May 2015): 212–228.

7. Roderick A. Smith, "The Japanese Shinkansen: Catalyst for the Renaissance of Rail," *The Journal of Transport History* 24, no. 2 (2003): 222–237.

8. Richard Truett, "The Toyopet Crown: Rocky start for a future giant," *Turning Points: 25 Pivotal Decisions in Toyota's 50 Years*, supplement, *Automotive News* (Detroit), Oct. 29, 2007; "After Toyopet trauma, Corona got Toyota up to speed in U.S.," *Automotive News* (Detroit), Oct. 29, 2007; "The Creators of Toyota's DNA," *Assembly*, accessed October 19, 2020, https://www.assemblymag.com/articles/84596-the-creators-of-toyota-s-dna.

9. "Development History of Japanese Automobile Industry," Car From Japan, accessed October 19, 2020, https://carfromjapan.com/article/industry-knowledge/development-history-japanese-automotive-industry/.

10. Michael S. Vaughn, Frank F. Y. Huang, and Christine Rose Ramirez, "Drug Abuse and Anti-Drug Policy in Japan: Past History and Future Directions," *The British Journal of Criminology* 35, no. 4 (Autumn 1995): 494–501; H. Richard Friman, "Gaijinhanzai: Immigrants and Drugs in Contemporary Japan," *Asian Survey* 36, no. 10 (Oct. 1996): 966; "Drugs and Crime Facts," Bureau of Justice Statistics, accessed October 19, 2020, https://www.bjs.gov/content/dcf/enforce.cfm.

11. "The Japanese do garbage better," *Science News* (Washington, D.C.), Jan. 2, 1988.

12. Charles Lane, "A View to a Kill," *Foreign Policy* 148 (May-June 2005): 37–42; Mai Sato, *The Death Penalty in Japan: Will the Public Tolerate Abolition?* (Wiesbaden: Springer Fachmedien Wiesbaden, 2013), 183–87.

13. Yukiko Koshiro, "Race as International Identity? 'Miscegenation' in the U.S. Occupation of Japan and Beyond," *Amerikastudien/American Studies* 48, no. 1 (2003): 64, 67, 69, 76; Martyn David Smith, *Mass Media, Consumerism and National Identity in Postwar Japan* (London: Bloomsbury Academic, 2019), 82.

Chapter 23

1. Shunya Yoshimi, "1964 Tokyo Olympics as Post-War," in "The Olympic Games in Japan and East Asia: Images and Legacies," special issue, *International Journal of Japanese Sociology* 28, no. 1 (March 2019): 80–95; Wendelken, 197.

2. Kurumi Aizawa, Ji Wu, Yuhei Inoue, Miki-hiro Sato, "Long-term impact of the Tokyo 1964 Olympic Games on sport participation: A cohort analysis," *Sport Management Review* 21, no. 1 (Feb. 2018): 86–97; Yoshikuni Igarashi, *Bodies of Memory: Narratives of War in Postwar Japanese Culture, 1945–1970* (Princeton: Princeton University Press, 2012), 144–45; Smith, 78.

3. Smith 61, 80–88.

4. Hasan Topacoglu, *Hawai "Meiji hyakunen-sai" ibento (1968 nen) to nikkei amerikajin no kioku* ハワイ「明治百年祭」イベント（1968年）と日系アメリカ人の記憶 [The 1968 Meiji Centennial Event in Hawai'i and the Recollections of Americans of Japanese Descent]. *Nihon komyunikēshon gakkai* 日本コミュニケーション学会 [Japan Communication Association] 46, no. 1 (2017): 61–80; Nick Kapur, "The Empire Strikes Back? The 1968 Meiji Centennial Celebrations and the Revival of Japanese Nationalism," *Japanese Studies* 38, no. 3 (2018): 305–328.

5. Yuko Kawanishi, *Mental Health Challenges Facing Contemporary Japanese Society: The "Lonely People"* (Kent: Global Oriental, 2009), 110, 115, 141.

6. Kawanishi, 63–4, 88–90; Jelonek, 103–9.

Chapter 24

1. Yasunari Kawabata, "Japan, the Beautiful and Myself," The Nobel Prize, accessed October 19, 2020, https://www.nobelprize.org/prizes/literature/1968/kawabata/lecture/; Yoshio Iwamoto, "The Nobel Prize in Literature, 1967–1987: A Japanese View," in "The Nobel Prizes in Literature 1967–1987: A Symposium," supplemental, *World Literature Today* 62, no. 2 (Spring 1988): 217–221.

2. Cardullo, 67.

3. Masami Sasaki, "Aspects of Autism in Japan Before and After the Introduction of TEACCH," *International Journal of Mental Health* 29, no. 2 (Summer 2000): 4.

4. Philip Brasor and Masako Tsubuku, "Automatic Dishwasher: The Square Peg in the Round Hole of Japanese Kitchens," *Japan Times* (Tokyo), Feb. 10, 2012.

5. Chris Burgess, "Unmanned Vegetable Stalls: Reflection of an Honest Society?" A British Prof in Japan, accessed October 19, 2020, http://abritishprofinjapan.blogspot.com/2017/07/unmanned-vegetable-stalls-trusting-society.html; Yoko Saito, Hisamitsu Saito, "Motivations for Local Food Demand by Japanese Consumers: A Conjoint Analysis with Reference-Point Effects," *Agribusiness: An International Journal* 29, no. 2 (Spring 2013): 147–161.

6. Chen Liu, Yasuhiko Hotta, Atsushi Santo, Matthew Hengesbaugh, Atsushi Watabe, Yoshiaki Totoki, Desmond Allen, and Magnus Bengtsson, "Food waste in Japan: Trends, current practices and key challenges," *Journal of Cleaner Production* 133, no. 1 (October 2016): 557–564; Atsushi Watabe, Chen Liu, Magnus Bengtsson, "Uneaten Food:

Emerging Social Practices Around Food Waste in Greater Tokyo," in *Food Consumption in the City: Practices and Patterns in Urban Asia and the Pacific*, eds. Marlyne Sahakian, Czarina Saloma, and Suren Erkman (Milton Park, UK: Routledge, 2016), 61–79.

7. Masako Tanaka, Yumi E. Suzuki, Ikuko Aoyama, Kota Takaoka, Harriet L. MacMillan, "Child sexual abuse in Japan: A systematic review and future directions." *Child Abuse & Neglect* 66 (April 2017): 31–40; "Josei senyōsha 女性専用車," RJ Essential, accessed October 19, 2020, http://rail-j.com/esse/ index.php?%BD%F7%C0%AD%C0%EC%CD%D1%BC%D6.

8. "Statistics of Film Industry in Japan," Motion Picture Producers Association of Japan, Inc., accessed October 19, 2020, http://www.eiren.org/statistics_e/; Cardullo, 67, 76.

Chapter 25

1. Tadokoro, 99–101; Johnson, 294–96.

2. Thomas R.H. Havens, *Fire Across the Sea: The Vietnam War and Japan, 1965–1975* (Princeton: Princeton University Press, 1987), 3–6.

3. Johnson, 292–94.

4. Nakanishi Hiroshi, "Overcoming the Crises: Japanese Diplomacy in the 1970s," in *The Diplomatic History of Postwar Japan*, ed. Makoto Iokibe, trans. Robert D. Eldridge (London: Routledge, 2011), 116–117; Havens, 244.

5. Ajay Kamalakaran, "When Akira Kurosawa brought the Russian Far East to the silver screen," *Russia Beyond* (Moscow), Dec. 25, 2015.

6. Philip Brasor and Masako Tsubuku, "Pricey family graves a fading tradition in aging Japan," *Japan Times* (Tokyo), Aug. 10, 2018.

7. "Japan—Urban population as a share of total population," Knoema, accessed October 19, 2020, https://knoema.com/atlas/Japan/Urban-population; Chauncy D. Harris, "The Urban and Industrial Transformation of Japan," *Geographical Review* 72, no. 1 (Jan. 1982): 52.

8. Koji Matsushita and Kunihiro Hirata, "Forest Owners' Associations," in *Forestry and the Forest Industry in Japan*, ed. Yoshiya Iwai (Vancouver: UBC Press, 2002), 54; Atsushi Takayanagi, "Treatment of Forests and Wildlife in Modern Society," in *Forestry and the Forest Industry in Japan*, ed. Yoshiya Iwai (Vancouver: UBC Press, 2002), 302; Richie, 199; Yuko Tsunetsugu, Bum-Jin Park, and Yoshifumi Miyazaki, "Trends in research related to 'Shinrin-yoku' (taking to the forest atmosphere or forest bathing) in Japan," *Environmental Health and Preventative Medicine* 15 (2010): 28.

9. Ken'ichi Miyamoto, "Japanese Environmental Policy: Lessons from Experience and Remaining Problems" in *Japan at Nature's Edge: The Environmental Context of a Global Power*, eds. Ian Jared Miller, Julia Adeney Thomas, and Brett Walker (Honolulu: University of Hawai'i Press, 2013), 227; Jonathan Hopfner, "Power of the Powerless: On ritual, protest and the art of

self-defence," *Dark Mountain*, accessed November 18, 2020, https://dark-mountain.net/power-of-the-powerless/; Nakanishi, 123; Johnson, 283–84.

Chapter 26

1. Murata Koji, "The Mission and Trials of an Emerging International State: Japanese Diplomacy in the 1980s" in *The Diplomatic History of Postwar Japan*, ed. Makoto Iokibe, trans. Robert D. Eldridge (London: Routledge, 2011), 145–148.

2. Murata, 147–48.

3. Murata, 143, 147.

4. Robert S. Boynton, *The Invitation-Only Zone: The True Story of North Korea's Abduction Project* (New York: Farrar, Straus, and Giroux, 2016).

5. Mark Ravina, "State-Building and Political Economy in Early-modern Japan," *The Journal of Asian Studies* 54, no. 4 (Nov. 1995): 997–1022.

6. Ulv Hanssen, *Temporal Identities and Security Policy in Postwar Japan* (London: Routledge, 2020), 103–121; Murata, 147–50, 152–53, 168.

Chapter 27

1. "Imperial Rescript: The Great Principles of Education, 1879," Children and Youth in History, accessed November 11, 2020, https://chnm.gmu.edu/cyh/items/show/134.

2. Yoshio Sugimoto, *An Introduction to Japanese Society* (Cambridge: Cambridge University Press, 1997), 123.

3. Martyn David Smith, 115–116; Colin P.A. Jones, "Seven lessons from a Japanese morality textbook," *Japan Times* (Tokyo), August 7, 2019.

4. Jonathan D. Mackintosh, *Homosexuality and Manliness in Postwar Japan* (London: Routledge, 2010), 2–3.

5. Tadashi Uchino, "Images of armageddon: Japan's 1980s theatre culture," *The Drama Review* 44, no. 1 (Spring 2000), 85–96.

6. James Welker, "From Women's Liberation to Lesbian Feminism in Japan: *Rezubian Feminizumu* within and beyond the *Ūman Ribu* Movement in the 1970s and 1980s," in *Rethinking Japanese Feminisms*, eds. Julia C. Bullock, Ayako Kano, and James Welker (Honolulu: University of Hawai'i Press, 2018), 50–52; Chris McMorran, "Liberating Work in the Tourist Industry," in *Rethinking Japanese Feminisms*, eds. Julia C. Bullock, Ayako Kano, and James Welker (Honolulu: University of Hawai'i Press, 2018), 119; Barbara Hartley, "Feminist Acts of Reading," in *Rethinking Japanese Feminisms*, eds. Julia C. Bullock, Ayako Kano, and James Welker (Honolulu: University of Hawai'i Press, 2018), 155.

7. Zack Beauchamp, "Japan's demographic time bomb, in one chart," Vox, accessed October 19, 2020, https://www.vox.com/2016/4/13/11421162/japan-oecd-chart; John W. Traphagan, "Interpretations of Elder Suicide, Stress, and Dependency

among Rural Japanese," *Ethnology* 43, no. 4 (Autumn 2004): 315–329.

8. Takashi Oshio and Satoshi Shimizutani, May 2011, "Disability Pension Program and Labor Force Participation in Japan: A Historical Perspective," NBER Working Paper 17052, National Bureau of Economic Research, Cambridge, MA; Chris B. Roberts, Yoshimune Hiratsuka, Masakazu Yamada, Lynne M. Pezzullo, Katie Yates, Shigeru Takano, Kensaku Miyake, and Hugh R. Taylor, "Economic Cost of Visual Impairment in Japan," *Archives of Ophthalmology* 128, no. 6 (June 2010): 766–771; Misa Kayama, Wendy Haight, Tamara Kincaid, Kelly Evans, "Local implementation of disability policies for 'high incidence' disabilities at public schools in Japan and the U.S.," *Children and Youth Services Review* 52 (May 2015): 34–44; Oshio.

Chapter 28

1. Michal Daliot-Bul, "Reframing and reconsidering the cultural innovations of the anime boom on U.S. television," *International Journal of Cultural Studies* 17, no. 1 (2014): 75–91; Akira Kurosawa 黒澤明, *Yumi wa tensai de aru* 夢は天才である [Dreams are Genius] (Tokyo: Bungeishunju, 1999), 195.

2. Karen A. Smyers, "'My Own Inari': Personalization of the Deity in Inari Worship," *Japanese Journal of Religious Studies* 23, no. 1 (Spring 1996): 85–116.

3. "Japanese Kids to Learn How to Farm on Abandoned Land," Japan For Sustainability, accessed October 19, 2020, https://www.japanfs.org/en/news/archives/news_id029225.html.

4. Gabriel Johnson, "Can the Japan-Korean Dispute on 'Comfort Women' Be Resolved?," *Korea Observer* 46, no. 3 (Autumn 2015): 1–27.

5. *A Message From Akira Kurosawa: For Beautiful Movies*, directed by Hisao Kurosawa, DVD (2000; New York: The Criterion Collection, 2015).

Chapter 29

1. Kurosawa to Bergman, Open Culture, accessed November 11, 2020, https://www.openculture.com/2013/12/akira-kurosawa-to-ingmar-bergman.html#:~:text=Bergman%2C,more%20wonderful%20movies%20for%20us.

2. *Making of Dreams: A Movie Conversation Between Akira Kurosawa and Nobuhiko Obayashi*, directed by Nobuhiko Obayashi, Blu-ray (1990; New York: The Criterion Collection, 2016).

3. Mark Vallen, "Nagasaki Nightmare: Art of the Hibakusha (Atom Bomb Survivors)," Art For a Change, accessed October 19, 2020, https://www.art-for-a-change.com/Atomic/atomic.htm.

4. Kurt W. Tong, "Korea's Forgotten Atomic Bomb Victims," *Bulletin of Concerned Asian Scholars* 23, no. 1 (1991): 31–37.

5. Neal Krause, Berit Ingersoll-Dayton, Jersey Liang and Hidehiro Sugisawa, "Religion, Social

Support, and Health Among the Japanese Elderly," *Journal of Health and Social Behavior* 40, no. 4 (Dec. 1999): 405–21.

6. Jane H. Yamashiro, *Redefining Japaneseness: Japanese Americans in the Ancestral Homeland* (New Brunswick: Rutgers University Press, 2017), 2–3, 43, 54.

Chapter 30

1. Sarah Fay, "Kenzaburo Oe, The Art of Fiction No. 195," *The Paris Review* 183 (Winter 2007).

2. Kenzaburo Oe, "Japan, the Ambiguous, and Myself," The Nobel Prize, accessed October 19, 2020, https://www.nobelprize.org/prizes/literature/1994/oe/lecture/.

3. Rachel DiNitto, *Uchida Hyakken: A Critique of Modernity and Militarism in Prewar Japan* (Cambridge: Harvard University Press, 2008), 252; T.R. Reid, "WWII re-fought, revised in Japanese media," *The Washington Post* (Washington, D.C.), August 14, 1995.

4. H.D. Harootunian, "Introduction: The Sense of an Ending and the Problem of Taishō," in *Japan in Crisis: Essays on Taishō Democracy*, eds. Bernard S. Silderman and H.D. Harootunian, 3–28 (Princeton: Princeton University Press, 1974), 15–16; DiNitto, 26–29.

5. DiNitto, 6.

6. Paul McCarthy, "Modern cat tales echo former feline fiction," *Japan Times* (Tokyo), May 31, 2014; *Woodlands Dark and Days Bewitched: A History of Folk Horror*, directed by Kier-La Janisse, online screening (2021; Los Angeles: Severin Films, 2021).

Epilogue

1. Jonathan Sprague, "They Changed Our Lives," CNN, accessed October 20, 2020, http://www.cnn.com/ASIANOW/asiaweek/features/aoc/aoc.intro.html.

2. Sato, *My Life in Cinema*; Kurosawa, *Yumi wa tensai de aru*, 175.

3. "Pop-Culture Diplomacy," Ministry of Foreign Affairs of Japan, accessed October 21, 2020, https://www.mofa.go.jp/policy/culture/exchange/pop/index.html; Koichi Iwabuchi, "Pop-culture diplomacy in Japan: soft power, nation branding and the question of 'international cultural exchange,'" *International Journal of Cultural Policy* 21, no. 4 (2015): 419–20.

4. *Kurosawa's Way*, directed by Catherine Cadou, Blu-ray (2011; New York: The Criterion Collection, 2016).

Bibliography

Books and Book Chapters

Akiyama, Nobumasa. "Disarmament and the non-proliferation policy of Japan." In *Routledge Handbook of Japanese Foreign Policy,* edited by Mary M. McCarthy, 173–87. London: Routledge, 2018.

Anderson, Joseph L. and Donald Richie. *The Japanese Film: Art and Industry.* Rutland: C.E. Tuttle Co., 1959.

Ball, W. Macmahon. *Japan: Enemy or Ally?* New York: The John Day Company, 1949.

Boynton, Robert S. *The Invitation-Only Zone: The True Story of North Korea's Abduction Project.* New York: Farrar, Straus, and Giroux, 2016.

Cardullo, Bert, ed. *Akira Kurosawa Interviews.* Jackson: University Press of Mississippi, 2008.

De Mente, Boye. *Passport's Japan Almanac.* Lincolnwood, IL: Passport Books, 1987.

Di Marco, Francesca. *Suicide in Twentieth-Century Japan.* London: Taylor & Francis, 2016.

DiNitto, Rachel. *Uchida Hyakken: A Critique of Modernity and Militarism in Prewar Japan.* Cambridge: Harvard University Press, 2008.

Dore, Ronald. *Shinohata: A Portrait of a Japanese Village.* New York: Pantheon Books, 1978.

Dore, R.P. *Land Reform in Japan.* Rev. ed. New York, Schocken Books, 1985.

Dower, John W. *Embracing Defeat: Japan in the Wake of World War II.* New York: W.W. Norton & Co./New Press, 2000.

Foster, Michael Dylan. *Pandemonium and Parade: Japanese Monsters and the Culture of Yōkai.* Berkeley: University of California Press, 2008.

Fujita, Kuniko and Richard Child Hill. *Japanese Cities in the World Economy.* Philadelphia: Temple University Press, 1993.

Fukumoto, Kunio 福本邦雄. *Kanryō* 官僚 [Bureaucrats]. Tokyo: Kobundo, 1959.

Galbraith, Stuart. *The Emperor and the Wolf: The Lives and Films of Akira Kurosawa and Toshiro Mifune.* New York: Faber & Faber, 2003.

Haitani, Kanji. *The Japanese Economic System: An Institutional Overview.* Washington, D.C.: Lexington Books, 1977.

Hanssen, Ulv. Temporal Identities and Security Policy in Postwar Japan. London: Routledge, 2020.

Harley, Barbara. "Feminist Acts of Reading." In Rethinking Japanese Feminisms. Edited by Julia C. Bullock, Ayako Kano, and James Welker, 154–69. Honolulu: University of Hawai'i Press, 2018.

Harootunian, H.D. "Introduction: The Sense of an Ending and the Problem of Taishō." In *Japan in Crisis: Essays on Taishō Democracy.* Edited by Bernard S. Silderman and H.D. Harootunian, 3–28. Princeton: Princeton University Press, 1974.

Hasegawa, Kenji. Student Radicalism and the Formation of Postwar Japan. Singapore: Palgrave Macmillan, 2019.

Havens, Thomas R.H. *Fire Across the Sea: The Vietnam War and Japan, 1965–1975.* Princeton: Princeton University Press, 1987.

Hirano, Kyoko. *Mr. Smith Goes to Tokyo: The Japanese Cinema Under the American Occupation.* Washington: Smithsonian Institution Press, 1992.

Hornfischer, James. *The Fleet at Flood Tide: America at Total War in the Pacific, 1944–1945.* New York: Random House, 2016.

Hotta, Eri. *Pan-Asianism and Japan's War, 1931–1945.* New York: Palgrave Macmillan, 2007.

Igarashi, Yoshikuni. *Bodies of Memory: Narratives of War in Postwar Japanese Culture, 1945–1970.* Princeton: Princeton University Press, 2012.

Ito, Osamu. "The International Environment and Domestic Structure of Postwar Japan's Rapid Growth." In *Japanese Economy and Society Under Pax-Americana,* edited by Hiroshi Shibuya, Makoto Maruyama, and Masamitsu Yasaka. Tokyo: University of Tokyo Press, 2002.

Johnson, Chalmers. *MITI and the Japanese Miracle: The Growth of Industrial Policy, 1925–1975.* Stanford: Stanford University Press, 1982.

Kawanishi, Yuko. *Mental Health Challenges Facing Contemporary Japanese Society: The "Lonely People."* Kent: Global Oriental, 2009.

Kurosawa, Akira. *Something Like an Autobiography.* Translated by Audie E. Bock. New York: Vintage Books, 1983.

Kurosawa, Akira 黒澤明. *Yumi wa tensai de aru* 夢は天才である [Dreams are Genius]. Tokyo: Bungeishunjū, 1999.

Lebra, Joyce Capman. "Women in an All-Male

Industry: The Case of *Sake* Brewer Tatsu'uma Kiyo." In *Recreating Japanese Women, 1600–1945*, edited by Gail Lee Bernstein, 131–48. Berkeley: University of California Press, 1991.

Lenz, Ilse. "From Mothers of the Nation to Embodied Citizens." In *Gender, Nation and State in Modern Japan*. Edited by Andrea Germer, Vera Mackie, and Ulrike Wohr, 211–229. London: Routledge, 2014.

Matsushita, Koji and Kunihiro Hirata. "Forest Owners' Associations." In *Forestry and the Forest Industry in Japan*. Edited by Yoshiya Iwai, 41–66. Vancouver: UBC Press, 2002.

McMorran, Chris. "Liberating Work in the Tourist Industry." In *Rethinking Japanese Feminisms*. Edited by Julia C. Bullock, Ayako Kano, and James Welker, 119–32. Honolulu: University of Hawai'i Press, 2018.

Metzler, Mark. *Capital as Will and Imagination: Schumpeter's Guide to the Postwar Japanese Miracle*. Ithaca: Cornell University Press, 2013.

Metzler, Mark. *Lever of Empire: The International Gold Standard and the Crisis of Liberalism in Prewar Japan*. Berkeley: University of California Press, 2007.

Mitsubishi Corporation, The. *Japanese Business Language: An Essential Dictionary*. Rev. ed. London: Routledge, 2011.

Miyake, Yoshiko. "Doubling Expectations: Motherhood and Women's Factory Work Under State Management in Japan in the 1930s and 1940s." In *Recreating Japanese Women, 1600–1945*, edited by Gail Lee Bernstein, 267–95. Berkeley: University of California Press, 1991.

Miyamoto, Ken'ichi. "Japanese Environmental Policy: Lessons from Experience and Remaining Problems." In *Japan at Nature's Edge: The Environmental Context of a Global Power*, edited by Ian Jared Miller, Julia Adeney Thomas, and Brett Walker, 222–252. Honolulu: University of Hawai'i Press, 2013.

Murata, Koji. "The Mission and Trials of an Emerging International State: Japanese Diplomacy in the 1980s." In *The Diplomatic History of Postwar Japan*. Edited by Makoto Iokibe, 143–172. Translated by Robert D. Eldridge. London: Routledge, 2011.

Nagy, Margit. "Middle-Class Working Women During the Interwar Years." In *Recreating Japanese Women, 1600–1945*, edited by Gail Lee Bernstein, 199–216. Berkeley: University of California Press, 1991.

Nakanishi, Hiroshi. "Overcoming the Crises: Japanese Diplomacy in the 1970s." In *The Diplomatic History of Postwar Japan*. Edited by Makoto Iokibe, 108–142. Translated by Robert D. Eldridge. London: Routledge, 2011.

Nollen, Scott Allen. *Takashi Shimura: Chameleon of Japanese Cinema*. Jefferson, N.C.: McFarland, 2019.

Nolte, Sharon H., and Sally Ann Hastings. "The Meiji State's Policy Toward Women, 1890–1910." In *Recreating Japanese Women, 1600–1945*, edited

by Gail Lee Bernstein, 151–74. Berkeley: University of California Press, 1991.

Ogino, Miho. "From Natalism to Family Planning: Population Policy in Wartime and the Post-War Period" In *Gender, Nation and State in Modern Japan*. Translated by Leonie Stickland. Edited by Andrea Germer, Vera Mackie, and Ulrike Wohr, 198–210. London: Routledge, 2014.

Prince, Stephen. *The Warrior's Camera: The Cinema of Akira Kurosawa*. Princeton: Princeton University Press, 1991.

Richie, Donald. *The Films of Akira Kurosawa*. Rev. ed. with additional material by Joan Mellen. Berkeley: University of California Press, 1984.

Rodd, Laura Rasplica. "Yosano Akiko and the Taishō Debate over the 'New Woman.'" In *Recreating Japanese Women, 1600–1945*, edited by Gail Lee Bernstein, 175–98. Berkeley: University of California Press, 1991.

Ryang, Sonia. *Japan and National Anthropology: A Critique*. New York: Routledge, 2004.

Sakamoto, Kazuya. "Conditions of an Independent State: Japanese Diplomacy in the 1950s." In *The Diplomatic History of Postwar Japan*. Edited by Makoto Iokibe, 50–80. Translated by Robert D. Eldridge. London: Routledge, 2011.

Sato, Mai. *The Death Penalty in Japan: Will the Public Tolerate Abolition?* Wiesbaden: Springer Fachmedien Wiesbaden, 2013.

Saxonhouse, Gary R. "Country Girls and Communication Among Competitors in the Japanese Cotton-Spinning Industry." In *The Pacific in the Age of Early Industrialization*, edited by Kenneth Pomeranz, 41–69. London: Routledge, 2009.

Schaller, Michael. *The American Occupation of Japan: The Origins of the Cold War in Asia*. New York: Oxford University Press, 1985.

Smith, Martyn David. *Mass Media, Consumerism and National Identity in Postwar Japan*. London: Bloomsbury Academic, 2019.

Snelling, Dennis. *Lefty O'Doul: Baseball's Forgotten Ambassador*. Lincoln: University of Nebraska Press, 2017.

Sugimoto, Yoshio. *An Introduction to Japanese Society*. Cambridge: Cambridge University Press, 1997.

Tadokoro, Masayuki. "The Model of an Economic Power: Japanese Diplomacy in the 1960s." In *The Diplomatic History of Postwar Japan*, edited by Makoto Iokibe, 81–107. Translated by Robert D. Eldridge. London: Routledge, 2011.

Tai, Michael. *China and Her Neighbors*. London: Zed Books, 2019.

Takayanagi, Atsushi. "Treatment of Forests and Wildlife in Modern Society." In *Forestry and the Forest Industry in Japan*. Edited by Yoshiya Iwai, 292–306. Vancouver: UBC Press, 2002.

Takemae, Eiji. *Inside GHQ: The Allied Occupation of Japan and its Legacy*. Translated by Robert Ricketts and Sebastian Swann. London: Continuum, 2002.

Tanaka, Junichi. "Japanese Tea Breeding History

and the Future Perspective." In *Global Tea Breeding: Achievements, Challenges and Perspectives.* Edited by Liang Chen, Zeno Apostolides, and Zong-Mao Chen, 227–39. Berlin: Springer Berlin, 2012.

Thomas, Jolyon Baraka. *Faking Liberties: Religious Freedom in American-Occupied Japan.* Chicago: Chicago University Press, 2019.

Townsend, Susan. *Yanaihara Tadao and Japanese Colonial Policy.* East Sussex: Psychology Press, 2000.

Watabe, Atsushi, Chen Liu, and Magnus Bengtsso. "Uneaten Food: Emerging Social Practices Around Food Waste in Greater Tokyo." In *Food Consumption in the City: Practices and Patterns in Urban Asia and the Pacific,* edited by Marlyne Sahakian, Czarina Saloma, and Suren Erkman, 61–79. Milton Park, UK: Routledge, 2016.

Watanabe, Tsuneo. *Japan's Backroom Politics: Factions in a Multiparty Age.* Translated by Robert D. Eldridge. Washington, D.C.: Lexington Books, 2013.

Weinberg, Bennett Alan and Bonnie K. Bealer. *The World of Caffeine: The Science and Culture of the World's Most Popular Drug.* London: Routledge, 2001.

Welker, James. "From Women's Liberation to Lesbian Feminism in Japan: *Rezubian Feminizumu* within and beyond the *Ūman Ribu* Movement in the 1970s and 1980s." In *Rethinking Japanese Feminisms.* Edited by Julia C. Bullock, Ayako Kano, and James Welker, 50–67. Honolulu: University of Hawai'i Press, 2018.

Wendelken, Cherie. "Aesthetics and Reconstruction: Japanese Architectural Culture in the 1950s." In *Rebuilding Urban Japan After 1945,* edited by Carola Hein, Jeffry M. Diefendorf, and Ishida Yorifusa, 188–209. Hampshire: Palgrave Macmillan, 2003.

Westgeest, Helen. *Zen in the Fifties: Interaction in Art Between East and West.* Zwolle: Waanders Publishers, 1997.

Yamashiro, Jane H. *Redefining Japaneseness: Japanese Americans in the Ancestral Homeland.* New Brunswick: Rutgers University Press, 2017.

Yasaka, Masamitsu. "American Impacts on Agriculture and Foods." In *Japanese Economy and Society Under Pax-Americana,* edited by Hiroshi Shibuya, Makoto Maruyama, and Masamitsu Yasaka, 336–366. Tokyo: University of Tokyo Press, 2002.

Yoshimoto, Mitsuhiro. *Kurosawa: Film Studies and Japanese Cinema.* Durham: Duke University Press, 2000.

Articles and Essays

"After Toyopet trauma, Corona got Toyota up to speed in U.S." *Automotive News* (Detroit), Oct. 29, 2007.

Aizawa, Kurumi, Ji Wu, Yuhei Inoue, and Mikihiro Sato. "Long-term impact of the Tokyo 1964 Olympic Games on sport participation: A cohort analysis." *Sport Management Review* 21, no. 1 (Feb. 2018): 86–97.

Ampiah, Kweku. "Japan at the Bandung Conference: The Cat Goes to the Mice's Convention." *Japan Forum* 7, no. 1, 15–24.

Beauchamp, Zack. "Japan's demographic time bomb, in one chart." Vox. Accessed October 19, 2020. https://www.vox.com/2016/4/13/11421162/japan-oecd-chart.

Brasor, Philip and Masako Tsubuku. "Automatic Dishwasher: The Square Peg in the Round Hole of Japanese Kitchens." *Japan Times* (Tokyo), Feb. 10, 2012.

Brasor, Philip and Masako Tsubuku. "Pricey family graves a fading tradition in aging Japan." *Japan Times* (Tokyo), Aug. 10, 2018.

Brown, Roger H. "Yasuoka Masahiro's 'New Discourse on *Bushidō* Philosophy': Cultivating Samurai Spirit and Men of Character for Imperial Japan." *Social Science Japan Journal* 16, no. 1 (2013): 107–129.

Burgess, Chris. "Unmanned Vegetable Stalls: Reflection of an Honest Society?" A British Prof in Japan. Accessed October 19, 2020. http://abritishprofinjapan.blogspot.com/2017/07/unmanned-vegetable-stalls-trusting-society.html.

Calder, Kent E. "Linking Welfare and the Developmental State: Postal Savings in Japan." *The Journal of Japanese Studies* 16, no. 1 (Winter, 1990): 31–59.

Conrad, David. "'The Greatest Good for the Greatest Number': American Land Redistribution in East and Southeast Asia, 1945–1969." PhD diss., The University of Texas at Austin, 2016. Texas ScholarWorks (2152/39700).

Creighton, Millie. "Consuming Rural Japan: The Marketing of Tradition and Nostalgia in the Japanese Travel Industry." *Ethnology* 36, no. 3 (Summer 1997): 239–54.

Daliot-Bul, Michal. "Reframing and reconsidering the cultural innovations of the anime boom on US television." *International Journal of Cultural Studies* 17, no. 1 (2014): 75–91.

Davis, Winston. "Buddhism and the Modernization of Japan." *History of Religions* 28, no. 4 (1989): 304–39.

Edwards, Walter. "Something Borrowed: Wedding Cakes as Symbols in Modern Japan." *American Ethnologist* 9, no. 4 (Nov. 1982): 699–711.

Fairchild, William. "Shamanism in Japan." *Folklore Studies* 21 (1962): 1–122.

Fay, Sarah. "Kenzaburo Oe, The Art of Fiction No. 195." *The Paris Review* (New York), Winter 2007.

Friman, H. Richard. "Gaijinhanzai: Immigrants and Drugs in Contemporary Japan." *Asian Survey* 36, no. 10 (Oct. 1996): 964–77.

Fujimoto, Tetsuya and Won-Kyu Park. "Is Japan Exceptional? Reconsidering Japanese Crime Rates." *Social Justice* 21, no. 2 (1994): 110–135.

Galvan, Patrick. "Sanshiro Sugata: The Deleted Scenes." Toho Kingdom. Accessed May 10, 2021.

https://www.tohokingdom.com/blog/sanshiro-sugata-the-deleted-scenes/.

Harris, Chauncy D. "The Urban and Industrial Transformation of Japan." *Geographical Review* 72, no. 1 (Jan. 1982): 50–89.

Hirakawa, Hiroko. "Maiden Martyr for 'New Japan': The 1960 Ampo and the Rhetoric of the Other Michiko." *U.S.-Japan Women's Journal* 51 (2017): 12–27.

Hoffman, Michael. "The long road to identity." *Japan Times* (Tokyo), Oct. 11, 2009.

Hopfner, Jonathan. "Power of the Powerless: On ritual, protest and the art of self-defence." *Dark Mountain.* Accessed November 18, 2020. https://dark-mountain.net/power-of-the-powerless/.

Horioka, Charles Yuji. "Why is Japan's Household Saving Rate so High?: A Literature Survey." *Journal of the Japanese and International Economies* 4, no. 1 (Mar. 1990), 49–92.

Hymans, Jacques. "Veto Players, Nuclear Energy, and Nonproliferation: Domestic Institutional Barriers to a Japanese Bomb." *International Security* 36, no. 2 (2011): 154–189.

Imazoto, Satoshi. "Household Fee Ranking System and Clans' Social Order Change in a Japanese Village in Nagano Prefecture." Journal of Rural Studies 13, no. 1 (2006): 13–24.

Ishijima, Ayumi. "The Discourse of Mistress in Modern Japan." 이화여자대학교 아시아여성학센터 학술대회자료집 [Ewha Womans University Asian Women's Studies Center Academic Conference Materials] (2006): 79–89.

Iwabuchi, Koichi. "Pop-culture diplomacy in Japan: soft power, nation branding and the question of 'international cultural exchange.'" International Journal of Cultural Policy 21, no. 4 (2015): 419–32.

Iwamoto, Yoshio. "The Nobel Prize in Literature, 1967–1987: A Japanese View." In "The Nobel Prizes in Literature 1967–1987: A Symposium," supplement. *World Literature Today* 62, no. 2 (Spring 1988): 217–221.

Iyer, Pico. "*Ikiru* Many Autumns Later." Insert for *Ikiru.* New York: The Criterion Collection, 2015. DVD.

James, John A. and Isao Suto. "Early Twentieth-Century Japanese Worker Saving: Precautionary Behaviour Before a Social Safety Net." *Cliometrica* 5, no. 1 (Jan. 2011): 1–25.

"The Japanese do garbage better." *Science News* (Washington, D.C.), Jan. 2, 1988.

"Japan's Citizen Kane." *Economist* (London), Dec. 22, 2012.

Jelonek, Barbara. "Rethinking Gender, Rethinking Migration: Statistical trends and law regulations of Japanese marriage." *Miscellanea Anthropologica et Sociologica* 17, no. 3 (2016): 103–9.

Johnson, Gabriel. "Can the Japan-Korean Dispute on 'Comfort Women' Be Resolved?" *Korea Observer* 46, no. 3 (Autumn 2015): 1–27.

Jones, Colin P.A. "Japan's discriminatory koseki registry system looks ever more outdated." *Japan Times* (Tokyo), Jul. 10, 2016.

Jones, Colin P.A. "Seven lessons from a Japanese morality textbook," *Japan Times* (Tokyo), August 7, 2019.

Kamalakaran, Ajay. "When Akira Kurosawa brought the Russian Far East to the silver screen." *Russia Beyond* (Moscow), Dec. 25, 2015.

Kapur, Nick. "The Empire Strikes Back? The 1968 Meiji Centennial Celebrations and the Revival of Japanese Nationalism." *Japanese Studies* 38, no. 3 (2018): 305–328.

Kawabata, Yasunari. "Japan, the Beautiful and Myself." The Nobel Prize. Accessed October 19, 2020. https://www.nobelprize.org/prizes/literature/1968/kawabata/lecture/.

Kayama, Misa, Wendy Haight, Tamara Kincaid, and Kelly Evans. "Local implementation of disability policies for 'high incidence' disabilities at public schools in Japan and the U.S." *Children and Youth Services Review* 52 (May 2015): 34–44.

Kimura, Junko and Russell Belk. "Christmas in Japan: Globalization Versus Localization." *Consumption Markets & Culture* 8, no. 3 (2005): 325–38.

Knight, John. "Competing Hospitalities in Japanese Rural Tourism." *Annals of Tourism Research* 23, no. 1 (1996): 165–80.

Koshiro, Yukiko. "Race as International Identity? 'Miscegenation' in the U.S. Occupation of Japan and Beyond." *Amerikastudien/American Studies* 48, no. 1 (2003), 61–77.

Krause, Neal, Berit Ingersoll-Dayton, Jersey Liang and Hidehiro Sugisawa. "Religion, Social Support, and Health Among the Japanese Elderly." *Journal of Health and Social Behavior* 40, no. 4 (Dec. 1999): 405–21.

Kuriyama, Midori 栗山 緑. *Nihon no "ashi bunka" no takakuteki kōsatsu—nihonjin no "hakimono" no chakudatsu* 日本の「あし文化」の多角的考察-日本人の「はきもの」の着脱 [A multifaceted consideration of Japanese "foot culture"—Japanese people's taking on and off of "footwear"]. *Journal of Japanese Culture* 70 (Aug. 2016): 41–55.

Kurosaki, Akira. "Japanese Scientists' Critique of Nuclear Deterrence Theory and Its Influence on Pugwash, 1954–1964." *Journal of Cold War Studies* 20, no. 1 (2018): 101–139.

Lane, Charles. "A View to a Kill." *Foreign Policy* 148 (May-June 2005): 37–42.

Liu, Chen, Yasuhiko Hotta, Atsushi Santo, Matthew Hengesbaugh, Atsushi Watabe, Yoshiaki Totoki, Desmond Allen, and Magnus Bengtsson, "Food waste in Japan: Trends, current practices and key challenges," *Journal of Cleaner Production* 133, no. 1 (October 2016): 557–564.

Luce, Henry R. "The American Century." *Time.* February 17, 1941, 61–65.

Mackintosh, Jonathan D. *Homosexuality and Manliness in Postwar Japan.* London: Routledge, 2010.

McCarthy, Paul. "Modern cat tales echo former feline fiction." *Japan Times* (Tokyo), May 31, 2014.

Metzler, Mark. "Capitalist Boom, Feudal Bust:

Long Waves in Economics and Politics in Pre-Industrial Japan." *Review* 17, no. 1 (Winter 1994), 57–119.

Metzler, Mark. "Woman's Place in Japan's Great Depression: Reflections on the Moral Economy of Deflation." *Journal of Japanese Studies* 30, no. 2 (2004): 315–52.

Miyawaki-Okada, Junko. "The Japanese Origins of the Chenggis Khan Legends." *Inner Asia* 8, no. 1 (2006): 123–134.

Oda, Ernani. "Family narratives and transforming identities: three generation of Japanese Brazilians living between Brazil, Japan and beyond." *Social Identities* 16, no. 6 (2010): 775–790.

Oe, Kenzaburo. "Japan, the Ambiguous, and Myself." The Nobel Prize. Accessed October 19, 2020. https://www.nobelprize.org/prizes/literature/1994/oe/lecture/.

Ōgai Tokuko. "The Stars of Democracy: The First Thirty-Nine Female Members of the Japanese Diet," English Supplemental. U.S.-Japan Women's Journal 11 (1996): 81–117.

Oshio, Takashi and Satoshi Shimizutani. May 2011. "Disability Pension Program and Labor Force Participation in Japan: A Historical Perspective." NBER Working Paper 17052, National Bureau of Economic Research, Cambridge, MA.

Prince, Stephen. "A Career Blooms." Liner notes for *Sanshiro Sugata*. New York: The Criterion Collection, 2010. DVD.

Prince, Stephen. "Doing His Part." Liner notes for *The Most Beautiful*. New York: The Criterion Collection, 2010. DVD.

Ravina, Mark. "State-Building and Political Economy in Early-modern Japan." *The Journal of Asian Studies* 54, no. 4 (Nov. 1995): 997–1022.

Reid, T.R. "WWII re-fought, revised in Japanese media." *The Washington Post* (Washington, D.C.), August 14, 1995.

Robert, Chris B., Yoshimune Hiratsuka, Masakazu Yamada, Lynne M. Pezzullo, Katie Yates, Shigeru Takano, Kensaku Miyake, and Hugh R. Taylor. "Economic Cost of Visual Impairment in Japan." *Archives of Ophthalmology* 128, no. 6 (June 2010): 766–771.

Russell, Catherine. "A Princess and Three Good Men." Insert for *The Hidden Fortress*. New York: The Criterion Collection, 2014.

Saito, Yoko and Hisamitsu Saito. "Motivations for Local Food Demand by Japanese Consumers: A Conjoint Analysis with Reference-Point Effects." *Agribusiness: An International Journal* 29, no. 2 (Spring 2013): 147–161.

Sasaki, Masami. "Aspects of Autism in Japan Before and After the Introduction of TEACCH," *International Journal of Mental Health* 29, no. 2 (Summer 2000): 3–18.

Sedensky, Eric C. "Pachinko Passion." *Japan Quarterly* 39, no. 4 (Oct. 1992): 457–64.

Smith, Roderick A. "The Japanese Shinkansen: Catalyst for the Renaissance of Rail." *The Journal of Transport History* 24, no. 2 (2003): 222–237.

Smyers, Karen A. "'My Own Inari': Personalization of the Deity in Inari Worship." *Japanese Journal of Religious Studies* 23, no. 1 (Spring 1996): 85–116.

Sprague, Jonathan. "They Changed Our Lives." CNN. Accessed October 20, 2020. http://www.cnn.com/ASIANOW/asiaweek/features/aoc/aoc.intro.html.

Takagi, Emiko, Merril Silverstein, and Eileen Crimmins. "Intergenerational Coresidence of Older Adults in Japan: Conditions for Cultural Plasticity." *The Journals of Gerontology: Series B* 62, no. 5 (Sep. 2007): S330-S339.

Takayama, Noriyuki. "The Japanese Pension System: How It Was and What It Will Be." Paper presented at *International Conference on Pensions in Asia: Incentives, Compliance and Their Role in Retirement, Tokyo, Hitotsubashi Collaboration Center, Hitotsubashi University, Feb. 2004*. Tokyo: Institute of Economic Research, Hitotsubashi University, https://hdl.handle.net/10086/14318.

Tanaka, Masako, Yumi E. Suzuki, Ikuko Aoyama, Kota Takaoka, and Harriet L. MacMillan. "Child sexual abuse in Japan: A systematic review and future directions." *Child Abuse & Neglect* 66 (April 2017): 31–40.

Tong, Kurt W. "Korea's Forgotten Atomic Bomb Victims." *Bulletin of Concerned Asian Scholars* 23, no. 1 (1991): 31–37.

Topacoglu, Hasan. *Hawai "Meiji hyakunen-sai" ibento (1968 nen) to nikkei amerikajin no kioku* ハワイ「明治百年祭」イベント（1968年）と日系アメリカ人の記憶 [The 1968 Meiji Centennial Event in Hawai'i and the Recollections of Americans of Japanese Descent]. *Nihon komyunikēshon gakkai* 日本コミュニケーション学会 [Japan Communication Association] 46, no. 1 (2017): 61–80.

Traphagan, John W. "Interpretations of Elder Suicide, Stress, and Dependency among Rural Japanese." *Ethnology* 43, no. 4 (Autumn 2004): 315–329.

Truett, Richard. "The Toyopet Crown: Rocky start for a future giant." In *Turning Points: 25 Pivotal Decisions in Toyota's 50 Years*, supplement. *Automotive News* (Detroit), Oct. 29, 2007.

Tsunetsugu, Yuko, Bum-Jin Park, and Yoshifumi Miyazaki. "Trends in research related to 'Shinrinyoku' (taking to the forest atmosphere or forest bathing) in Japan." Environmental Health and Preventative Medicine 15 (2010): 27–37.

Tsushima, Masahiro and Koichi Hamai, "Public Cooperation with the Police in Japan: Testing the Legitimacy Model." *Journal of Contemporary Criminal Justice* 31, no. 2 (May 2015): 212–228.

Uchino, Tadashi. "Images of armageddon: Japan's 1980s theatre culture." *The Drama Review* 44, no. 1 (Spring 2000), 85–96.

"The Unlikeliest Shoe Empire." *Los Angeles Times* (Los Angeles), Feb. 13, 1992.

Vaugh, Michael S., Frank F. Y. Huang, and Christine Rose Ramirez. "Drug Abuse and Anti-Drug

Policy in Japan: Past History and Future Directions." *The British Journal of Criminology* 35, no. 4 (Autumn 1995): 491–524.

Wildes, Harry Emerson. "The Postwar Japanese Police." *Journal of Criminal Law, Criminology & Police Science* 43, no. 5 (1953): 655–71.

Wilson, Sandra. "War, Soldier and Nation in 1950s Japan." *International Journal of Asian Studies* 5, no. 2 (2008): 187–218.

Yoshimi, Shunya. "1964 Tokyo Olympics as Post-War." In *The Olympic Games in Japan and East Asia: Images and Legacies.* Special issue, *International Journal of Japanese Sociology* 28, no. 1 (March 2019): 80–95.

Yoshioka, Eiji, Yasuaki Saijo, and Ichiro Kawachi. "An analysis of secular trends in method-specific suicides in Japan, 1950–1975." *Popular Health Metrics* 15, no. 14 (2017).

Documentaries

Cadou, Catherine. *Kurosawa's Way.* 2011; New York: The Criterion Collection, 2016.

Imamura Shōhei 今村 昌平. *Nippon Sengoshi— Madamu Onboro no seikatsu* にっぽん戦後史— マダム おんぼろの生活 [*History of Postwar Japan as Told by a Bar Hostess*], 1970.

Janisse, Kier-La. *Woodlands Dark and Days Bewitched: A History of Folk Horror,* 2021. Los Angeles: Severin Films, 2021.

Kurosawa and the Censors. 2007; New York: The Criterion Collection, 2007.

Kurosawa, Hisao. A *Message From Akira Kurosawa: For Beautiful Movies,* 2000; New York: The Criterion Collection, 2015.

Nogami, Teruyo. *Akira Kurosawa: It is Wonderful to Create.* 2002; New York: The Criterion Collection, 2003.

Obayashi, Nobuhiko. *Making of Dreams: A Movie Conversation Between Akira Kurosawa and Nobuhiko Obayashi.* Blu-ray. 1990; New York: The Criterion Collection, 2016.

Sato, Shizuo, dir. *Akira Kurosawa: My Life in Cinema.* DVD. 1993; New York: The Criterion Collection, 2006.

Other Sources

"Bloody May Day (May 1, 1952)." Cross Currents. Accessed May 26, 2021. http://www.cross currents.hawaii.edu/content.aspx?lang=eng& site=japan&theme=work& subtheme=UNION &unit=JWORK007.

"The Creators of Toyota's DNA." *Assembly.* Accessed October 19, 2020. https://www.assembly mag.com/articles/84596-the-creators-of- toyota-s-dna.

"Development History of Japanese Automobile Industry." Car From Japan. Accessed October 19, 2020. https://carfromjapan.com/article/ industry-knowledge/development-history- japanese-automotive-industry/.

"Drugs and Crime Facts." Bureau of Justice Statistics. Accessed October 19, 2020. https://www.bjs. gov/content/dcf/enforce.cfm.

"Imperial Rescript: The Great Principles of Education, 1879." Children and Youth in History. Accessed November 11, 2020. https://chnm.gmu. edu/cyh/items/show/134.

"Japan—Urban population as a share of total population." Knoema. Accessed October 19, 2020. https://knoema.com/atlas/Japan/Urban- population.

"Japanese Kids to Learn How to Farm on Abandoned Land." Japan For Sustainability. Accessed October 19, 2020. https://www.japanfs.org/en/ news/archives/news_id029225.html.

Joint Chiefs of Staff. *Basic Initial Post-Surrender Directive.* JCS1380/15. Washington, D.C.: Joint Chiefs of Staff, 1945. Accessed October 14, 2020. https://www.ndl.go.jp/constitution/e/ shiryo/01/036/036tx.html#t003.

"Josei senyōsha" 女性専用車. RJ Essential. Accessed October 19, 2020. http://rail-j.com/esse/ index.php?%BD%F7%C0%AD%C0%EC%CD% D1%BC%D6.

Kitamoto, Asanobu. "Digital Typhoon: Typhoon Damage List." Accessed October 15, 2020. http://agora.ex.nii.ac.jp/cgi-bin/dt/disaster. pl?lang=en&basin=wnp&sort=dead_or_ missing &order=dec&stype=number.

Kurosawa, Akira. Kurosawa to Bergman. Open Culture. Accessed November 11, 2020. https://www. openculture.com/2013/12/akira-kurosawa-to- ingmar-bergman.html#:~:text=Bergman%2C, more%20wonderful%20movies%20for%20us.

McGee, Scott. "Sanshiro Sugata Part 2." TCM. Accessed October 26, 2020. https://www.tcm. com/tcmdb/title/491264/sanshiro-sugata-part- 2#articles-reviews?articleId=290058.

Natural Park Act. Act No. 161 of 1959. http://www. env.go.jp/en/laws/nature/law_np.pdf (accessed October 15, 2020).

"Natural Resources and Japan: Gold, Timber, Urban Mining and Metal Thieves." Facts and Details. Accessed October 15, 2020. http:// factsanddetails.com/japan/cat24/sub159/item 932.html.

Newsreel. *The Quiet Duel,* DVD. 1949; Newbury Park, CA: BCI Eclipse Company, 2006.

"1949 Dainippon Beer is split up." Sapporo Beer. Accessed October 14, 2020. https://www. sapporobeer.jp/english/company/history/1949. html.

Pergrams, Oliver R.W. and Patricia A. Zaradic. "Evidence for a fundamental and pervasive shift away from nature-based recreation." Accessed October 15, 2020. https://www.ncbi.nlm.nih. gov/pmc/articles/PMC2268130/pdf/zpq2295. pdf.

"Personal Saving Rate in the United States from 1960 to 2019." Statista. Accessed October 18, 2020. https://www.statista.com/statistics/ 246234/personal-savings-rate-in-the-united- states/.

"Pop-Culture Diplomacy." Ministry of Foreign Affairs of Japan. Accessed October 21, 2020. https://www.mofa.go.jp/policy/culture/exchange/pop/index.html.

"Statistics of Film Industry in Japan." Motion Picture Producers Association of Japan, Inc. Accessed October 19, 2020. http://www.eiren.org/statistics_e/.

Vallen, Mark. "Nagasaki Nightmare: Art of the Hibakusha (Atom Bomb Survivors)." Art For a Change. Accessed October 19, 2020. https://www.art-for-a-change.com/Atomic/atomic.htm.

Index

Numbers in *bold italics* indicate pages with illustrations